DEVELOPMENT CENTRES

Latest titles in the McGraw-Hill Training Series

TOTAL QUALITY TRAINING
The Quality Culture and Quality Trainer
Brian Thomas   ISBN 0-07-707472-6

CAREER DEVELOPMENT AND PLANNING
A Guide for Managers, Trainers and Personnel Staff
Malcolm Peel   ISBN 0-07-707554-4

SALES TRAINING
A Guide to Developing Effective Sales People
Frank S. Salisbury   ISBN 0-07-707458-0

CLIENT-CENTRED CONSULTING
A Practical Guide for Internal Advisers and Trainers
Peter Cockman, Bill Evans
and Peter Reynolds   ISBN 0-07-707685-0

TRAINING TO MEET THE TECHNOLOGY CHALLENGE
Trevor Bentley   ISBN 0-07-707589-7

IMAGINATIVE EVENTS Volumes I & II
Ken Jones   ISBN 0-07-707679-6 Volume I
                      ISBN 0-07-707680-X Volume II
                      ISBN 0-07-707681-8 for set of Volumes I & II

LEARNING THROUGH SIMULATIONS
A Guide to the Design and Use of Simulations in Business and Education
John Fripp   ISBN 0-07-707588-9

MEETINGS MANAGEMENT
A Manual of Effective Training Material
Leslie Rae   ISBN 07-707782-2

WORKSHOPS THAT WORK
100 Ideas to Make Your Training Events More Effective
Tom Bourner, Viven Martin
and Phil Race   ISBN 07-707800-4

TRAINING FOR PROFIT
A Guide to the Integration of Training in an Organization's Success
Philip Darling   ISBN 07-707785-7

THE HANDBOOK FOR ORGANIZATIONAL CHANGE
Strategy and Skill for Trainers and Developers
Carol A. O'Connor   ISBN 07-707693-1

Details of these and other titles in the series are available from:

The Product Manager, Professional Books, McGraw-Hill Book Company Europe,
Shoppenhangers Road, Maidenhead, Berkshire SL6 2QL, United Kingdom.
Telephone: 0628 23432. Fax: 0628 770224

Development centres

Realizing the potential of your employees through assessment and development

Geoff Lee
David Beard

McGRAW-HILL BOOK COMPANY

London · New York · St Louis · San Francisco · Auckland
Bogotá · Caracas · Lisbon · Madrid · Mexico · Milan
Montreal · New Delhi · Panama · Paris · San Juan · São Paulo
Singapore · Sydney · Tokyo · Toronto

Published by
McGRAW-HILL Book Company Europe
Shoppenhangers Road, Maidenhead, Berkshire SL6 2QL, England
Telephone: 0628 23432
Fax: 0628 770224

British Library Cataloguing in Publication Data
Development Centres: Realizing the
Potential of Your Employees Through
Assessment and Development. –
(McGraw-Hill Training Series)
I. Lee, Geoff   II. Beard, David
III. Series
658.3

ISBN 0-07-707785-7

Library of Congress Cataloging-in-Publication Data
Lee, Geoff
    Development centres: realizing the potential of your employees
through assessment and development / Geoff Lee, David Beard.
        p.   cm. — (The McGraw-Hill training series)
    Includes bibliographical references and index.
    ISBN 0-07-707785-7
    1. Employees—Training of—Case studies.   2. Employee training
directors—Case studies.   I. Beard, David.   II. Title.
III. Series.
HF5549.5.T7L426   1993
658.3'124—dc20   93-5287
                                                                           CIP

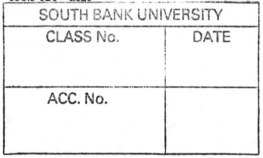
12345 CL 9654

Typeset by Book Ens Limited, Baldock, Herts.
Printed and bound in Great Britain by Clays Ltd, St Ives plc

We wish to dedicate this book to all the managers who have gone through or assisted us on programmes. We would like to thank them for their perseverance, tolerance and good humour

Contents

Series preface

Training and development are now firmly centre stage in most organizations, if not all. Nothing unusual in that—for some organizations. They have always seen training and development as part of the heart of their businesses—but more and more must see it that same way.

The demographic trends through the nineties will inject into the marketplace severe competition for good people who will need good training. Young people without conventional qualifications, skilled workers in redundant crafts, people out of work, women wishing to return to work—all will require excellent training to fit them to meet the job demands of the 1990s and beyond.

But excellent training does not spring from what we have done well in the past. T&D specialists are in a new ball game. 'Maintenance' training—training to keep up skill levels to do what we have always done—will be less in demand. Rather, organization, work, and market change training are now much more important and will remain so for some time. Changing organizations and people is no easy task, requiring special skills and expertise which, sadly, many T&D specialists do not possess.

To work as a 'change' specialist requires us to get to centre stage—to the heart of the company's business. This means we have to ask about future goals and strategies, and even be involved in their development, at least as far as T&D policies are concerned.

This demands excellent communication skills, political expertise, negotiating ability, diagnostic skills—indeed, all the skills a good internal consultant requires.

The implications for T&D specialists are considerable. It is not enough merely to be skilled in the basics of training, we must also begin to act like business people and to think in business terms and talk the language of business. We must be able to resource training not just from within but by using the vast array of external resources. We must be able to manage our activities as well as any other manager. We must share in the creation and communication of the company's vision. We must never let the goals of the company out of our sight.

In short, we may have to grow and change with the business. It will be hard. We shall not only have to demonstrate relevance but also value for money and achievement of results. We shall be our own boss, as accountable for results as any other line manager, and we shall have to deal with fewer internal resources.

The challenge is on, as many T&D specialists have demonstrated to me over the past few years. We need to be capable of meeting that challenge. This is why McGraw-Hill Book Company Europe have planned and launched this major new training series—to help us meet that challenge.

This series covers all aspects of T&D and provides the knowledge base from which we can develop plans to meet the challenge. They are practical books for the professional person. They are a starting point for planning our journey to the twenty-first century.

Use them well. Don't just read them. Highlight key ideas, thoughts, action pointers or whatever, and have a go at doing something with them. Through experimentation we evolve; through stagnation we die.

I know that all the authors in the McGraw-Hill Training Series would want me to wish you good luck. Have a great journey into the twenty-first century.

ROGER BENNETT
Series Editor

About the series editor

Roger Bennett has over 20 years' experience in training, management education, research and consulting. He has long been involved with trainer training and trainer effectiveness. He has carried out research into trainer effectiveness and conducted workshops, seminars, and conferences on the subject around the world. He has written extensively on the subject including the book *Improving Trainer Effectiveness*, Gower. His work has taken him all over the world, and has involved directors of companies as well as managers and trainers.

Dr Bennett has worked in engineering, several business schools (including the International Management Centre, where he launched the UK's first masters degree in T&D), and has been a board director of two companies. He is the editor of the *Journal of European Industrial Training* and was series editor of the ITD's *Get In There* workbook and video package for the managers of training departments. He now runs his own business called The Management Development Consultancy.

About the authors

Editors   **David Beard**

David Beard is People Development Manager for Global Customer Service Operations in BT, where he uses competency-based assessment and development centres to select and develop senior managers who are responsible for looking after global business customers.

He previously managed a small specialist unit in BT Training which designed and helped implement development centres for business units throughout the company. In this role he pioneered the design of development centres for use across different national cultures in the BT regions. He also managed the design of a programme for 1000 specialist UK sales staff and the company's high potential development centre programme.

David Beard has undertaken consultancy work for large multinational corporations in the United Kingdom, India, China, Hong Kong and Sweden. He was educated at the London School of Economics, and has published a number of articles on development centres, training and management development.

Geoff Lee

Geoff Lee has been a training professional for 18 years. After a short spell in the steel industry, he completed masters' degrees at Cambridge and Warwick Universities and two postgraduate professional diplomas. Geoff then lectured in higher education in Manchester—working on subjects ranging from retail marketing to organization theory and psephology, as well as publishing widely in journals and books and working as a consultant.

He joined BT in 1982 as a trainer, designed several portfolios and worked as an internal process consultant. Geoff founded the Development Centres group, and from 1988 to 1992 he managed core management training in BT, managing 60 training professionals. He is now working on management development processes in Group Personnel's Development Strategy group.

Geoff is a fellow of two professional institutes and a registered psychometrician. He has represented BT in the United Kingdom on government bodies and in Europe and the Far East.

Contributors

Keith Coaley

Keith Coaley is a chartered psychologist and a member of the British Psychological Society's sections of occupational psychology, developmental psychology and counselling psychology. He is a member of the Association of Teachers of Psychology and of the Institute of Training and Development. Keith has a first-class honours degree and an MSc in psychology, in addition to a degree in physics. During his career Keith has worked as journalist, teacher and lecturer in psychology, and as an occupational psychologist in industry. He is a trained counsellor. In his present post Keith is involved in the design and management of development centres and in competency-based approaches to personnel processes.

Anne Guymer

Anne Guymer is a training specialist in BT's global customer service operations, where she manages the complex cross-cultural training needs of senior service managers who are assigned to BT's major global customers. Anne has used development centres on an extensive basis for a number of specialists, and is particularly interested in the techniques for gaining line manager commitment to their use.

During the past nine years Anne has worked as a computer specialist and operational manager, as well as managing different training and development functions within BT. Anne managed the implementation of a development centre programme which was recently used for 1000 BT sales staff, including implementation throughout the Far East.

Bridget Hogg

Bridget Hogg is an occupational psychologist with expertise in researching and defining managerial competences, both in the United Kingdom and in Europe. Bridget has worked with senior managers in several large European organizations, determining the important competences for the European manager of the future. Bridget's background includes an MSc in occupational psychology and research interests in cultural influences on management styles. Bridget currently works on the design and implementation of development centre programmes. She is a registered user of psychometric tests.

Ray Knightley

Ray Knightley has worked in the training field for 19 years. He has worked as a job analyst and course designer for the Post Office, a principal training adviser for the Distributive Industry Training Board and principal officer in local government. Since joining BT in 1968, he has worked as a management tutor, organizational development consultant and, most recently, as a development centre designer and project manager, in which field he has been published. He holds the professional examinations of the Institute of Personnel Management, and is a member of both the IPM and ITD. He is a registered user of psychometric tests.

Chris Latham

Chris Latham is a graduate of Birkbeck College, London University and holds an honours degree in psychology; a certificate in education and a diploma in internal audit from City University Business School. He is a member of the British Psychological Society; a BPS registered user of psychometrics and a member of the Institute of Training and Development. Prior to joining BT Chris worked in the Civil Service as a manager and trainer of managers. He joined BT in 1988 as a consultant in the Management Consultancy Unit in BT Training Division. He then moved into interpersonal skills training and is now a management development consultant specializing in development and assessment centre design and applications in the United Kingdom and overseas.

Tricia Marchbank

Tricia Marchbank is a graduate of the London School of Economics and holds an honours degree in the economics of industry and trade. She is a member of the Institute of Training and Development and holds the ITD Diploma in Training Management. Since joining BT in 1983, she has worked as a sales executive, sales planning manager and sales training officer with the BT sales force. She moved into management training in 1988, designing and delivering interpersonal and evaluative skills courses. She currently works as a senior project manager/tutor and holds the British Psychological Society's statement of competence in occupational testing. She trains assessors in all aspects of selection and has worked as an assessor since 1988, most recently on development centres in the United Kingdom and Hong Kong. She is currently project-managing the design of a selection centre for global account service managers in BT. Tricia has six years of operational and training management experience.

Sandy Schofield

Sandy is currently studying for her Master's in Business Administration and holds a postgraduate diploma in health education and a teacher's certificate. She is a member of the Association for Management Education and Development (AMED) and the Institute of Training and Development (ITD). Sandy is a British Psychological Society registered user of psychometric tests.

Sandy began her career as a teacher in a high school before moving on to work in the NHS in health education, where she eventually managed the service as a district officer for Ealing Health Authority. Her next move in 1986 was with BT as a management development tutor in the Management College. Since then she has been involved in a variety of training and management development projects: project manager—total quality management; facilitator training; implementation manager in personal development planning; management consultancy; project manager and designer of development/selection centres in the United Kingdom and overseas.

Preface

During the 1980s and 1990s considerable attention has been given to the 'international manager' and the search for these flexible, resilient people who can lead their organizations, not merely into Europe but beyond into 'global' trading environments.

At the same time the need to measure the quality of the 'stock' of their managers has led organizations to concentrate on 'competences' and their application in personnel systems, such as performance management. A natural corollary is the use of competences in development centres, to identify differing career and development paths. This book sets out to explore some of the ways this has been implemented.

Chapter 1 begins with a clarification of the terminology, the history of this approach and the linkage of development centres to business objectives. The development of middle managers in Swedish Telecom is used as a case study to illustrate the application.

Chapter 2 then goes into considerable depth on competences, the bedrock of the approach. Definitions of competences and their use in centres is reviewed, and the Woolwich Building Society's integrated approach is described.

Chapter 3 is a practitioner's guide to the design of the main components of a development centre, with an illustration from Norwich Union Insurance. Chapter 4 is a natural accompaniment, detailing the methods for defining competences and exercises, by different types of interviews and biographical questionnaires. Again, our purpose is to provide easy-to-understand instruments for practitioners.

Chapter 5 addresses the use of psychometric tests in centres, covering the current debate on the different types and illustrating their application in a large project: the entire BT UK sales force. Chapter 6 follows another of the most sensitive areas—the provision of effective feedback and carry-through by the use of development logs.

Chapter 7 deals with the practical issues of implementing centres and the high-skill activity of training senior line managers as assessors. As in the previous chapter, we call upon the experience of ICI Pharmaceuticals, as well as an Indian Government example.

Chapter 8 is given over to a wide range of case studies, to show the different applications: including manufacturing, the global financial services sector and education in the United Kingdom.

As we implemented these processes, we found that cultural adaptations were required in different parts of the world. Assessment and development centres are primarily an Anglo-Saxon device and care is needed when exporting methods to other parts of an international company. We cite our experience in BT Asia-Pacific in Chapter 9.

Chapter 10 examines the essential tasks of validating the centres to ensure that they are achieving their objectives, and evaluation to prove their worth to the business.

We conclude by looking at some trends from the debate on discriminatory practices and ethical aspects. Trends to computerize such diagnostic systems are reviewed in brief and their possible wider use among shop-floor workers is discussed. The book ends with an integrative case study from Wang (UK) Ltd.

Acknowledgements

We would like to thank all the contributors of case studies; they enhance the book considerably. For case studies in the specified chapters we thank the following people and organizations: Chapter 1, Televerket and Peter Kennedy of ICL; Chapter 2, The Woolwich Building Society; Chapter 3, Martin Woods and Norwich Union Insurance Group; Chapter 5, Keith Coaley of British Telecom; Chapter 6, Helen Carter and ICI Pharmaceuticals; Chapter 7, Ambrish Agarwal and the Advanced Level Telecommunications Training Centre, India; Helen Carter and ICI Pharmaceuticals; Chapter 8, ICI Pharmaceuticals; BT employees; Howard Green and the National Educational Assessment Centre; Edward Zawisza and the Rover Group; Melanie Stopeck, Perkins Williamson and American Express; Chapter 9, John Postins, Director of Sales for BT Asia-Pacific; Chapter 10, Keith Coaley and BT; Chapter 11, Francis Nichols and Wang (UK) Ltd.

We owe a great deal to Matthew Grace and Mike Cavill for helping us with graphics and proformas. Like the authors, they gave up their own time to assist us. For the use of some of the BT sales data we would like to express our gratitude to Director, Alan Cunningham. Similarly, Example 1 in Chapter 1 comes from a BT Group Personnel report (1992). Tony Shuttleworth, Senior Management Development Consultant, Pilkington plc, spoke at the Third Annual Forum on Developing Effective Business-Led Management Training and Development, arranged by IRR Ltd, 1 March 1991 and is responsible for Example 2.

And finally, we are grateful to our senior line managers in the Executive Development and Resourcing Division in BT, notably Peter Merry and Dr John Taylor, who in 1992 gave us permission to publish.

1 Definitions and applications of development centres

Geoff Lee

Introduction

This book contains three key messages. Firstly, that development centres are one of the most useful tools for accurately pinpointing the gaps between an individual's abilities and those required of a particular job. They provide accurate data on individual skills and abilities at one level, and a skills audit of the participant population at an organizational level. More than that, they provide a mechanism for empowering individuals to take appropriate action to develop their abilities and close the gap between current ability levels and the performance levels needed for a particular job or role.

Organizations that operate development centre programmes are convinced of the benefits that accrue in terms of enhanced workplace performance leading to better business performance. A number of case studies are included from such organizations, illustrating the utility value of development centre programmes, and Chapter 10 provides guidance on techniques to measure the benefits of development centre programmes.

The second message is that development centres are comparatively straightforward to design and implement. They do not contain any mystical elements that can only be unravelled by personnel specialists or psychologists. The most effective development centres are simply designed within the companies that operate them, and are managed by operational managers. They can be designed by competent line managers, trainers or personnel staff, using simple guidelines which are contained in subsequent chapters of this book.

The third message relates to cost. A frequent response to any proposal for running development programmes within a company is that the cost would be prohibitive. This proposition is not entirely accurate. As this book demonstrates, it is possible for staff within an organization to design and implement a programme of development centres without the use of costly external consultants. Furthermore, a programme which is designed in this way is likely to reflect more accurately the needs of the organization. Recent calculations by a large British company in the service sector demonstrated that the full opportunity cost of designing and implementing a development centre programme for 1000 of its sales staff amounted to less than £165 000. This represents £165 per person for a three-day residential workshop, held in a hotel, and leading to personal development plans for all participants.

There are four key success criteria for implementing a development centre programme: clear objectives; organizational support; good communications; and a development centre which accurately identifies development needs of individual participants and links these into effective developmental action in the workplace.

Clear objectives

An organization may need to identify and improve the abilities of particular groups of people for different reasons. These reasons should be clarified before the design and implementation stages. Chapter 8 discusses some of the applications of a development centre, and some of the possible objectives. Chapter 10 looks at the need for clear objectives for validation and evaluation purposes.

Organizational support

Development centres require considerable resources in order to work effectively. Consequently the design stages need to be completed as part of a wider strategy for implementation. Chapter 7 explores some of the implementation issues and provides practical guidance on project management.

Communications

An accurate and consistent message needs to be communicated to everyone involved with the development centre programme. This includes participants and their line managers, people who run the development centre, senior managers, and training and personnel staff. A poorly executed communications strategy often leads to apprehension among participants which affects their commitment, motivation and performance. It also leads to badly briefed line managers who may not take responsibility for managing subsequent developmental activity. Consequently, full benefits are not realized.

The need for an effective communications strategy is shown in Chapter 7, which discusses implementation, and in Chapter 6, which looks at feedback to participants.

A well-designed development centre

This book is a practical guide, and most of the chapters discuss design issues. Chapter 2 looks at methods for establishing competences, the criteria for effectiveness against which the participants are measured. Chapters 3, 4 and 5 look at measuring instruments such as simulations and exercises (Chapter 3), interviews (Chapter 4) and psychometric tests (Chapter 5). Chapter 6 looks at the design of feedback and development planning systems, and Chapter 9 looks at issues which are relevant to the use of development centres by people from different cultures.

This theme is developed further in Chapter 11, which discusses legal and ethical issues, and explores new developments in the application of development centre techniques. A well-designed development centre programme needs skilled people to run it. Guidance on training is given in Chapter 7.

This first chapter provides an introduction to development centres, concentrating on general definitions, explanations and applications. It is divided into several short sections:

- Introduction
- What is a development centre?
- Development centres and assessment centres
- History of use
- Current applications
- Demonstrating the business benefits
- Development centres and strategic business objectives
- Case study: using competences to develop middle managers in Swedish Telecom
- Checklist
- References and further reading

What is a development centre?

Development centres are workshops which measure the abilities of participants against the agreed success criteria for a job or role. Key characteristics of a development centre are as follows:

1 Observations in the centre are based on key dimensions or 'competences' which differentiate between successful and less successful performance.
2 Observations are arrived at by a skills analysis, described in detail in Chapter 2, which may include the following methods:
    (a) Interviewing managers performing in the job about how they structure their time and which activities are critical.
    (b) Observation of people doing the job.
    (c) Using a repertory grid methodology to lead managers to differentiate between successful and less successful individuals and therefore behaviours.
    (d) Collecting a wide range of information by the use of an appropriately designed job analysis questionnaire.
3 Development centres measure the abilities of participants by simulating a job or role situation which requires them to demonstrate abilities in the relevant competences in them. The simulations or exercises, such as negotiation or in-tray, may be linked by a common theme so that they simulate a 'day in the life' of the person in the target job or role. Development centres used by the Canadian Civil Service are linked thematically in this way.
4 Exercises are designed according to certain criteria:
    (a) The ability of the exercise to bring out the required behaviour.
    (b) The level of education, ability and experience of the participants.

(c) The relative importance of the different competences based on the job content of the target job or role.

(d) The need to observe the participants in a variety of situations.

(e) The need to observe the demonstration of competences in different exercises.

(f) The time and money available for the centre.

5 Rating of participant performance is undertaken by trained assessors, who have undergone a course of familiarization and skill training. The essentials of this are the following:

(a) Familiarization with all the exercises by pre-testing.

(b) Experience of reaching a common agreed understanding of the assessment criteria.

(c) Skill and knowledge acquisition of behavioural observation, behavioural categorization and behavioural rating.

6 They involve one-to-one feedback interviews with participants, during which the strengths and development that have been highlighted by performance on the centre are discussed. Data that have been collected by the trained assessors may also be pooled with those produced prior to the centre by peers, subordinates, and line manager, who have completed job performance questionnaires for the participant.

7 Assessors' assessments are collated and distilled into a written report before the one-to-one feedback interview. This often involves a plenary discussion in which assessors who have assessed the same individual in different exercises discuss the overall performance of that individual by reviewing all of the evidence.

Development centres and assessment centres

There is often some confusion over the difference between development centres and assessment centres, leading to concerns about the use of the former. This is understandable since some of the assessment techniques are common to both activities.

Similarities between development and assessment centres

The main similarities are seen in the principles of assessment. Both activities are designed to measure the abilities of those who take part. Both activities use trained people who observe and assess performance against competences, as participants complete tasks which simulate real activities associated with a particular role or job.

Differences between development and assessment centres

The differences are greater than the similarities. The main differences were catalogued by Kerr and Davenport (1989) and identified as follows.

Purpose

Development centres are used to identify the personal development and training needs of people who already work in an organization, either in their current role or for a future role. Assessment centres are used for selecting job applicants.

Outcomes　　Information about performance and ability of candidates in an assessment centre is used to make a decision on selection or rejection. While the final decision is generally communicated to the candidate, details of the individual's performance and ability at the assessment centre are not usually discussed.

The range and quality of data about an individual's performance in a development centre are fed back to the participant. Lengthy discussions normally take place between a development centre observer and each participant during which the feedback is discussed and interpreted, and a mutually agreed action plan is devised to improve performance. This results in considerable dialogue between assessors and participants in a development centre.

Development centres frequently include aspirations interviews where participants can discuss career intentions and seek career guidance. Most development centres now include personality testing which, again, encourages the individual to discuss work and career plans.

The outcome of a development centre is a personal development plan for each participant. Typically this includes:

- Targeted training
- Coaching
- Mentoring
- Project-based learning
- Job change
- Job enlargement
- Self-development, e.g. by seeking feedback from peers.

Process　　Assessment centres are analytical tools of assessment in which the assessors remain detached and neutral so that they do not influence the performance of those that they assess. Development centres encourage a climate of experimentation in which it is 'OK' to make mistakes, and where assessors are drawn into the learning process. Participants are able to use different approaches to dealing with work tasks, and to discuss and consult with the assessors. The emphasis is on learning. This requires high trust levels between assessors and participants, which can be encouraged by social contact outside the assessed activities. Development centres are generally longer than assessment centres, and test abilities against a greater number of competences. Development centres often incorporate workplace performance feedback, using questionnaires which are completed before the workshop by the participant, the line manager and workplace colleagues or subordinates.

Other differences　　Development centre programmes are clearly explained with briefings for participants prior to and at the beginning of the development centre workshop. Line managers are also briefed. This may not be the case with assessment centres. A further difference relates to language. The skilled people who run assessment centres are usually referred to as 'assessors', while on development centres they are frequently called 'observers'. People who attend assessment centres are usually 'candidates', while for development centres they are often referred to as 'participants'.

Given that 'assessor' is a term more widely used and understood throughout the world, rather than 'observer' which may carry connotations of lack of analytical rigour, we will adhere to the term assessor throughout this book.

The ways in which confusion and movement between the two types of centre can occur are illustrated by the two examples below. They arrived at the same objectives by different routes.

Example 1: BT Trainer Development Centre

After running the first series of development centres for 46 trainers in 1987, a thorough evaluation was carried out using quantitative and qualitative data which indicated that they were seen as follows:

- Heavily assessment orientated, with most time spent on this and little time for feedback and development planning.
- Feedback was not provided during the event but at a subsequent meeting which could take place up to four months later. The 'unfreezing' of participants on the workshop and their receptiveness were consequently wasted. Participants were left to internalize self-perceived needs or rationalize and reject development needs in the time between leaving the centre and receiving feedback.
- The assessors were assessors and not trained in counselling or feedback skills. They tended to focus on verbal behaviour, looking for micro detail and not themes. They were less skilled in identifying development themes, providing constructive feedback and co-working with participants on development steps.
- An environment for learning was missing: trust was not built between assessors and participants, and the skills of giving and receiving feedback were not built incrementally. In this respect the event functioned as an assessment centre. Typically the assessors stayed detached from delegates, for reasons of objectivity and because their busy schedules kept them apart—even at mealtimes. But by doing so the opportunity was lost to reassure, to build networks and to pass on key messages on behalf of the company.
- Line manager interest and involvement was poor, as intimated earlier.
- On the positive side, the centre was seen as relevant, fair and accurate.
- The problems were rectified by building the feedback into the centre, providing 'icebreaker' non-assessed exercises, and increasing the proportion of reviews and discussions and the number of applications from 25 to 60 per cent. The assessors who were unable to acquire the new skills to run the event were not used again on the programme.

Example 2: Pilkington Executive Development Programme

- This was a respected course run for the major glass-making company which contained outdoor development. It was decided in 1989 to include a non-judgemental development centre to capitalize on the supportive culture, to make financial and time savings, and to identify far more clearly the development needs of young managers.
- They were aware of the risks of information ownership, and potentially changed attitudes towards the programme.
- In the 'workshops' feedback is given by 'coaches' immediately after exercises. Former participants return as coaches who are also counsellors and mentors who work with people during and after the workshops. Coaches are trained over two days in running the exercises giving feedback. Coaches can only give feedback when they have hard, factual evidence to substantiate it, whether positive or negative.
- The 'contract' with the directors was that information would be used only to open doors, not close them, that it would be updated as development occurred and participants could withhold any information. This did not occur—managers want their development needs addressed, if they believe in the integrity of the process.
- Feedback from the workshop is only part of the data collected, as participants also collect feedback—pre-course, from their manager, peers and subordinates and during the course from the colleagues they worked with in the outdoor exercise and a business simulation.
- All the feedback is analysed by the participant on Day 2 of the workshop. It is then that they write (a) a skills report and (b) a development plan.
- The major benefit to the programme has been to give it a sharper focus—a more quantifiable and useful method for participants to use the learning and self-awareness they gain from the whole event.

Other confusions   Similar boundaries have to be recognized between development centres, which are run for business units with their line managers in a supportive but assessing role, and the following workshops:

1 **Organizational Development [OD] workshops**. These are part of a consultancy intervention, where changes to work practices may be on the agenda. And, far from being in control, the senior managers may be receiving sensitive upward feedback about themselves.

2 **Teambuilding workshops**. These may be open workshops where managers are trained in skills and techniques to return and practise at the workplace. Delegates may well leave leadership or interpersonal skills courses with similar 'action plans'. At this point it has to be seriously addressed whether repetitions of feedback on behaviour, via upward feedback data, reviews on courses and the use of 'learning styles', 'team type' and psychometric 'personality' profiles lead to a diagnostic overkill and disempower managers if they leave with too many 'action plans'. Evidence shows that the success factor with

open-to-all events is minimal. There is often no support back at the workplace for change.

3 **Working teams**. Teambuilding workshops which encompass real working teams, including outdoor management training, can have considerable positive benefits—in terms of respect, confidence, understanding and support—which can be transferred to the workplace. Here competency measurement is not overt or formally undertaken.

4 **Career development workshops**. Experience has taught us that running open versions of such events often fails for most participants, though individuals may receive benefit through focusing on their problem, or from individual counselling. The rest tends towards awareness/education about opportunities, life-goals and planning, usually following diagnosis by more analytical tools. Again the absence of the line manager and the company's manpower and succession planning is critical. If a work group were to undertake such a workshop, it would move towards consultancy because of the mix of individual organizational needs.

If a workshop were run for a workplace team, using skill measures, such as competences, it would be moving into the development centre area, but without researched and validated exercises.

The use of development centres

The general objectives of development centres can include:

- diagnosing the strengths and weaknesses for development;
- providing participant feedback, to produce change or teambuilding;
- identifying and planning the development of people already deemed to have higher potential;
- succession planning;
- career planning, leading to organizational planning and development, through the summation and analysis of findings, aiding:
  —manpower planning;
  —the development of evaluative skills in line managers;
  —the development of performance evaluation and feedback among participants;
  —evaluation of training.

As discussed above, the way that development and assessment centres are conducted differ. This will be illustrated below by two examples that arrived at the same conclusion by different means.

Key issues and problems

Boundaries

The division of development and assessment work can be unclear. Some early BT experiences (in 1986) saw some total quality trainer development centres and senior management development programme workshops set out on a developmental course but selection intruded as informal and formal decisions were reached about individuals. Conversely, some assessment centres for skills audit and competency identification purposes had to move to development planning in order to maintain morale. We found that one indiscreet remark by a senior manager could undo all the briefing and reassurances in written and introductory briefings.

Ownership and confidentiality

Ownership of data about individual participants needs to be made explicit, specifically about who has access to information arising from the development centre. If it is left to the individual to decide what to reveal to line managers, questions can be raised about the organization's need to know—in order to appraise and develop managers to achieve results. Yet any direct transference to the formal appraisal system of centre material, especially any link to promotability or performance-related pay, alters the basis of the centre towards assessment and changes the mood and behaviours within it.

Line manager involvement

As the natural developers of their people, line managers should be involved before and after the centre. Not all line managers can be relied upon to provide a supportive, committed or catalytic role, even if a post-development centre interview format is prescribed and an observer is present.

Development displacement

Line managers and participants can make false assumptions that their development is now being planned and undertaken by someone else on their behalf. Line managers may be tempted to pass on 'difficult' individuals for career planning elsewhere.

Selection

Issues of elitism or preferential treatment occur if access to separate development and training is opened to some but not others. It raises questions of pre-selection mechanisms and nominated 'favourite sons', and can lead to a situation where all of a participant population are offered development, but some get more development than others.

Expectations

A communications strategy is needed in order to structure expectations about the outcome of development centre programmes. An accurate and realistic explanation of what will happen after the programmes, together with messages that participants are responsible for their own development, will help to avoid frustrations and disappointments.

History of use

The war years

The consensus of opinion is that work in Germany and Britain prior to and during the Second World War formed the basis for the assessment centre as it is used today.

German research had been proceeding along many lines of enquiry since the reconstitution of its forces in 1927. Psychological testing was employed extensively in selection but was based more on soldierly traits than on technical ability even for tank drivers, radio operators, pilots and other specialists. Officer selection, though rigorous, was based on similar 'soldierly' qualities, with the addition of intellectual ability tests. What was sought was a picture of the personality as a whole. Assessment was based on subjective opinions and very little scoring was used.

In 1941 the shortcomings of British Army officers' selection by interview alone were apparent, and some of the German techniques were employed, including psychiatric interviews and intelligence tests. By 1942 War Office Selection Boards (WOSBs) had been set up. These used a mixture of military officers, psychiatrists and psychologists to assess candidates' performance both in formal testing and socially, as one of the military assessors lived and ate with participants during the selection process. The tests included group discussions, short lectures, obstacle courses, leaderless group tasks designed to bring out social skills under stress, as well as initiative, leadership and cooperation. Results from all these tests were then discussed by all members of the Board before a decision was made. One can see here the structure of today's assessment processes.

The methods were adopted by the United States after it entered the War, and the Office of Strategic Studies (OSS) drew upon British, German and American tests to define the nine dimensions it regarded as critical for the selection of agents and operatives. This was published as *Assessment of Men* (OSS, 1948).

Post-war developments

The British Civil Service

In 1945, as recruitment to permanent posts in the Civil Service began, the WOSB model was adopted in the form of the Civil Service Selection Board (CSSB). The short-term validation was so good in 1948 that the method was introduced in parallel with the usual examination and interview.

America: the AT&T experience

In 1956 the American Telephone and Telegraph Company set up its management Progress Study under Douglas Bray. The original aim was to gain insight into the management process and in particular to identify the criteria related to success. This required identifying a baseline personality in newly selected managers, followed by a later check on what, if anything, had changed after several years. Significantly, the centre was designed for research purposes rather than operational use, and the projections made of potential were locked away and could not be contaminated by use of the information for selection or promotion. Even in its early stages, the use of the assessment centre so impressed people in AT&T that within two years subsidiary companies set up centres for operational use. For example, Michigan Bell used its centre to assess the potential of non-managerial staff for managerial positions.

Others soon followed—Standard Oil of Ohio, IBM, Sears, and J. C. Penny all contributed to the published work.

The 1970s   The 1970s saw a rapid growth in the use of assessment centres in the United States—estimates vary from 300 to 2000. American companies introduced them into their overseas subsidiaries, and others took to them on a more limited scale.

Current applications   Figures on the use of development centres in the United Kingdom vary from between 4 and 20 per cent of companies, with the main purposes being graduate recruitment or to facilitate promotion from within. Many UK companies are using competency-based systems for performance measurement and the development of managers—some of these are referred to in Chapter 2. Here we will merely cite a few examples of companies employing assessment centres, development centres or hybrids.

1 W. H. Smith has long been using assessment centres and profiling, based on a set of competences derived from senior management. This enables the company to target training at managers in a systemic way. The company has since moved more to the 'developmental' use of centres.
2 National Westminster Bank adopted a set of 11 high potential competences developed in America by H. Schroeder. These were also used on the assessment centre for entry to the Warwick University MBA which is supported by several major UK companies. National Westminster Bank gradually developed its own competency language.
3 National & Provincial Building Society has designed a competency-based organization derived from its mission, goals, strategy, management philosophy and values. These were fitted into the 400 roles required, and were evaluated and ordered into one simple, market-competitive and competency-based benefits system. The emphasis is on individual contributions, team contributions, and cross-organizational flexibility. Every person has been assessed against the framework work and the company is in a position to identify development needs, moves to other roles and recruitment requirements. This is a prime example of the link to strategic business objectives which will be covered later in this chapter. Extensive use is made of their work in the Open University MBA module 'Human Resource Strategies'.
4 ICL was using assessment centres as early as 1979 for graduate recruitment, and has continued to do so. Company staff developed their own design and implementation skills to the point where assessment centre techniques were widely adopted for all selection, promotion and career changes. By the early 1980s, ICL was redefining performance criteria and appraisals and linking them with competences used for selection and development.

Demonstrating the business benefits   Development centres are costly programmes to design and implement, and most companies require more than just an article of faith that they will yield tangible benefits. The management development or training manager who advocates development centres as a solution to development or training problems frequently struggles with a complex range of approaches to show that the effort is worth while.

There is no definitive right or wrong way to prove the worth of a development centre programme, and the most effective proof is often in terms of the company's own value systems: what data are needed to convince key decision makers within the company of the benefits of such a programme? An additional complicating factor is that most development centre programmes are not designed to be evaluated. Evaluation data are often cobbled together quickly in order to provide *post hoc* proof of value.

Much has been written about the validation of assessment centres and about the evaluation of training programmes, but very little has been written about techniques which apply specifically to development centres. This section reviews some of the current thinking on validation and evaluation, and provides some practical guidance on calculating the benefits. It starts by defining terms and then looks at techniques. A more detailed discussion of evaluation is contained in Chapter 10.

Most development centre programmes are implemented for a specific reason. They are diagnostic instruments which are designed for a defined group of people within a company, with the objective of accurately identifying training and development needs of both the group as a whole and individuals within the group. The ultimate aim of the process is to increase the effectiveness of these people in carrying out their work within the company.

Validity

Validity is a measure of the accuracy and effectiveness of a development centre. A good development centre measures performance against relevant criteria, using accurate measuring instruments and is run by skilled assessors who share a common understanding of effective performance and apply the same standards of assessment.

Consequently, validity can be demonstrated in three ways:

1 Content-related validity, or proving the link between what is measured on a development centre and what is required in a job.
2 Criterion-related validity, or proving that a true relationship exists between performance on a development centre and performance in a job.
3 Inter-rater reliability, or proving that different assessors have applied the same standards in assessing the same behaviours.

Content validity can be demonstrated by a simple content analysis of the job in order to show that the competences which are tested on the development centre are identical to those which are needed to complete the job to an effective level of performance. Criterion validity can be demonstrated by comparing workplace assessment of performance, such as annual appraisals and attainment of objectives, with development centre performance. Inter-rater reliability can be demonstrated by a simple test in which assessors are asked to mark the same draft answers from a development centre exercise. High levels of reliability and validity show that the results of a development centre programme can be used with some confidence.

Evaluation

Development centre programmes are usually adopted by a company as a means to an end. They are diagnostic instruments which identify precise development needs by revealing a gap between the current abilities of participants and the standard of performance required in a particular job. This gap needs to be closed by providing some additional activity such as coaching, development or training. In most cases, the programmes are prompted by a feeling that a workplace problem exists, that the performance gap is wide, that it needs to be quantified, and that remedial action needs to be carefully targeted.

This provides the basis for evaluation. The performance gap which exists before the development centre programme needs to be identified through critical incident interviewing and careful data collection. A pre-development centre failure cost can then be calculated. A similar approach can be adopted after the programme has been completed, and a calculation made on the extent to which the failure costs have been eliminated. This will produce a cost savings figure which can be deducted from the cost of running the development centre programme and providing the follow-up development activity. Recent experience with the British Telecom sales force indicates that dramatic savings of over £60 million can be made by development centre programmes, and that these savings can be demonstrated to senior managers.

Development centres and strategic business objectives

As we shall see in Chapter 2, development centres are processes which are designed to measure abilities against competences. Competences are often defined with only a single group, task or role in mind, such as 'high flyers', middle managers or sales staff. Most managers are quick to realize that the precision of definition and the rigour of measurement used in competency-based development centres often make other company processes on objective-setting, appraisal and succession planning look blunt, clumsy and subjective.

Consequently, organizations often find themselves moving into competency-based training and development by two routes. Firstly, through the use of development centres on an *ad hoc* basis because of their previous experience with assessment centres for recruitment. This happened in British Telecommunications plc during the 1980s, after the company was sold into private ownership, which began to use its management trainers and psychologists to design and run programmes. Widespread use of development centres generated discussion about the use of resources for these activities, and the need for a company policy. Meanwhile, line managers involved in running the programmes noticed the inextricable link between performance ratings for development purposes, and the potential for the company to obtain a much sharper picture of the abilities and potential of its valuable 'human resources'. This generated a need to standardize the different measures and procedures which had evolved through local design and implementation initiatives.

A frequently used second route emerges when organizations adopt a new competency approach, after perhaps some experience of competency-based selection, and decide upon a step change to integrate their approaches to organizational and individual development. In these circumstances the companies often incorporate development centres into their new systems or they make use of competences in other, related ways. Some of these approaches are outlined below.

ICI   ICI, the British chemicals company, use competences in its management development and training programmes. The initial design was created with the help of an American-based training company, Development Dimensions International (DDI). The work of both these companies will be examined later.

Mars Electronics   The Mars Group has a clearly defined common culture expressed in five principles: mutuality, responsibility, efficiency, quality and team working. Each has a set of competences which allow managers to review their performance and next set of objectives annually.

Cadbury Schweppes   Cadbury Schweppes, the British confectionery and soft drinks company, initially adopted a set of generic competences devised by an external consultant. These were then developed into a company-specific set which are used in selection, succession planning and management development.

Courtaulds Textiles plc   Courtaulds Textiles plc, the British textiles and polymers group, has developed 'competencies' from the work by Richard Boyatzis. Originally, they were applied to organizational development and are now actively used in recruitment (particularly graduate recruitment), self-development, appraisals, coaching and management development. Specific competency-based training courses using a 'Seeing', 'Doing', 'Actioning & Influencing Others' model have also been developed.

Unilever   Unilever, the Anglo-Dutch conglomerate, developed a competency language incrementally over time in the light of experience. The first four dimensions—vital energy, sense of reality, helicopter quality and analytical ability—were derived from work by a Dutch consultant—Van Lenep. Other items, such as 'warmth' and 'humour' were gradually dropped in favour of newer competences which were closely linked to the company's business strategy, a key one being 'tolerance of ambiguity'. Other dimensions derived by Dr Cobern and his Unilever colleagues include creativity, leadership, vision/communication and integrity. These are used widely, but there is no standard, mandatory, company-wide competency language.

BT   BT, the British telecommunications company, was an early pioneer of competences, using them for recruitment and selection. In the 1980s BT developed a competency-based training system, using a personal development planner (PDP)—a process by which the individual and line manager systematically planned the individual's development. Specialist competences could be added to a generic set of management competences.

The PDP competences were first defined in 1988 using data derived from 100 repertory grid interviews with junior managers. This initial research phase was augmented by additional diagnostic interviews with over 200 middle and senior managers.

BT conducted research to compare the management competences used in five other European countries. As a result of this work, six more competences were added to the PDP set in order to help define skills, knowledge, behaviour and performance levels for the 'international manager'.

Most companies modify their competency frameworks over time so that the content and language reflect business strategy, roles, technology and markets. Successful implementation depends on the relevance, usefulness and user-friendliness of the competency systems to line managers. In this respect, the increasing use of development centres helps in convincing them.

Case study: Using competences to develop middle managers in Swedish Telecom

Swedish Telecom use a middle management development centre programme for identifying people with potential for middle and senior management roles. The programme is run in four regional centres, Göteborg, Malmo, Stockholm and Umea, and each telecom area has local responsibility for selecting and briefing development centre participants. Data from the programmes are then used by local personnel units as one factor in making decisions about promotion. Participants can be sponsored by their own unit or can apply to attend the programme if they have a combination of educational attainment and work experience in Swedish Telecom. Additionally, a 'green card' or promotability marking from the development centre is the basic requirement for attending certain middle management training such as the leadership programme.

The competences measured on the development centre programme are standard behavioural, trait and skills-based competences, as shown in Table 1.1 on page 16.

Each development centre is attended by five participants and consists of two days of simulated workplace activities and role plays. These reflect various managerial problems which are relevant to the current and future requirements of managers in Swedish Telecom. Participants are observed by a group of trained observers who assess performance of each participant against the competences, and make judgements about their suitability for higher level work. The observers are usually senior and experienced line managers.

Assessors produce descriptive and non-evaluative reports of behaviours exhibited by participants after each exercise has been completed. At the end of the two-day workshop, participants each complete a personal evaluation form, outlining their perceived performance on the event.

Development centres

Table 1.1 *Competences measured on Swedish Telecom development centre programme*

Competences used in the selection of directors	Competences used in the selection of middle managers
Job motivation	*Engaging and motivating others*
1 Commitment 2 Inner professional ethics	1 Level of activity 2 Social sensitivity 3 Ability to impress others
Communication ability	*Communication ability*
3 Verbal presentation 4 Argumentational ability	4 Verbal presentation
Understanding of human behaviour	*Influencing others and creating results*
5 Leadership 6 Negotiation 7 Social sensitivity 8 Impression 9 Independence	5 Negotiation ability 6 Leadership 7 Results orientation 8 Personal development
Problem-solving ability	*Problem-solving ability*
10 Information collection 11 Information analysis 12 Decision-making quality 13 Decisiveness 14 Personal development 15 Work structuralization 16 Planning ability	9 Information collection 10 Information analysis 11 Overall vision 12 Decision-making quality 13 Decisiveness 14 Work structuralization 15 Planning ability
Adaptability	*Ability to deal with changes*
17 Flexibility 18 Preparedness to take risks 19 Stress tolerance 20 Insecurity tolerance	16 Flexibility 17 Preparedness to take risks 18 Independence 19 Stress to tolerance 20 Insecurity to tolerance

Before leaving the development centre, they also agree a date for the follow-up feedback interview. Assessors meet after the development centre workshop has ended in order to complete a detailed assessment and report on the abilities of each participant. About two weeks after the workshop, participants and observers carry out one-to-one meetings in order to discuss the outcomes. Feedback data are owned by the participants, who take responsibility for their own development planning. The only formal feedback received by the sponsoring unit who sent the participant is a 'green card' if the participant was identified as ready for promotion. Participants are, however, encouraged to discuss outcomes and plan development with their line managers.

Checklist

1 Be clear that you have senior management commitment.
2 Ensure that their ownership and involvement is linked to business objectives.
3 Specify whether development and/or assessment is the objective.
4 Adhere to best practice on design, feeedback and confidentiality.

References and further reading

Boehm, V.R. (1985) 'Using assessment centres for management development—five applications', *Journal of Management Development*, 4 (4), 40–53.

Bray, D.W. (1985) 'Fifty years of assessment centres: a retrospective and prospective view', *Journal of Management Development*, 4 (4), 4–12.

Byham, C. (1980) 'The assessment center as an aid in management development', Training and Development Journal, 25 (12), 10–23.

Goodge, P.M. (1987) 'Assessment centres: time for deregulation', *Management Education and Development*, 18, Part 2.

Griffiths, P.J. and Allen, B. (1987) 'Assessment centres: breaking with tradition', *Journal of Management*, 6 (1).

Kennedy, P. (1991) 'Effective Strategies for Defining, Identifying and Applying competences.' A paper to the IRR conference in London, 13 June 1991.

Kerr, S. and Davenport, H. (1989) 'AC or DC: A Wolf in Sheep's Clothing?', *British Psychological Society*, 5 (5), 1.

MacKinnon, D.W. (1980) *How Assessment Centers Were Started in the United States: The OSS Assessment Program*. Development Dimensions International, Pittsburgh.

OSS Assessment Center (1948) *Assessment of Men*, Johnson Reprint Corp. (Harcourt Brace & Jovanovich Inc.) New York.

Sackett, P.R. and Ryan, A.M. (1985) 'A review of recent assessment centre research', *Journal of Management Development*, 4 (4), 13–27.

Smith, M. and Robertson, I. (1990) *Advances in Selection and Assessment*, John Wiley, Chichester.

Stewart, A. and Stewart, V. (1981) *Tomorrow's Managers Today*, Institute of Personnel Management, London.

2 Competences

Bridget Hogg, David Beard and Geoff Lee

Introduction

Competence is a word used in everyday life to refer to a person's ability or capacity to undertake a particular task. So we might hear someone referred to as a 'competent musician' or a 'competent speaker' and understand that he or she is in some way good at performing this role.

Training providers and recruitment experts are now using the term 'competence' to refer to the capacity of personnel to fulfil certain skill-based job requirements. It is becoming common to hear discussion of potential job candidates, or promotees, in terms of their competence or capacity to undertake certain specific aspects of the job. One of the attractions of the competency approach is that it focuses on what a person 'can do' rather than on what he or she knows.

This chapter provides an overview of the current debate surrounding the use of competences for assessment and development. It is based on experience of defining and working with competences to aid management development. It is aimed at both trainers and personnel professionals, who desire to implement a competence-based system of assessment, and all managerial students who are desirous of getting to grips with the many issues surrounding the competence debate.

The chapter is divided into the following sections:

- Introduction.
- What is competence?—a discussion of the definition of 'competence' as applied to management assessment and performance.
- Current debate about the use of competences—a description of the main issues, differences, and controversies both in the academic debate and the practitioners' use of competence-based assessment.
- Meta-competences and the learning organization—definition and discussion of the emerging emphasis on meta-competences and the learning organization concept.
- Techniques for competency definition—a practical guide to the most well-used techniques.
- Management competences in the future.

- Measuring competence in a development centre—a practical guide to competence assessment in the development centre context.
- Case study: an integrated approach to competences—the Woolwich Building Society.
- Checklist.
- References and further reading.

What is competence?

1 **Competence is what a person can do**. Some of the various definitions of competence express the desire to see specific work-related behaviours very clearly:

an observable skill or ability to complete a managerial task successfully . . .

(Jacobs, 1989)

underlying characteristic of a manager causally related to superior performance on the job.

(Evarts, 1987)

the ability to perform effectively the functions associated with management in a work situation.

(Hornby and Thomas, 1989)

Although there are many varied definitions of competence, broadly speaking, the majority incorporate three interrelated elements (Beard *et al.*, 1988):

(a) positive attributes of the job holder;
(b) the job being effectively done;
(c) the positive attributes of the job holder (i) being responsible for the job being effectively done (ii), by way of the job holder's behaviour.

The many different definitions of competency encompass terms such as: ability, skill, behaviour, underlying characteristic, and capacity. It is a feature of some of these descriptions that the possession of competency is not necessarily known to the person to whom it is attributed.

Based on a literature review and consideration of the complexity of the managerial role, the author (Hogg) has developed a definition of management competencies, which is as follows:

Competencies are the characteristics of a manager, that lead to the demonstration of skills and abilities, which result in effective performance within an occupational area. Competence also embodies the capacity to transfer skills and abilities from one area to another.

2 **Competence is underlying**. This definition acknowledges that competence is that which underlies and facilitates the demonstration of appropriate and skilled behaviours. Competence is not performing a set of tasks like a robot and it is not an underlying capacity which is never demonstrated.

3 **Competence includes motivation and self-knowledge**. This definition implies that there is a motivational level to competence, as highlighted

by Boyatzis (1982). That is, that within the notion of competence comes the desire or willingness, and the ability, to demonstrate effective performance. In addition, this definition encompasses a measure of self-knowledge. Such self-knowledge aids the transfer of skills, abilities and knowledge from one situation to another, although such transfer can begin unconsciously.

4 **Competence is effective performance**. This definition is similar to many others in that competence is seen as leading to effective performance in an occupational area, rather than superior performance. This is what Boyatzis (1982) refers to as a threshold competency. A threshold competency is 'essential to performing a job, but is not causally related to superior job performance.' (Boyatzis, 1982, p. 23).

The current debate about the use of competences

Competence is in itself a very complicated concept. On the one hand it is said to relate to effective performance, and is thus definable and measurable. On the other hand it can refer to underlying characteristics of a person which are not easily measured. The many studies which have attempted to define and quantify competence have had to recognize and tackle this complexity.

Some competence approaches, however, do not seem to have fully embraced the complexity of competences and hence do not formally address issues of:

- level of competence (skill level versus underlying characteristics);
- specificity of competence (generic versus specific);
- degree of competence (effective versus superior performance).

Competence approaches fall loosely into two categories: those that primarily value the measurement and definition of competence; and those that primarily value the underlying characteristics which lead to behavioural demonstration of a competence.

The ensuing discussion illustrates both types of approach, discussing the main controversies and issues which these different approaches highlight, and attempting to introduce clarity into the debate by answering some of the questions posed.

Are management competences generic?

There is an underlying debate as to whether competences are unique to a particular job or organization, or whether they are generic. Some competency approaches have concentrated on defining competence for a particular company, others have attempted to define a generic set of competences. In other words 'Does "management" require the same sets of behaviours to be demonstrated, irrespective of the organization, job function, location, etc., of the managers?'

The Training Enterprise and Education Directorate of the UK Employment Department (formerly the Training Agency), started from the premise that management competence is generic. It has attempted to draw up a list of generic management competences, based on extensive research with British managers.

The Training Enterprise and Education Directorate's approach stands out for its thoroughness and attention to detail. It was a proponent of the belief that managerial competence has to be precisely defined and measurable. The Training Enterprise and Education Directorate, funded by the government, attempted to define precisely which behaviours were required to perform managerial jobs. It concentrated on generic competences, irrespective of functional specialism or industry sector.

The Management Charter Initiative (MCI) is now identified as the lead body for management competence standards in Britain. It is responsible for encouraging the implementation of the Training Enterprise and Education Directorate's competence standards in British organizations and for providing necessary support.

The history of the approach of the Training Enterprise and Education Directorate of the UK Employment Department

In 1990 the Training Enterprise and Education Directorate (then the Training Agency) produced its 'Field Trial of Draft Standards' for supervisors, junior managers and middle managers. It defined extensive lists of the performance criteria required for these three occupational levels. These performance criteria were developed from interviews and workshops designed to elicit the views of current practising managers in Britain. The Training Enterprise and Education Directorate emphasizes that its focus is not on 'excellent practice' nor 'with what is simply adequate' but on 'what you might realistically expect a good manager to be able to do' (Training Agency, 1990).

Following feedback from organizations that trialled the competences during 1990, the management standards were revised to form standards for two levels of management instead of three. The previous 'supervisor' level remained as level one, and the junior and middle manager levels were combined into level two, as the competences for each were reported to be very similar by organizations during the trials.

KEY PURPOSE
(overall description of the outcomes expected of a manager)
↓
Unit of competence
↓
(a cluster of activities which forms a significant part of a manager's work)
↓
Element of competence
(an activity)
↓
Performance criteria
(the descriptions of what competent performance looks like)
↓
Range statements
(the range of products services, customers, etc., to which the competence relates)

The Training Enterprise and Education Directorate's competence model (see page 21) works from broad key purposes, breaking these down into constituent parts (units and elements of competence) until performance criteria and range statements are defined.

An illustration of this, applied to one of the middle manager competences, is taken from the MCI (Management Charter Initiative) Standards on Training and is given below.

Key purpose. To sustain and enhance the performance of the organization to meet its objectives.

Unit of competence (M11). Exchange information to analyse problems and make decisions.

Element of competence (M11.1). Lead meetings and group discussions to analyse problems and make decisions.

Performance criteria (M11.1a). The purpose of the meeting is clearly established with others from the outset (M11.1h). Any decisions taken fall within the group's authority.

Range statements. This covers type and size of meeting (informal or formal); content of the meetings (e.g. group decision making); and attendees.

Advantages and disadvantages of the Training Enterprise and Education Directorate approach

It is evident that this is a very detailed approach to competence identification and assessment. The benefit of this is seen in terms of objective measurement of behaviour and the opportunity to consider many areas of a manager's activity.

However, such an approach has considerable drawbacks, not least that it appears to approach managerial assessment with the assumption that managing is a series of discrete tasks performed to a certain level, and that competence is always observable (i.e. at the behavioural level).

Managing does not appear to be merely the sequential exercise of discrete competences, and 'shopping lists' of competences at best may simply illuminate different elements of what is, at the end of the day, a complex whole.

There has been an increasing awareness of underlying factors pertaining to the demonstration of competences (more detailed discussion of these factors follows). The Training Enterprise and Education Directorate, perhaps influenced by this strengthening ground swell of opinion, took steps to address the area of personal competence in the final standards.

Personal competence is viewed as part of the other competences, underlying their demonstration. In addition the Training Enterprise and Education Directorate has produced information on the minimum knowledge and understanding requirements for successful demonstration of these competence standards.

Conclusion to the Training Enterprise and Education Directorate approach

Originally the Training Enterprise and Education Directorate set out to define a generic set of management competences which would apply to all junior and middle managers, irrespective of their organization and job function. More recently some revision of the original competence standards has felt to be in order as organizations are applying these management standards.

The series of possible range statements (areas of application of the competences) is almost infinite, and companies have written their own range statements to reflect their procedures and situation, without changing the standards. This implies that, although there are generic competences applicable to every manager regardless of industry sector, there are differences in terms of the areas of application of these competences. In other words, while the same competences may be needed by managers they may require a different level of skill in these competences.

In order to provide further for these sorts of differences the Training Enterprise and Education Directorate developed a subset of the competences required of a manager at level one. This is for use by organizations whose managers at this level do not need to work across the full range of activities cited in the standards.

The changes that the Training Enterprise and Education Directorate has made to the initial model would indicate that there are some important differences between British organizations' competence requirements.

Competence qualifications

The Management Charter Initiative (MCI), which joined forces with the Employment Department to become the lead body on competence standards, is concerned with the development of management in general, starting at the level of the organization and then identifying the needs of the individual. One of the aims of the MCI is to rationalize management qualifications in Britain, introducing a new certificate of competence in management. Nine areas of knowledge and skill necessary for new managers have been identified through consultations with senior managers in organizations involved in the MCI (Hornby and Thomas, 1989). These nine areas are:

1 Identification of the management task
2 Personal skills
3 Effective management
4 Information management
5 Environment of the manager
6 Managing people
7 Managing resources
8 Client/customer relations
9 Personal effectiveness

These nine areas comprise elements of understanding, awareness and observable ability. For example, the successful completion of area (1) 'Identification of the management task', involves competence to describe (showing understanding):

- the management functions performed at the candidates' level of responsibility;
- the contribution that each function makes to the effective working of the organization;
- the levels of responsibility above and below in whatever hierarchies exist;
- how responsibilities change at different levels.

Candidates would need to show awareness of different management styles and need the ability to:

- draw any valid conclusions as to implications for management effectiveness;
- identify and devise a 'map' indicating boundaries of responsibilities within their own organization.

This approach is not unlike many other approaches to assessing competence. The most obvious difference is that the focus here appears to be slanted more towards knowledge elements than observable behaviour. The innovative element of the MCI approach, however, lies in the fact that the definition of competence standards will be independent of the method of learning. This means that the new certificate of competence can be pursued by many different routes including the recognition of prior learning and learning through the workplace.

Competence assessment, therefore, will not always be course based. Candidates will not be required to attend courses covering subjects they are already familiar with in order to gain the new certificate. The MCI approach, therefore, primarily differs from other management education accreditation courses on offer in that it recognizes accreditation of prior learning as a valid means of assessment.

This enlightened approach has also recently been adopted by the Certificate in Management programme within British Telecom. Students on the programme are assessed on competence attainment by a variety of means (not merely written coursework) including the accreditation of prior learning.

Management competence standards in Europe

The Training Enterprise and Education Directorate (then the Training Agency) commissioned a report from Golding *et al.* (1989) to look at standards of management competence in France, Germany, Italy and Spain. The authors found the concept of competence to be relatively unknown in these countries, and discovered no examples of competence standards that could be compared to the work of the Training Enterprise and Education Directorate in Britain. It seems that there is no direct comparison between these European countries and British managerial competences, and hence no evidence for the supposed generic nature of management competences.

Recent competence-based research in European telecommunications companies (Hogg, 1991) also concludes that 'the question concerning the possible generic nature of competences remains unsolved'. Evidence was found to suggest that although threshold competences (those typically needed for effectiveness) were broadly similar across Europe, significant differences were discovered between competences regarded as most vital to effective performance.

Hogg concludes (p. 324) 'The differences observed (between competences regarded as vitally important to effectiveness) could be interpreted as an indication that competence isn't generic across Europe. These differences may reflect differential values and/or differential competence requirements . . . competence could be said to be culture specific rather than generic.'

This research serves to highlight one important point: namely, that threshold competences may be generic whereas competences needed for superior performance may be culture specific, and differ with respect to organization, job function and national culture. This point will be referred to again later in discussion of the possible generic nature of competences that lead to superior performance.

A similar approach to that of the Training Enterprise and Education Directorate was taken by the American Management Association (AMA). AMA has drawn up a list of generic management competences based on extensive research by Boyatzis.

Boyatzis—the McBer research

The competency approach was devised in the 1970s by the US company McBer to identify those personal characteristics which result in effective and/or superior performance within a job. The impetus for the research came from the American Management Association (AMA), the largest management related organization in the United States, with approximately 90 000 members (Powers, 1989). AMA commissioned McBer to find out what makes managers competent and to design a programme where managers could learn these competencies.

This research is documented by Boyatzis (Boyatzis, 1982), who was the President and Chief Executive Officer of McBer Company. McBer studied a sample of 2000 managers, in 41 different types of jobs, in a dozen different organizations, to determine the competences needed by a manager (Evarts, 1987). McBer used the job competence assessment method to determine these competencies (described on pages 34–5).

The objective of the McBer research was to generate a list of every competence that had been shown to relate to effectiveness as a manager, regardless of the specific job and the organization.

Previous job competency assessment studies undertaken by McBer were examined and 'a list was developed' (Boyatzis, 1982, p. 26) of competencies related to effective performance. These competences (a) distinguished (with statistical significance) effective performance in a job, and (b) were not unique to the specific product or service that the organization provided (Boyatzis, 1982, p. 26). This analysis produced a list of 21 types of characteristics which were grouped into six clusters:

- Goal and action management cluster
  —concern with impact
  —diagnostic use of concepts
  —efficiency orientation
  —proactivity

- Leadership cluster
  —logical thought
  —self-confidence
  —use of oral presentations
  —conceptualization

- Human resource management cluster
  —use of socialized power
  —positive regard
  —managing group process
  —accurate self-assessment

- Directing subordinates cluster
  —developing others
  —use of unilateral power
  —spontaneity

- Focus on others cluster
  —self-control
  —perceptual objectivity
  —stamina and adaptability
  —concern with close relationships

- Specialized knowledge
  —memory
  —specialized knowledge

The McBer research found that 12 of these characteristics were found to relate to managerial effectiveness: concern with impact, diagnostic use of concepts, efficiency orientation, proactivity, conceptualization, self-confidence, use of oral presentations, managing group process, use of socialized power, perceptual objectivity, self-control and stamina and adaptability. These were called competencies.

In addition, 'seven characteristics were found to be threshold competencies' (i.e. essential to the job but not causally related to superior performance): use of unilateral power, accurate self-assessment, positive regard (middle level managers only), spontaneity, logical thought, specialized knowledge and developing others (Boyatzis, 1982, p. 229).

At first glance these findings would seem to offer positive evidence for the belief that competences are generic. They even offer support for the view that both threshold competences and competences needed for superior performance are generic. However, the McBer research has a number of limitations which must be considered before one can accept these competencies (and threshold competences) as being generic.

Limitations of the McBer research

Firstly, neither the organizations, nor the managers, in the sample were randomly selected. The sample McBer used was comprised of managers at various levels across 41 functions, from 12 public and private organizations in the United States. There was a distinct bias towards large organizations (four Federal departments in the US government, eight organizations on the Fortune 500 list) which could have affected the results. This biased sample means that generalization to managers in small companies (or other countries) must be undertaken with extreme caution.

Secondly, the McBer study did not obtain information from all 2000 managers at each of the research stages. Some of the analyses were based on small sample sizes which may call the conclusions drawn from them into question. For example, examination of the 'mean skill level' results by managerial level of the sample (Boyatzis, 1982, p. 272) shows that there were only 36 'entry' level managers in the sample, 142 'middle' managers and 75 'executives', totalling 253 managers.

Thirdly, the research analyses then attempted to measure differences between poor, average and superior performers at each managerial level. This resulted in analyses comparing very small sample sizes to each other (i.e. six poor performers to four superior performers at the entry level), and some unreliable results (Boyatzis, 1982, p. 273). Additionally, exploration of the findings within managerial level and function was not segregated by sector (i.e. public vs private sector); therefore, some differences due to level and function may have been obscured resulting in the appearance of a generic model.

Finally, the research lacked an absolute measure of managerial performance against which all managers could be compared. Managers were assessed, as being either 'poor', 'average', or 'superior' by some rather unreliable methods (such as supervisory ratings) against standards prevailing in their own organization. Hence, an 'average' performer, as rated by supervisor A in organization A, may have been rated as 'poor' or 'superior' by supervisor B in organization B. Coupled with the small numbers in some analyses, mentioned above, the reliability and validity of these measures and the conclusions reached can be disputed.

Boyatzis himself (Boyatzis, 1982, p. 48) admits that 'caution in generalizing from these findings and conclusions must be exercised. The findings and conclusions should be considered exploratory not definitive.'

However, the American Management Association used the competencies outlined by the McBer research as the basis for devising a competency training programme designed to teach practising managers to become more effective (Evarts, 1987).

In conclusion, it appears that there is a ground swell of belief in the fact that management competence is generic, but some modifications to the Training Enterprise and Education Directorate's generic model have had to be made in order to accommodate managers in all companies. This suggests that subtle differences exist in competence requirements between British companies. Anecdotal evidence to support this view comes from the observation that managers from one company, although mobile, need a settling-in period when they join another company, and that some large British and multinational companies, including British Telecom, have attempted to research and define competences specific to managers within their own company, defined by their organization's requirements.

Additional evidence suggests that generic competences (on an international dimension) may be those that are typically needed but not directly related to superior performance. It may be that competences which most closely relate to superior performance are those which are most diverse across cultures.

Are threshold competences more generic than competences which lead to superior performance?

Threshold competences Boyatzis (1982) has drawn a distinction between a threshold competency and competencies. This illustrates the difference in approach between the Training Enterprise and Education Directorate (which includes threshold competences in their work) and other competence approaches which concentrate on superior performers. Boyatzis defines a threshold competency as:

a person's generic knowledge, motive, trait, self-image, social role or skill which is essential to performing a job, but is not causally related to superior job performance.

A threshold competency, then, can be summarized as a quality that a person needs in order to do a job, such as the ability to speak the native language. The Training Enterprise and Education Directorate's competence definitions would seem to fall within this definition.

A competency, on the other hand, is an underlying characteristic that differentiates superior performance from average and poor performance (Boyatzis, 1982). This is the sort of competence that many companies are trying to identify to improve performance and results.

In addition to the distinction between a threshold competence and competencies, Boyatzis distinguishes three different levels of a competency. Each competency may exist within the individual at different levels:

* Motives (unconscious), e.g. desire to achieve goals.
* Self-image (conscious), e.g. I am a forward planner.
* Skills (behavioural), e.g. ability to state a goal, form a plan.

It is the authors' opinion that the many different studies involving competence have not made explicit whether they are referring to competence in terms of a 'threshold' competence or in terms of 'that which leads to superior performance'. In addition, most competence approaches concentrate their focus on the skill level of a competence largely at the expense of motive and self-image levels.

It is likely, in the authors' opinion, that threshold competences are largely generic, that is, they will be essentially the same in different companies in Britain (not necessarily globally generic). A basic illustration of this is the need for the ability to be able to communicate in the English language for most jobs in Britain, such language ability or competence is a threshold competence. Managerial competences such as decision making may also fall into this category. Such competences are thought to be generic for two reasons:

1 Many such competences are either presumed by recruiters (English language) of the job incumbents, or appear in the published competency lists (or equivalents, i.e. recruitment criteria, etc.) of many British companies.

An initial literature review by the author (Hogg, 1989) found that certain competencies do appear time and time again in various lists of management criteria or competences. The author found that the most frequently mentioned competences or criteria included: analysis, communication, creativity, decision making, delegation, development of subordinates, judgement, specialist knowledge, leadership, managing people and resources, negotiation, oral presentation, planning and organizing, problem solving, social skills and team membership.

While there are undoubtedly differences in the terminology used, and perhaps also in the behavioural specifics a company would list for each of these, it is not unreasonable to hypothesize that the underlying construct or competence which they are all trying to assess is the same. Early support for this is found in the generic approach of the Training Enterprise and Education Directorate/Management Charter Initiative (1990) and in the work of Dulewicz (1989).

Dulewicz states (1989, p. 59) that 'with more research and some unity of purpose, it should be possible to produce a universal model to explain the majority of common variance between managerial competence at both middle and senior levels'.

2 The underlying need for these managerial competences from different companies is possibly a function of the types of task required of managers. The types of tasks required should be expected to influence the competences required.

If in Britain there is a common managerial culture (as well as individual company cultures) which influences similar tasks to be required of managers (as a function of working in common ways in common situations) it is not surprising that the same threshold competences are specified. Admittedly there are a number of 'ifs' in this argument which would need substantiation before one could be conclusive about this hypothesis. However, it is the same argument commonly used when we hypothesize that management differences exist between countries as a function of the culture of the country. Hofstede (1980) for one has shown that different work values and goals can explain some of the differences and similarities between personnel in different countries.

Competences leading to superior job performance

There are additional complications when considering whether competences which lead to superior job performance may be generic. Such critical competences (identified as crucial or critical factors to job success via critical incident interviewing, for example) may differ between companies. They may be more dependent upon what is unique to the business rather than on what is similar. One example of this type of competence might be awareness of international ways of approaching business deals, which may be needed by only a few managers in a few companies. Ricks (1983) has shown how lack of this competence has contributed to some very critical and costly incidents in the past.

The generic properties of competences leading to superior performance are more difficult to determine. The author would hypothesize that they are not generic, in that they apply to all managerial jobs. They may, however, apply to many managers at the same level or in the same type of job across different companies and hence, in this more limited sense, could be said to be generic. It may be that these competences are the ones which make a real difference both between companies and between managers in different countries.

It is of great use to an organization to determine which competences its managers typically use and need and which are most important to effective performance. Extending this further, before an organization undertakes competence-based assessment it needs to determine a level of focus: whether on typically needed competences or competences needed for superior performance. Organizations with a global focus might also like to consider the generic nature, or otherwise, of their competences, across a range of their managers from different countries, to determine if there are national cultural differences in valued competences, or whether the company culture takes precedence.

Levels of competence

The competencies outlined by the McBer research are, by Boyatzis' definition, underlying characteristics. For each of these competencies the McBer research identified behavioural characteristics expressed at the skill level. In some instances these competences are also identified in terms of the motive or trait level or the social role or self-image dimensions (Powers, 1989).

Recognition of these different levels of competence (or competency) may help to explain differences in research findings. Although most competence studies focus on the observable skills (i.e. the behavioural level of competence) there is an increasing awareness of the conscious and unconscious levels of competence in the work of more progressive researchers and organizations, such as those seeking the label of 'learning organization'.

Advanced competency approaches have taken up the challenge to view managerial competence as the interaction of behaviours and the cognitive processes which underlie them (both conscious and unconscious). These attempts to describe more fully the indefinable essence of effectiveness form some of the more advanced competence approaches of the 1980s and 1990s. Such approaches, founded on the principles of the learning organization, value the underlying characteristics of competences rather than merely their behavioural (and observable) expression. These approaches fall into the second of the two categories outlined on page 33.

Meta-competences and the learning organization

The learning organization concept has grown in popularity in Britain since the 1970s, and now exercises a growing influence among line and human resource managers. The origins of the learning organization can be traced back to Schan's Reith lectures in 1970, in which he outlined a new flexible, ethical and experimental organization with a structure allowing strategy to be formulated and modified as a result of experience. This theme was developed by many other writers, most recently by Garratt (1990) and by Pedler *et al.* (1990).

Companies are heeding the call to be a 'learning company—a company which facilitates the learning of all its members and continually transforms itself' (Pedler *et al.*, 1989). Following this lead, and the increasing emphasis on the learning company, forward-thinking companies are considering competence in relation to personal development. They are moving away from peer and boss ratings, to self-assessment of competence and development needs as part of a continuous learning cycle. Successful managers are those who have not only a repertoire of competences, knowledge and skills, but also the ability to learn from situations, to adapt to changing circumstances, to transfer their competence and to choose and follow a development path for themselves.

Burgoyne defined three categories of competence.

1 Basic knowledge and information:
    (a) command of basic facts, i.e. goals and plans of the organization and product knowledge;
    (b) knowledge of basic management principles and theories;
    (c) technical/professional knowledge.
2 Skills and attributes:
    (a) continuing sensitivity to events;
    (b) analytical/problem-solving/decision-making skills;
    (c) social skills;
    (d) emotional resilience;
    (e) proactivity.
3 Meta-qualities:
    (a) creativity;

(b) mental agility;
(c) balanced learning habits and skills;
(d) self-knowledge.

Burgoyne's argument was that lower level competencies were dependent upon higher level competencies and meta-qualities. Burgoyne emphasized that the priority in managerial development should be to cultivate meta-qualities from which other competences would flow.

- **Meta-competence**—balanced learning habits and skills.
- **Skill/attribute**—continuing sensitivity to events.
- **Basic knowledge and information**—organizational knowledge.

This holistic view of competence is now particularly highly regarded within management development for its consideration of both the complexity of competence and the individuals to whom it is attributed. It demonstrates what Green describes when he says 'Skills are important bricks, but a pile of bricks is no building' (Green, 1986). It is a feature of the latest competence theories that managerial competence is viewed as a product of the whole as much as it is the discrete elements.

Garratt looked at the implications of business trends for senior corporate strategists and executives. He argued that increased competition, cost cutting and the need for quick and flexible responses were affecting management styles and creating a need for different management skills. He saw a need for flexibility, learning and analysis at corporate levels and suggested that a 'learning organization' approach was one way to promote this. He outlined three overlapping levels of learning within an organization: individual learning, group learning and organizational learning. He advocated structures and processes which allowed situations to be assessed, actions to be planned and implemented, outcomes to be reviewed, and learning points to be identified and fed back into subsequent cycles of analysis, action and implementation.

Pedler *et al.* (1989) provide a discussion of the historical evolution of the learning organization. They see it as a rejection of radical action and 'quick fix' approaches adopted by many organizations since the 1960s in response to changing markets, entrenched structures and alienated employees. For Pedler *et al.* the learning organization is experimental, providing a pragmatic and incremental response to change, avoiding radical shifts in corporate direction and policy, and incorporating the views and experiences of an organization's stakeholders into the formulation of corporate strategy. They offer illustrations with a series of 'glimpses' into contemporary applications. The true learning organization probably exists in theory only, and there is little evidence of an example in the pure form which is advocated by the academic writers such as Pedler *et al.*

If a learning organization is experimental, flexible and learns from experience, this places new requirements on the abilities of its workers. The competences for a learning organization are likely to include the following:

1 Learning ability (deutero-learning—Bateson, 1973). This breaks down into three elements: creativity, mental agility and balanced learning habits. These three together allow individuals to fully understand situations, generate creative solutions and learn from experience.
2 Personal flexibility (Pedler *et al.*, 1986). This ability allows people to take on and quickly master new tasks, and respond effectively to changing situations and requirements.
3 Forecasting (Morgan, 1988). This ability incorporates strategic, analytical and forward thinking to anticipate the future.

Morgan writes of the need to identify 'fracture lines' or portents of change in the macro business environment. These might include political, consumer and economic changes.

Learning organization competences include 'softer' skills and behaviours and are sometimes referred to as 'meta-competences'. These are frequently described as the enabling skills, behaviours and attitudes which underpin overall effectiveness. Meta-competences are seen by writers such as Burgoyne as a major contribution to competency-based development and training. They can be used to describe effective behaviours but do not encourage the pursuit of tightly defined micro behaviours at the expense of overall effectiveness. The meta-competency approach assumes that there are many routes to effectiveness. It is receiving growing attention as a counter to current competency definitions which focus attention on details of behaviour, skills and knowledge, often at the expense of overall effectiveness and outcomes. The meta-competency approach is very useful in situations of ambiguity and change. Practical applications have been developed by soft systems methodologists such as Beer (1988).

The development of meta-competences (balanced learning habits and transference of knowledge) should be a priority for companies that wish to lead the field in management development, and utilize their management potential to the full. As a successful manager owes his or her success to ability to learn, so does a successful company. The 'learning company' must also have the ability to learn from past situations, to adapt to change and to follow a path of development. Greater emphasis must be placed on learning and development if a company is to achieve this goal and become a learning organization of the future.

'The problem is to get people to see that the process of development is key to their survival and that of their organisation. All the learning invested and accumulated in many parts of the organisation is of no use unless the people in the middle and at the top of that organisation can value it and turn it into the good of the whole. They have the ability to control, often unknowingly, the climate for, and the flow of, learning in their organisation' (Garratt, 1990, p. 15).

Garratt argues that such middle and senior managers may fail to recognize their strategic role and hence can block the learning cycle. He suggests that in the future the real challenge for 'learning leaders' will be in balancing the management of power groupings (the company's owners, the consumers, the providers and the public) (Garratt, 1990, p. 89). As a learning organization depends for success on its people, the old adage 'people are our chief asset' will need to receive more than lip service in a learning organization. Learning leaders will need to develop a successful relationship with each of the power groupings.

These relationships will need to focus on areas such as: the quality of business performance, to satisfy the owners; the quality of customer service and products, to satisfy the consumer; the relationship between the organization and the physical environment, to satisfy the public; and the quality of working life 'in terms of the balance we can achieve between body, mind, and spirit both at work and at home', to satisfy the providers of the service (Garratt, 1990, p. 90).

The learning organization may depend for its success on the demonstration of competences such as learning, development, quality focus, successful development of customer relationships, and the adoption of a balanced approach to working and personal life. It is interesting to speculate to what extent these competences are demonstrated in the most economically successful and prosperous companies. To date no study has tackled this issue, perhaps because of its enormity, although Moss Kanter (1991, p. 16) claims that, in a recent worldwide survey of companies in 25 countries, she found the most successful organizations 'put the people factor foremost. Growth, profits and expansion were strongly linked to job satisfaction and highly rated skills.'

Techniques for competency definition

The job competence assessment method

The competency approach was devised in the 1970s by the US company McBer. McBer used the job competence assessment method to determine these competencies. This involves the following five stages (Boyatzis, 1982, p. 42):

1 Determination of the appropriate measure of job performance to identify top performers, and collection of job performance data. McBer used three criterion measures of job performance: work output measures; supervisory nominations or ratings; and peer nomination ratings.
2 Job element analysis. This involves generating a list of characteristics perceived to lead to effective/superior performance. Ratings are then obtained from managers to produce a weighted list of distinguishing characteristics, which are then analysed into clusters.
3 Use of the critical incident interview to obtain detailed descriptions of an individual's managerial performance which is then coded, classified and related to job performance data.

4 Choice and use of tests/measures to assess competencies identified in the prior two steps. Relation of scores to job performance data.
5 Integration of the results from steps 2–4, determining (statistically and theoretically) causal relationships between the competencies and between competencies and job performance. This results in a validated competency model.

The objective of the McBer research was to generate a list of every competence that had been shown to relate to effectiveness as a manager, regardless of the specific job and the organization.

Recent approaches to defining competences in British organizations use similar techniques to those listed above, but do not necessarily use all of them. A pragmatic approach to producing company-specific validated competency definitions is described below.

Defining competences

As discussed in Chapter 1, there are four elements that are crucial to an effective development centre:

1 Appropriate criteria (competences) against which to measure participants.
2 Instruments (interviews, exercises and tests) which accurately measure abilities against the appropriate criteria.
3 Skilled assessors who can recognize effective performance as defined by the appropriate criteria.
4 A process for feeding back and using development centre data in order to improve individual and organizational performance.

This section deals with the first of these issues, the identification and definition of the appropriate criteria. Specifically, it explains the various methods for researching and defining competences.

Competency-based training and development has become widespread during the 1980s and 1990s, promoted by the work of the American Management Association and by the Training Enterprise and Education Directorate in Britain. There are many sets of well-researched and valid competences which are readily available. Commercial organizations such as Development Dimensions International (DDI) and government-sponsored bodies such as the training agencies can provide ready-made sets of competences. The advantages of using these as the criteria for measuring performance in a development centre are clear to see:

• Cheap and easy to acquire
• Well researched
• Validated as accurate indicators of effective performance
• Universal applications, used in many different organizations

Commercially produced competences also have their limitations:

• General competences and definitions may not meet the specific needs of an organization which uses them.
• Competency language may not be appropriate for the user organization, e.g. may not support company values and culture.

- Incompatibility with other competency systems used by the organizations, e.g. competences for recruitment or appraisal.
- Static definitions which do not evolve as company needs change.

Many organizations buy commercially developed competency sets from external suppliers because of time and resource constraints, but then experience some of the limitations which are listed above. National Westminster Bank is a typical example, starting with DDI competences and then establishing an internal competency unit to develop the commercially produced set in order to reflect corporate culture, values and business needs in a language which was used throughout the bank. Other organizations such as British Telecom have developed company-specific competency sets using internal experts who have acquired skills of competency research through collaboration with external consultants.

In practice, competency definition is straightforward, and can be carried out by using a few simple techniques. Most professional trainers and personnel managers would already be familiar with these. The rest of this chapter describes processes and techniques for researching and defining company-based competency sets. A fully structured framework can be built, and an example of how this might look is shown in Figure 2.1. This shows one dimension and its competencies and behavioural anchors.

Step 1   Preparation   If competences are descriptions of effectiveness for a particular organization, against which people within that organization can be measured, certain issues need to be addressed before the competency research can begin.

1 What is the target population for whom the development centre programme is intended?
2 Why is the development centre programme being used for this population?
3 Who can give an authoritative statement on what constitutes effective performance for the target population?
4 Are the behaviours and performance which are valued as effective now the same behaviours and performance which will be valued in the future?

Questions 3 and 4 are frequently difficult to answer, and company-based competency research programmes usually overcome them by adopting the following methodologies:

- Identifying people to be interviewed who are widely recognized as 'successful' and 'effective' within the organization. These would usually consist of a range of people: senior managers who can provide a strategic view of effectiveness at the level of the target population; line managers of the target population; representatives of the target population.
- Using interviews to obtain data from these people about what constitutes effectiveness among the target population, both now and in the future.

ANALYSIS AND PLANNING

- Understands the work component parts of issues & processes.
- Can identify relevant themes and patterns which explain and interpret a set of facts.
- Able to define appropriate courses of action.
- Understands process and systems approaches and applies them logically and appropriately so that results meet success criteria.
- Can design efficient and effective systems, methods and procedures, defining priorities and realistic milestones and deadlines.

• Identifies and recommends changes to improve effectiveness.
• Understands processes, procedures and systems affecting own activities.
• Able to analyse issues and problems, and to plan work effectively.

Operational Managers	Managers of Managers	Senior Managers	Directors
Is well-organized & produces plans that work.	Helps customers & colleagues to clarify issues & problems.	Able to identify critical factors effecting performance.	Sets direction of analytical research.
Able to distinguish relevant information.	Makes decisions based upon relevant information.	Prioritizes evidence & finds source of problems & workable solutions.	Sets diagnostic challenges for BT management in line with BT vision.
Employs minimum resources to solve problems.	Clearly defines priorities.	Coordinates systems and process activities within & across functions.	Leads understanding & awareness of people, processes, systems & technology requirements.
Able to integrate systems & procedures.	Sets milestones & deadlines for self & team.	Examines & reviews systems.	Produces workable global strategies.
Helps customers & colleagues to clarify issues & problems.	Works within available resources.	Produces operational plans to achieve function's objectives.	Systematically increases the network's influence & power.
Makes decisions based upon relevant information.	Improves business processes & systems.	Understands relationship between people, processes & systems.	
Clearly defines priorities.	Coaches team to facilitate understanding of BT processes.	Leads effective development of systems & process performance.	
Sets milestones & deadlines for self & team.	Predicts performance accurately.	Predicts time scales & performance accurately.	
Works within available resources.	Ensures implementation plans work effectively.	Produces accurate forecasts.	
Improves business processes & systems.	Reviews progress & is able to adapt plans when necessary.	Quantifies opportunities & risk to BT business.	
Coaches team to facilitate understanding of BT processes.	Able to identify critical factors effecting performance.	Accurately assesses future business trends.	
Predicts performance accurately.	Prioritizes evidence & finds source of problems & workable solutions.	Produces business plans which produce results quickly.	
Ensures implementation plans work effectively.	Coordinates systems and process activities with & across functions.	Seeks fast routes to high performance.	
Reviews progress & is able to adapt plans when necessary.	Examines & reviews systems.	Seeks optimally to meet business requirements & add value.	
	Produces operational plans to achieve function's objectives.	Logically challenges assumptions & strengths corporate plans.	
	Understands relationship between people, processes & systems.	Integrates multi-business objectives.	
	Leads effective development of systems & process performance.	Determines the direction of process development.	
	Predicts time scales & performance accurately.	Creatively optimizes resources.	
	Produces accurate forecasts.	Evaluates best options & decides operational strategy.	

Figure 2.1 The structured findings of competency research for one dimension; analysis and planning

- Seeking ideas from successful senior managers for a strategic view of future skills, behaviours and effective performance levels.
- Seeking ideas from successful line managers of the target population on current effective skills, behaviours and performance levels.
- Seeking ideas from successful members of the target population on actual skills, behaviours and performance levels.

Before interviews are conducted, it is often useful to gain some agreement over which 'successful' people should be interviewed, and to brief them before the interviews take place. A letter or verbal explanation to explain the research project, how and why they were selected for interview, and the format of the interview is very helpful.

Step 2   Interviewing successful people   The purpose of the interviews is to obtain specific examples of effective skills, behaviours and performance required of the target population. The interview techniques should encourage interviewees to volunteer information and thereby reduce problems of interviewer bias. An example interview transcript is included in Figure 2.2, below.

Diagnostic Interview

Date: 19 June 1992   Duration: 40 minutes

What type of sales managers work for you?
Z Managers who manage X managers. I only have one working for me now, but have previously managed six ZM(XM)s. I have also managed units which had ZMs who supervised 'box' salesmen, selling switches and networks such as mega/kilo stream, private circuits, etc.

What are the skills needed to do a ZM(XM) job?

- STRATEGY—to see the sales opportunities in an account, to see the right level to go in at, and to take a long-term view of the customer's needs. I had a bloke (ZM) who worked for me and built up contacts in the 'farm' sector, took our sales from nothing to £2m in 18 months. He saw the opportunities— even in the current economic climate where the public sector operates—and he developed the right contacts. He built a reputation for reliability by delivering what he said he would, by ensuring quality and by offering the right price. Price is only one criterion (we can't be very flexible here and the competition will always undercut us) but we can offer reliability and quality. This bloke got on well with the decision making and provided objective advice on telecoms. He built up trust which led to the sales success over 18 months.
- KNOW THE CUSTOMER'S BUSINESS—what the customer needs to operate effectively and how we can meet that need. My bloke replaced the comms manager of the 'farm' authority by providing business advice on telecoms to the director.
- MAN MANAGEMENT—set clear standards for salesmen, providing coaching and support. He needs to go out with the salesman to the customer's premises and watch the bloke deal with the customer. Good ZMs will review the interaction with the salesman after the meeting with the customer and give coaching on the six steps, etc. My ZM goes out with a salesman once per week. Good ZMs will also arrange with the salesman about his own role in the meeting before they go into it so that the salesman's position with the customer is not undermined. The man management role also means dealing with poor performers. Most ZMs don't like to do this because they rely on the

salesman for bringing in the business and meeting targets—they don't want to antagonize.
- ANALYSIS—they need to be able to understand problems and issues—often complex ones. An understanding of the role of the buyer would be useful—we teach them selling skills but not buying skills and how to deal with them. The field ZM should act as devil's advocate in coaching staff.
- SENSE OF PURPOSE—they need to be able to drive things and take personal responsibility. My FZM had to fight the manager who managed the support staff and the engineering manager in order to get their people to deliver on time for the authority.

You mentioned that the FZMs don't like managing poor performers—what examples can you think of which illustrate this?
Last year I had an old field manager who had six 'box' salesmen. One of the salesmen was a maverick—did everything his own way, wanted the minimum effort. He'd offer discounts which he was not allowed to do and would make all sorts of promises but not deliver them. He made a promise to a solicitor's practice in Kent and then did nothing about it. The solicitor kept phoning the business sales office for information about progress but the salesman, who was out on the road, never responded. The support staff escalated it and eventually it came up to me. I looked into it and found that this bloke always operated in this way—I found six similar current examples of his work. He'd offered discounts contrary to sales policy. I got the field manager in and found that he knew about it but didn't want to do anything about it because:

(a) he did not want to confront the salesman—he was independent, loud and influential amongst other team members;
(b) he didn't know what to do about it.

The field manager just sat quiet and let it happen. He didn't want any trouble; targets were being met (but sales were falling off trees so there was little incentive). I then set up regular meetings with him to review his staff issues. I also called in the salesman and let him have it. I told him that the field manager was going to monitor him and review progress to me. I told him that if there was no improvement in two weeks, I'd have him in the sales office doing a desk job—so he wouldn't be needing his car or his Visa card any more. I knew I couldn't sack him because it would have to go up the line—to John Giles, and I'd have to justify it, but I knew I had the power to take him off the road. He said to me, 'You can't do that'. I said to him, 'Look at my eyes, laddie—do I look like a man who's having you on?' He improved after that.

You mentioned that the field manager didn't want to confront the salesman, was this due to lack of assertiveness on his part?
Yes, certainly. He'd always avoid conflict or dealing with difficult issues.

What did that little incident cost?
In the end we lost the customer's business, worth £1000. There was also time:

1 × support person	2 hours in dealing with an angry customer
1 × field manager	2 hours digging out the details on the salesman
1 × senior manager	2 hours sorting it out, putting in place monitoring systems
1 × salesman	1 hour sorting him out

In time terms that's about one day's work—£100.00.

How typical is this problem of lack of assertiveness?
I was responsible for the national role out of development training and got to see most field managers. About 40 per cent were like this—that is about 50–60. Throughout the UK probably £000s of income are lost through unauthorized

discounts and £000s of time wasted through complaints because field managers will not manage their people because of lack of assertiveness. God knows what else they are doing or not doing because of this.

Are there any other problems arising from lack of assertiveness?
One of the problems I have seen is managers driving themselves too hard. A friend of mine is a field manager—a very good one. He would work all hours, drive his staff by example—they really respected him. He had a heart attack at 44 and was off for two months. He's back now but has slowed down. You can't say that it was due to the job but there is a very strong link. I was a field manager with this bloke—we were in a team of four. Every one of us had heart problems in our forties. It starts with pains in the arms and chest. We all had time off work. I was off for two weeks. It also has a cost in terms of family life. The other week I was at a dinner with six other sales managers from Kent. We were all divorced.

Exercises
Thinks our ideas are OK but look at group exercise—is this realistic? ZMs don't discuss or negotiate targets—they are imposed. Think about another situation. Alternatively, have a coaching session for staff—taking them over the six steps of the sale on a one-to-one basis ('that way we'd find out if they know the six steps').

Group exercise team
Find out from a sales manager the sort of meetings which ZMs have to attend as part of their work, and design a short exercise around such a scenario. This will give us evidence of the inter-personnel/social skills with others in a group setting/persuasion context.

Figure 2.2   Diagnostic interview transcript

Interviewing senior managers for a strategic view   This is probably the most difficult aspect of the data-gathering process because it is often speculative, and senior managers are frequently remote from the target population. The interview usually begins with a brief explanation of the purpose and duration of the interview, and an overview of the interview format.

A useful technique to follow is listed below, and is based on the form which is illustrated in Figure 2.3.

1 Ask for a main or important area of skill or ability in which the target population will have to perform well, either now or in the future.
2 Ask for examples of behaviour which would illustrate that the target population had this skill or ability.
3 Ask for the desired business outcomes as a result of using this particular skill or ability.

Repeat the process until the senior manager has exhausted the list of main areas of skill or ability and then ask for an importance ranking of these areas. Finally, ask the senior manager to identify which main areas will be particularly important for the future, but which are less important now.

Interviewing line managers of the target population   The purpose of these interviews is to obtain information on the actual skills, behaviours

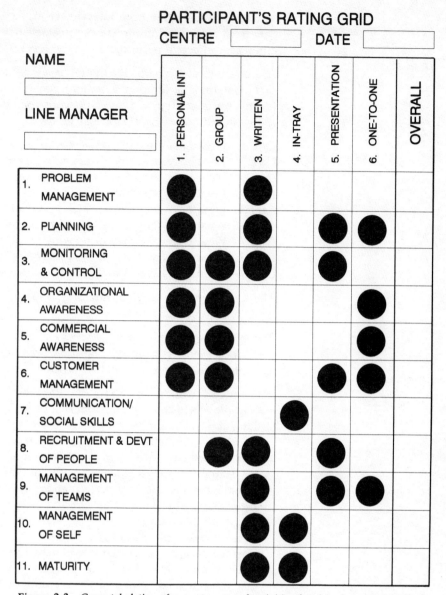

Figure 2.3 *Cross-tabulation of competences and activities (used in design and in final marking)*

and performance of the target population by talking to line managers who are recognized as having effective teams or people working for them. A technique called repertory grid interviews can be used.

Repertory grid interviewing techniques were developed by the American clinical psychologist, George Kelly in 1955. The interviewer remains neutral, asking a series of questions which allow the interviewee to volunteer information on key issues and rate their relative importance. From these data it is possible to understand the personal constructs of the interviewee: what he or she sees as good, bad, effective, ineffective, important, less important, and so on. Data which are generated in this way are relatively free from interviewer bias and can be pooled with the data from a number of interviews to establish a collective view of the criteria for effective performance at the level of the target population.

The interviewer prepares for the interview by producing nine cards, each containing a different statement. Small box index cards are ideal for this purpose. Typical statements contained on the numbered cards (Stewart and Stewart, 1977) are as follows:

Card 1   What have they done which was important?
Card 2   What have they done frequently/spent a lot of time on?
Card 3   What have they done which was important but unplanned?
Card 4   What have they done alone?
Card 5   What have they done which involved other people?
Card 6   What have they done which was important but took little time?
Card 7   What else have they done which was important?
Card 8   What else have they done which was time consuming?
Card 9   What else have they dealt with which was unplanned?

The statements can vary considerably, and will be influenced by the content of job descriptions.

The interviewer begins the interview by explaining the purpose, duration and process, and by emphasizing the confidentiality of the discussion. The interviewer then follows the guidance listed below:

1 Hand each card in turn to the line manager and ask for a specific example of effective action from one of his or her staff which illustrates the statement on the card. The example should be an ACTIVITY—something the individual has actually done. It should not be a responsibility or something that the individual is supposed to do. For example, for card 1: 'consistently met monthly sales target'. This statement is specific, behavioural and measurable, as opposed to more vague statements such as 'an effective sales representative'.
2 Ask the line manager to write the statement on the card. Move on to the next card and repeat the process.
3 Once each card has an example of actual performance written on to it, hand three cards to the line manager. Ask the line manager to say how the activities on two cards resemble each other but are different from the activity on the third card. For example, the line manager may say:

well, consistently meeting monthly sales targets [on card 1] and making regular visits to customers [on card 2] both take commitment and sense of purpose. Whereas coping with a sudden and unexpected lost sale [on card 3] requires personal resilience.

The interviewer would then record:

Commitment/sense of purpose—personal resilience

discussing customer's requirements [on card 5] and giving presentations [on card 6] both require good spoken communications. Whereas completing visit reports [on card 4] need good written communications.

The interviewer would record:

Spoken communications—written communications.

The interviewer can use a simple grid to ensure that the maximum combination of three different cards is used:

```
1  2  3
4  5  6
7  8  9
```

Possible combinations include 1,2,3   4,5,6   7,8,9   2,3,6   6,9,8   8,7,4   4,1,2   1,5,9   7,5,3   1,3,9   3,9,7   9,7,1   7,1,3, etc. In practice, the concentration of line managers begins to decline after about one hour, and the number of similarities/differences begins to be repeated.

If the interviewer is able to record between 12 and 20 similarities and differences per interview, there will be enough data to work with in the definition of competences.

Interviewing the target population   The purpose of these interviews is to cross-check data from the line managers' interviews to ensure that effective skills and behaviours used by the target population, which have not been identified by the line managers, are subsequently identified and incorporated in the competency framework.

Interviews with the target population can also be used to establish examples of the problems and issues which effective members of the target population actually face. These can then be used in designing exercises.

Critical incident interviews are used for the target population. These seek specific examples of significant events which the interviewee has had to deal with. The interviewee identifies them as significant, and then talks about how they were dealt with. The interviewer controls the interview and systematically explores each event by adopting the following procedure:

Situation   What was the situation faced by the interviewee?
Objectives   What was the interviewee supposed to do in this situation?
Action   What did the interviewee actually do?
Results   What did the interviewee achieve?

The interviewer needs to exercise a high level of sensitivity in managing this type of interview since the incidents could reflect on the interviewee's performance. Interviewers should start the interview by explaining the purpose, duration and process, and by emphasizing the confidentiality of the information.

Interviewers can move into critical incidents with questions such as:

Q 'What do you see as the most important part of your job?'
A 'Visiting customers in order to identify their needs, and explain how our products and services could meet their needs.'

Q 'What was the most memorable visit that you made to a customer?'

A 'I had to see the communications manager in XYZ Company Ltd.'

Q 'Why was this particularly memorable?'

A 'We had never managed to sell to this company before.'

Q 'What were your objectives for that first meeting?'

A 'I wanted to establish their requirements, whether they had a budget, who made the decisions to buy, and who influenced the decision maker.'

Q 'How did you prepare for this meeting?'

What constitutes a valid interview sample? It often proves difficult to identify a large number of interviewees and provide a large number of trained interviewers, and the size of the same interview population is often raised as a question. The answer depends on a number of factors:

1 The more homogeneous the work of the target population, the smaller the sample size which needs to be interviewed.
2 The nature of the competences will influence the research techniques, e.g. competences for future 'high fliers' will rely on interviews with senior managers and their assessment of future needs rather than on interviews with the target population to find out what work, skills and behaviours they are using at the moment.
3 The greater the differences between what the target population will be required to do in the future and what it does at the moment, the more select and restricted the research sample will be. In practice, an interview sample size of 30 people would be adequate.

Collecting data from other sources If members of the target population and line managers cannot be interviewed in order to establish data on what effective members of the target population actually do at the moment, competency research will have to consist of analysis of job descriptions of functional analysis.

Job description analysis consists of a careful reading of the job description of the target population, together with an assessment of the effective skills and behaviours which are necessary to complete the main activities.

Step 3   Classifying
the interview data

At this stage of the competency research there will be a number of interview transcripts from senior managers and lists of different skills requirements from the repertory grid interviews with line managers. These data need to be analysed, converted into tentative competences and tested for accuracy by a wider population.

The purpose of step 3 is to produce a tentative list of competences and a competency validation questionnaire. Ideally, this stage is carried out with the help of 5–6 people.

Task 1   The first task consists of copying each of the behaviours from the senior managers' interview transcripts (Figure 2.2 on pages

38–40) on to 'Post-it' stickers (small notelets with a sticky edge for easy adherence to walls, etc.), labelling them 'A'.

Task 2 The second task consists of copying each of the behaviours from the line managers' interviews (recorded by the interviewer) on to a 'Post-it' sticker, labelling them 'B'.

Task 3 The third task consists of copying each of the transcripts from the interviews with the target population, and asking the 5–6 people who are carrying out the work to write each skill or behaviour listed in the transcript on to a separate 'Post-it' sticker, labelling each one 'C'.

Task 4 The 5–6 people then group the 'Post-it' stickers into common themes which reflect the content of the stickers. These form the basis of main competence headings. Between 40 and 80 behavioural statements usually emerge. Writers such as Boyatzis have produced models for classifying competences.

Motives and traits

1 **Motives**. When people have a high achievement motive they respond to situations where performance can be measured and an outcome can be stated. Motives cover competences such as sense of purpose, commitment and motivation.

2 **Traits**. These include thought and psychomotor activity related to a general category of events. For example, when someone with the trait of efficacy encounters a problem or issue, they take initiative to understand the problem or resolve the issue. Traits cover competences such as initiative, flexibility and self-control.

Self-image and social roles

1 **Self-image**. This relates to an individual's self-perception and his or her evaluation of that self-perception. Evaluations are drawn from comparisons with others in the same environment. Self-image is both the concept of self and the labelling of the image in the context of values. Self-assessment might lead people to see themselves as creative and expressive. Their jobs might require them to be organized and self-disciplined. Consequently, as a result of feedback, they might then see themselves as too creative and expressive and with insufficient planning and self-discipline. The realism of the self-image encompasses competences such as personal maturity.

2 **Social roles**. The social role refers to the set of social conventions and norms which an individual perceives as acceptable within the social group(s) to which he or she belongs. The particular social role adopted by an individual is a combination of the characteristics which he or she possesses and of how others expect that person to act. This category includes competences such as communications, social skills and leadership skills.

Skills Skill is an ability to demonstrate a sequence of behaviours that are functionally related to attain a performance goal. Using a skill is not a single action, but consists of a series of actions which collectively contribute towards an individual's ability to function effectively within a given situation.

Skills include competences such as analysis of problems, imagination and creativity in identifying solutions, vision, planning and organizing, and commercial awareness. It is also important to differentiate between tasks and functions.

Boyatzis quotes the example of organizing resources, which requires multiple skills to perform effectively. It involves analytical and planning skills, together with communication and persuasion skills if the outcome is to be successful.

It is usual to emerge with between 6 and 10 main headings. More than 10 competences can cause difficulties of assessment in a development centre. It may also indicate a certain amount of duplication (non-orthogonal competences—competences which are not totally different and mutually exclusive).

The 'Post-it' stickers under each main heading of competence can be checked for duplication and overlap, and duplication can be removed.

Step 4   Draft competency definition

The main headings can then be defined in terms of a summary which explains the content of the 'Post-it' sticker messages listed below. For example,

Analysis—an ability to fully understand problems, issues and complex information. This is demonstrated by . . .

The main headings are the COMPETENCES or areas of competence.

Each 'Post-it' sticker item would then be expressed in terms of an observable outcome. For example,

distinguishing between the causes of problems and the symptoms of problems;

quickly understanding issues in face-to-face discussion.

These are the behavioural statements or behavioural anchors, sometimes called COMPETENCIES, which define each of the main competences.

Step 5   Validating interview data by questionnaires

The draft competency list now needs to be validated by a larger group of people, particularly by line managers of the target population and by senior managers. This is usually completed by using a frequency/importance questionnaire, in which respondents are asked to rate the frequency with which each item (draft competence) is performed by the target population and the importance of each item.

The questionnaire would normally have a key:

Frequency   5 Daily
             4 Weekly
             3 Monthly
             2 Quarterly
             1 Yearly/hardly ever

Importance   5 Vital
              4 Very important
              3 Quite important
              2 Not very important
              1 Not vital

NB   A five-point rating scale such as this should normally have equal strength opposite points, e.g. Vital–Not vital.

The items would normally be expressed in the following way:

Analysis   An ability to fully understand problems, issues and complex information. This is demonstrated by distinguishing between the causes of problems and the symptoms of problems.

              5   4   3   2   1
Frequency   _____

              5   4   3   2   1
Importance _____

In a frequency–importance questionnaire consisting of several stapled pages, it is often useful to photocopy definitions of the rating scale and instructions on to the back of each sheet for easy reference as respondents complete the questions. The questionnaire should also contain space for respondents to comment on the language of the competences and suggest any major omissions.

Many managers are often very busy and fail to complete questionnaires, and a response rate of 50 per cent is good. The response rate can often be increased by:

- making personal requests to respondents;
- providing clear instructions;
- explaining the importance/outcomes;
- setting a deadline for return;
- providing stamped-addressed envelopes;
- gaining visible support from senior managers.

Step 6: Questionnaire analysis

This is in two parts. Part 1 is a simple clerical task of collating scores for frequency importance. It is helpful to give a weighting to each score so that very important or frequent tasks are made more significant for the purposes of analysis. Typical weightings may be as shown in Table 2.1.

Data can be collated using the form in Figure 2.3 on page 41 and an average score calculated for each item. Items which receive a low overall average, say 5 or less, can be deleted.

Part 2 consists of an analysis of qualitative data from the comments contained on the questionnaires. Repeated comments or suggestions from a number of questionnaires indicate a need to amend the wording or content of a particular competence.

Table 2.1 *Questionnaire analysis collation*

Questionnaire score	Weighting
5	×5
4	×4
3	×3
2	×2
1	×1

Summary

At the end of this process, a set of viable company-based competences will have been developed, based on the language, culture and values of the organization. The interviews with successful people provided data on effective skills and behaviours. These were converted into a draft set of competences which were then tested by a questionnaire, completed by a larger population than the interviewees. The questionnaires provided qualitative and quantitative data about the draft competency list which could then be used to make amendments.

Company-based competences need to meet three main criteria:

1 They need to be accurate descriptions of effective behaviours, attitudes and skills, both now and for the future.
2 They need to be expressed in the everyday language of the organization.
3 They need to reflect the values and culture of the organization.

Some of these criteria change over time, and the competences need to be modified and developed in order to reflect organizational change and development.

Management competences in the future

The progress of competence work so far has been charted from the consideration of behaviours, knowledge and skills, to a growing awareness of attitudes, values and the importance of learning to learn. The former could be subject to formal 'objective' measurement, the latter rely more on informal self-assessment for managerial development. Pragmatic approaches to defining management competences for use in development centres have been described.

Competence seems to be moving in two directions simultaneously. The Training Enterprise and Education Directorate is extending its work on competences and attempting to define precise competence standards for most occupations. This very detailed approach is intended to form the basis of recognized qualifications from the National Council for Vocational Qualifications (NCVQ), and certificates of competence based on an assessment of what someone 'can do'.

The second direction follows the work of Burgoyne and emphasizes the importance of the 'learning company' and 'meta-competences', focusing not on formal assessment but on the learning capacities of the individual and the organization, and the self-monitoring of progress and development.

Both are important progressions in this very influential area of human resource activity.

Measuring competence in a development centre

In the course of defining competences and competencies/behaviours on the 'Post-its', we have begun to find potential measures of good and poor performance. The next step is to attach a rating scale to them to create sets of behaviourally anchored rating scales or BARS.

Rating scales need to be clear in their language and of the right length, i.e. not so short as to hinder differentiations of performance, nor so long as to complicate observers' markings. A typical scale would be that shown in Table 2.2.

Table 2.2 *Rating scale for a development centre*

Rating	Interpretation
6	Demonstrates a high level of attainment against the criteria
5	Demonstrates an acceptable level of attainment against the criteria
4	Demonstrates an acceptable level of attainment against the essential criteria, but with some minor development needs in less important/less desirable areas
3	Demonstrates development needs in essential areas in order to meet the criteria
2	Demonstrates development needs in all areas in order to meet the criteria
1	Criteria not met

In the scale in Table 2.2 there is no mid-point to attract observers towards a 'central tendency'. In an assessment centre one could well see '4' removed in order to force a decision.

An essential part of the training is to give the observers an understanding of the competences and behaviours and ensure that they practise using the scale so they converge in the ratings given.

It is also important that they take ownership of the behaviours by discussing them, amending and perhaps adding to them. It would take too long to evolve the behaviours in the training workshop itself, without the start given by those identified in the research. Experience has also taught us not to go through all the competences before practising—from the animated discussion of the first sets, it drops to 'we'll give a high mark if we see it and a low mark if we don't' as tiredness sets in. It is better to sequence practices using mock candidates with the competences that have been agreed, until the full set has been tested. Some sensitivity is needed in the early stages when marks can be wayward.

There has been some controversy about BARS. Jones (1989) dismissed them as based on faith not evidence, and he defined rater reliability in three ways: repetition by coaching; alternate form by different exercises of the same type; and internal consistency reliability, i.e. different exercises testing the same competences. But most research has been positive that BARS increase inter-rater reliability, though it does not eliminate halo and leniency effects.

The forms on which the observers record their findings should be divided, with sections for each of the competences for particular exercises. During the training it often helps to put a list of the behaviours in small print at the top of each box. When the observers have become familiar with these, they can be replaced for the real centres with 'evidence, comments, development suggestions'. Once observers are at the point of classifying as they record, these reminders help to keep them focused on the objectives of the centre. An example of an observer's comment sheet is appended in Figure 2.4.

If the guidance given in Chapter 3 is followed, it should not be a problem to find and rate behaviours. In the Trainer DC cited in Chapter 1, however, it became clear that 'adaptability' and 'helicopter vision' were conspicuous by their absence. Interviews with observers confirmed their difficulty. Hugh Davenport, a BT business psychologist, conducted a full statistical factor analysis which showed that there was clustering—some competences were acting as 'gatekeepers'. Performance on 'analysis' was necessary before participants could hope to show 'innovation' and 'listening skills' were needed before one could 'influence'. Observers were then asked about 'relatedness' to see how they thought they were differentiating between competences: pathfinder analysis then revealed that some observers thought there were 'families' while one observer (one of the editors!) believed all the competences to be separate and equal.

This clustering and the evaluation of performance in separate exercises rather than each competence separately in each exercise brings us to the 'Halo' effect. It is important who is doing the rating as well as what is being rated.

The problems of observer beliefs are well covered by Wexley and Youtz (1985). They first list the findings of earlier studies:

• Knowledgeable, complex raters are less lenient.
• Less leniency does not necessarily produce accuracy.

S M D C

SALES MANAGER DEVELOPMENT CENTRE
GROUP EXERCISE
Marking Frame Page 1 of 2

NAME   **OBSERVER**

PROBLEM MANAGEMENT:evidence/comments/devt suggestions

| rating |

COMMUNICATION/SOCIAL SKILLS:evidence/comments/devt suggestions

| rating |

MANAGEMENT OF TEAMS:evidence/comments/devt suggestions

| rating |

Figure 2.4   Example marking sheet

SALES MANAGER DEVELOPMENT CENTRE
GROUP EXERCISE
Marking Frame Page 2 of 2

NAME   **OBSERVER**

MANAGEMENT OF SELF:evidence/comments/devt suggestions

rating

MATURITY:evidence/comments/devt suggestions

rating

OTHER COMMENTS

rating

Figure 2.4 (continued)

- More accurate raters are more free from self-doubt, are less stressed, have investigative interests and are detail-conscious.
- Accurate raters are emotionally adjusted, have dramatic interests, self-insight and social empathy.
- Lenient observers, like people, are uncritical, self-confident, not highly ambitious and derive job satisfaction from rendering service.
- The better-performing are more reliable and the people-orientated more lenient.

They then applied a wide battery of psychological tests and multiple regression and concluded that rater beliefs about people affected both accuracy and leniency. The lenient have a good general view of people while observers who believe in the variability of people tend to rate more accurately and less leniently. But they confirmed that rater errors and accuracy are not necessarily linked. The study supports the view that raters committing halo and leniency errors may be as accurate.

The distortion seems to be most evident during the end-of-centre discussions and the formulation of overall ratings. Feltham (1988) concluded, after studying assessment centres for police constables, that the 'adjustment' process produced less valid and less efficient results when the results were collected judgementally rather than mechanically. This finding was corroborated by the study of a naval officers' centre and the designers tried to introduce improvements—fewer competences, rigorous assembling of data—to no avail in terms of improvements on predictive validity of overall ratings. They offer as explanations contamination of the competences, performance consistency (as assessors' minds wander from behaviours to 'expected' performance) or that underlying 'managerial intelligence' was being measured, especially in group discussions.

These problems have implications for the training of observers and validation which we will address in Chapters 3 and 7.

Case study: An integrated approach to competences— The Woolwich Building Society

Traditional strengths and values, such as long-standing commitment to give our customers a friendly, efficient quality service, helped to establish the Woolwich as one of the UK's leading building societies. However, increasing pressures brought about by external influences such as legislation, increased competition, reduced markets and the recession, meant that those strengths and values had to be maintained and refocused to help us accept the need to change and become more competitive, more diverse and more results- and achievement-orientated. In short, we needed quality people to manage and work in an increasingly quality-orientated organization.

Training and development has always played an important part in the Woolwich's success and its cradle-to-grave approach was one which fitted the expectations and needs of the organization. Linked to knowledge and understanding of a fairly simple product range and services, driven by inputs rather than linked to outputs, training and development were programme-based and primarily off-the-job and there existed little, if any, linkage to the other human resource (HR) processes. The one major ingredient which did not figure was any evidence of change in either individual or organizational performance or ability to demonstrate improvement in competence. In addition, the various HR processes had been developed by different people, in different parts of the organization, using different start-points—thereby creating misunderstanding and confusion among its internal customers.

To turn this around we needed to define what was expected of staff, in particular our managers, and to ensure that HR practices and processes were formulated to ensure coherence in how individuals contribute to organizational and personal performance competitiveness and success.

Using our own 'Competence Model for Effective Performance', we set about satisfying the requirements of the model—a clear definition of the behaviours required, the expectations and measures of a common set of criteria and a commitment to using them as a basis of an integrated HR approach.

This framework requires that the organization describes the inputs (characteristics, traits, etc.) which an individual must bring to the job as well as the outcomes which the role demands—enabling/personal and functional competences respectively. The former are necessary but not sufficient for effective performance as they merely focus on personal performance and describe the characteristics or behaviours that individuals need to possess. Functional competences are strategic, specify what the current and future role are about and are usually recognized as a benchmark for professional achievement.

In 1989 we started the process but realized that the HR function could not and should not work in isolation from its customers. Top-level support had to be gained for signing on to what was being planned and signing off the final outputs. Benefits had to be sold to line managers across the organization and their commitment to being involved, not merely interested onlookers, had to be gained.

Using the services of external consultants, our own in-house expertise and, most importantly, our internal customers we have achieved the following:

- We have defined generic core enabling/personal competences for junior, middle and senior managers.
- We have used these competences to develop and underpin a career appraisal programme to identify senior manager potential.
- We have built a computer model to create a structured interview format around the key competences in any job for selection purposes.
- We have used the managerial competences to underpin a new performance-related pay system, later defining additional competences for senior/middle technical and administrative staff and also for junior non-managerial staff. Each competence has agreed descriptors and performance criteria against which the individual is measured. Line

managers now have a basis for appraising their staff against the same criteria, which reduces inconsistency and increases objectivity.

- We have used the managerial competences to underpin management development and education programmes (some of which carry external accreditation).
- We have defined and developed functional standards of competence (including both technical and managerial) for district managers. These are linked where appropriate to national standards (Building Society Lead Body and Management Charter Initiative standards).
- We have defined and developed functional standards of competence (managerial) for head office middle managers, linked where appropriate to MCI standards.
- We have defined and developed standards of competence for the branch staff which include NVQ level 2 standards plus Woolwich specific standards.

While not allowing ourselves to be driven blindly by national developments, the standards are carefully reviewed and where they fit the outputs required of a particular role they will be used—customized with accepted Woolwich language if appropriate. Where they do not fit or exist we omit or develop our own.

In addition, a major strategic initiative currently underway is the introduction of personal development planning based on functional standards of competence. Designed as a management tool, the processes are used to develop new starters (either to the organization or the role), to identify and correct under-performance in existing staff and to link an individual's development with the performance appraisal process. The personal development planning system will also be aligned to national standards such as NVQs so that an individual, having successfully completed a Woolwich Personal Development Plan, can convert it to the appropriate level NVQ. This is being made possible by working closely with the external providers to ensure compatibility of evidence requirements.

A competence-based approach allows us not just to satisfy internal needs but, of increasing importance, to comply with new legislation for defining and continually assessing competence of staff who have direct contact with the customer in a sales and advisory capacity.

For the first time we now have a mechanism to identify what an individual needs to do in order to perform effectively and to what standard. This in turn assists in targeting training and development resources to facilitate the design and delivery of both work-based and off-the-job training (including open learning) based on outputs required for the current and future roles.

The next step is to set up a database to record the competence required for the various roles within the organization. As individuals are assessed and signed-off as competent this will be logged, allowing us to track who is competent and to what level. Not only will this allow line managers to provide more objective and constructive feedback to individuals on their development needs and potential, but as an organization we will be able to identify suitable candidates for positions and monitor existing or future skill shortages and requirements.

A competence-based approach provides a challenge not only to the HR function but to the line managers. Defining standards of competence is only the first step. A new dimension to the role of the line manager has been added—the coaching and development of staff is no longer an optional extra. Line managers have to be committed to the approach and trained and coached to recognize and assess competence against organizational and national standards.

While never pretending to be the answer to every prayer, competences are the skeleton on which the flesh and bones of the too often disparate HR processes and systems (from recruitment and selection, job profiling and evaluation, performance measurement and appraisal, career and succession planning, training and development and ultimately satisfying national requirements) can be built into a cohesive whole. The future challenge for the Woolwich is to continue to see this as a strategic and dynamic process which fits current and anticipated needs of the organization.

Competences provide a common language of currency. If the aim is to have a competent, quality workforce the currency must be spent wisely and this requires commitment from the top, understanding from those involved and a willingness to confront and change often devalued processes and practices.

Checklist

1 As the size and complexity of this chapter indicates, it is essential to be clear which levels and definitions are being employed.
2 There are many sources of competency sets ready to hand, but care needs to be taken that the constructs are derived from and are appropriate to an organization.
3 The future of computerized models and meta-competences focused on change may be enlivening—but most of us need to walk before we run for the frontier.

References and further reading

Bateson, G. (1973a) *Steps to an Ecology of Mind*, Paladin, Boulder, Colorado, USA.
Bateson, G. (1973b) 'Towards the Learning Company', *Management Education*, 20.
Beard, D. *et al.* (1988) 'Definitions of Competence', Unpublished internal documents.
Beer, S. (1988) *Diagnosing the System for Organisations*, John Wiley, Chichester.
Boyatzis, R.E. (1982) *The Competent Manager*, John Wiley, Chichester.
Burgoyne, J. (1990) 'Doubts about competences', in M. Divine (ed.) *The Photofit Manager*, Unwin Hyman, London.
Dulewicz, V. (1989) 'Assessment centres as the route to competence', *Personnel Management*, Nov., 6.

Evarts, M. (1987) 'The Competency Programme of the AMA', *Journal of Industrial and Commercial Training*, Jan/Feb.

Feltham, R. (1988) 'Validity of a police assessment centre', *Journal of Occupational Psychology*, 61 (2), 129–44.

Garratt, B. (1990) *Creating a Learning Organisation*, Director Books, Woodhead Faulkner, Cambridge.

Golding, *et al*. (1989) 'Management competence standards in Europe', Training Agency, Sheffield.

Green, S. (1986) 'A critical assessment of RVQ', *Personnel Management*, 18(7).

Hofstede, G. (1980) *Cultures Consequences*, Sage Publications Ltd., London.

Hogg, B. (1989) 'The AMA Competency Programme'.

Hogg, B. (1991) 'European Managerial Competences', MSc thesis, UMIST.

Hornby, D. and Thomas, R. (1989) 'Towards a Better Standard of Management', *Personnel Management*, January.

Jones, A. (1989) 'Assessment centres and measurement efficiency: evaluation of the need for change'. Paper presented at the Fourth Congress on the Psychology of Work and Organisation, Cambridge.

Morgan, G. (1988) *Riding the Waves of Change*, Jossey Bass, San Francisco.

Moss Kanter, R. (1991) 'Companies Need to Have a Global Perspective', *Personnel Management*, May, 16.

Pedler, M., Burgoyne, J. and Boydell, T. (1986) *A Manager's Guide to Self Development*, McGraw-Hill, Maidenhead.

Pedler, M., Boydell, T. and Burgoyne, J. (1989) 'Towards the learning company', *Management Education and Development*, 20, Part # 1, 1–8.

Pedler, M., Burgoyne, J. and Boydell, T. (1990) *The Learning Company*, McGraw-Hill, Maidenhead.

Powers, M. (1989) 'Enhancing Managerial Competence: the AMA Competence Programme', *Journal of Management Development*, 6 (4).

Ricks, D.A. (1983) *Big Business Blunders: Mistakes in Multinational Marketing*, Dow Jones-Irwin, Homewood, Illinois, USA.

Schon, D.A. (1971) *Beyond the Stable State*, Random House, London.

Stewart, A. and Stewart, V. (1977) *Tomorrow's Managers Today*, The Institute of Personnel Management, London.

Training Agency (1990) *MCI Standards on Training*, Training Agency, Sheffield.

Wexley, N. and Youtz, G. (1985) *Organisational Behaviour for the FLMI Insurance Education Program*, Dow Jones-Irwin, Homewood, Illinois, USA.

3 Designing an assessment process: constructing exercises, timetables and materials

David Beard

Introduction

This chapter discusses the techniques for designing a development centre, providing practical guidance for producing exercises and timetables. The guidance is derived from many years of experience in designing development centres for use in BT. This chapter is aimed at training and personnel managers who want ideas and help in designing programmes for use in their own organizations. While the chapter offers logical and structured steps for the design of each stage, it does not purport to be a definitive statement on design issues. There are many routes to effectiveness, and those who design development centre material will evolve their own techniques and processes which fit their own needs and the needs of their organizations. The key message of this chapter is that development centre design need not be difficult as long as three principles are adhered to:

1 Be clear of the objectives and desired outcomes of the development centre.
2 Plan the design carefully in a logical and systematic way before taking action.
3 Test exercises and timetables before general use, and be willing to make amendments in the light of experience.

The chapter is divided into eight sections:

- Introduction.
- Exercises and their uses—an explanation of the various types of development centre exercise that can be used for gaining evidence of participants' abilities.
- Developing exercises themes—a discussion of the sources of information and ideas to construct exercises.
- Exercise design—a practical guide to the way in which development centre exercises can be designed.

- Implementation issues—factors to consider at the design stage such as time limits and difficulty.
- Timetables.
- Case study: Practical applications at Norwich Union Insurance Group.
- Further reading.

Exercises and their uses

Types of exercises

This section looks at the commonly used types of exercise, pinpointing their applications and limitations. There is a finite variety of exercise types, and the main ones are listed below:

- Ice breaker exercises
- Group exercises
- Negotiation, selling and influencing exercises
- One-to-one discussion exercises
- Analysis–presentation exercises
- Planning exercises
- In-tray or in-basket exercises
- Written exercises

Each exercise is discussed in more detail later on in this section, and notes on designing main exercise types may be found on page 73. The problems contained in development centre exercises tend to fall into one of three categories:

1 **Crisis**. Participants are faced with problems which must be resolved within tight deadlines, and where implications of inaction or inappropriate action could be severe. Some in-tray, group and analysis–presentation, one-to-one exercises fall into this category.
2 **Exploitative**. Participants inherit a situation and have to develop or improve it. Some analysis–presentation, group, one-to-one and written exercises fall into this category.
3 **Creative**. Participants have to design, set something up or plan something new. Some planning, selling and negotiation exercises fall into this category.

It is useful to obtain a balance of these three categories in a development centre so that participants are not being asked to undertake the same intellectual activity, albeit in the guise of different problems.

Exercises and competences

The first stage in designing development centre exercises is to look at the competences against which the participants' abilities will be measured. Each exercise can be used to measure the effectiveness of participants against a range of competences, and different exercises provide better opportunities for gathering certain types of evidence than other exercises. A general rule is that group or one-to-one interactions can provide good evidence of social and communications skills, flexibility, sense of purpose and personal maturity. Analytical and planning exercises, often completed as individual activities, can provide good evidence of problem analysis, commercial skills, strategy and imagination.

The competency–exercise grid provides a summary of what each exercise type can be used to measure (see Table 3.1). While each exercise can be designed to provide evidence of ability against a number of different competences, a few rules should be observed:

1 Avoid overloading observers by asking them to obtain evidence against too many competences. A maximum of five competences tested by each exercise is manageable.
2 Ensure that each competence is tested by a development centre exercise.
3 Try to obtain evidence against each competence from at least two different exercises. This will increase the quality and accuracy of the evidence.
4 Prioritize the competences or use weightings to ensure that the most relevant competences for the work of the participant population are tested thoroughly.

Table 3.1 Competency and exercise summary grid

Competence area	Group	Negotiation	One-to-one	Analysis presentation	Planning	Written	In-tray
Analysis		X	X	X	X	X	X
Imagination		X		X	X		X
Strategy		X		X	X	X	X
Planning	X	X	X	X	X	X	X
Communication	X	X	X	X	X	X	
Social skills	X	X	X	X	X	X	
Persuasion	X	X	X	X		X	
Selling	X	X	X				
Commercial		X		X	X	X	X
Numerical				X	X		X
Maturity			X				
Sense of purpose	X	X	X				
Flexibility	X	X	X				
Self-control	X	X	X	X			

Exercise types and development centre objectives

The second stage in exercise design is to ensure that the choice of exercises matches development centres objectives. A development centre to measure the effectiveness of sales staff should include a selling exercise, a development centre for identifying redeployees should include an exercise that measures flexibility and the ability to learn and adapt.

Ice breaker exercises   As discussed in earlier chapters, development centres are designed to facilitate the personal discovery of skills and development needs and to foster a culture of independence in which participants will be motivated to plan and implement personal development activity. Development centres use the same approach as assessment centres, competency-based assessment by skilled observers of the performance of participants in job-related exercises. Consequently, it is useful to emphasize the differences between assessment centres and development centres. For a fuller discussion of the differences between assessment and development centres, refer back to Chapter 1.

An effective way to emphasize the differences is to start a development centre with a short session which covers giving and receiving feedback and the concept of the Johari window. The Johari window is explained in more detail in Chapter 6. This latter point can be referred back to during the one-to-one counselling and feedback session at the end of the development centre. An example of this type of session is contained at the end of the chapter. This type of session has a number of objectives:

1 To place in context the purpose and outcomes of the development centre.
2 To explain the event in terms of individual learning and development as well as an organizational skills audit.
3 To structure expectations and prepare participants for the type and style of feedback.

A short ice breaker exercise can then be used. This usually consists of a group activity and has a number of elements:

1 It should be fun and light-hearted.
2 It should be used to allow participants to get to know each other and the observers.
3 It should be non-assessed.
4 It should follow the general pattern of later exercises so that participants quickly become used to completing such activities.
5 It should enable participants to give and receive feedback about their performance from other participants or observers, and to analyse critically their own performance.

Group exercises   The purpose of a group exercise is to provide a basis for testing the ability of participants to interact effectively with others in order to achieve a desired outcome, and to establish a process which will allow group tasks or objectives to be met. The usual competence areas covered by this type of exercise are:

• communications and social skills;
• sense of purpose;
• flexibility;
• team and leadership skills.

There are several types of group exercise:

1 **Assigned roles**. Participants are given roles to provide clarity and to allow quicker discussion of content issues. Assigned roles can be used to encourage competition or entrenched positions within a discussion, and to see if participants will support difficult positions if forced into a role. Participants' behaviour may be influenced by the need to 'act', and different roles may also have different perceived powers which could also affect behaviour.

2 **Non-assigned roles**. Participants play themselves and normally behave as co-equals. This type of exercise places more emphasis on the need to clarify roles and processes before embarking on a discussion of content issues.

3 **Competitive group exercises**. These contain an element of persuasion, negotiation or selling, and require each participant to convince the others of a particular outcome. Participants generally have an individual brief from which they work, containing some information that is common to all group members and some that is specific to themselves. There may be 'winners' and 'losers' in this type of exercise. It can provide a basis for testing competences such as:
   (a) sense of purpose;
   (b) self-control;
   (c) negotiations skills.

4 **Consensus group exercises**. These require participants with potentially opposing views to come to a consensus decision. They provide an opportunity to test the abilities of participants to place group needs above personal needs, and participate in a discussion which has as its outcome a decision which is supported by all group members.

Negotiation exercises

These can be in the form of a dialogue between two individuals, either an assessor and a participant, two participants, or a role player who is not taking part and a participant. It can often be difficult for observers to participate in a discussion and still provide objective assessment of a participant's performance. This type of exercise can be used with alternative teams of participants. Most negotiation exercises are complex processes which require careful briefing and preparation time. The main competences which are tested by this type of exercise are:

- planning;
- selling, negotiating and persuading skills;
- analytical skills (particularly during discussions);
- sense of purpose;
- flexibility;
- self-control.

Types of negotiation exercise might include the following:

1 **Controlled pace negotiations**. These follow recognized stages (e.g. meet to identify positions, meet to make proposals, meet to respond and make counter-proposals. This type of exercise may require a long

time to complete but can offer observers an opportunity to obtain detailed evidence.

2 **Different outcomes**. Negotiation exercises can be structured to encourage consensus or win–lose outcomes. Consensus outcomes may provide evidence of:

(a) pragmatism;
(b) empathy;
(c) placing group or long-term goals above individual or short-term goals.

Win–lose outcomes may provide evidence of:

(a) planning;
(b) analysis;
(c) sense of purpose.

Most negotiation exercises include assigned roles, with each individual or party working from a slightly different brief.

One-to-one discussion exercises These exercises are usually role play and can provide evidence of an ability to interact effectively with another individual, often over a difficult issue, and to come to an amicable conclusion. The competences tested in this type of exercise may include:

• communications and social skills;
• listening skills;
• empathy;
• sense of purpose;
• maturity;
• persuasion;
• flexibility and self-control.

Two participants are usually given individual briefs in order to discuss a particular problem, which would normally fall into one of the following classifications.

1 **Diagnostic interviews**. These identify a point of view, a set of information or requirements. This type of exercise can be used for consultancy work, selling professional services or staff management skills (discipline, appraisals, etc.).
2 **Counselling**. This type of discussion exercise can be used to measure staff management skills such as coaching, objectives' setting or identifying and correcting substandard performance. The topic of discussion for this type of exercise would normally be a fictitious case study. With some care, real live issues can be used, but these are often difficult to manage in order to obtain consistent evidence of participants' skills.
3 **Instructing and feedback**. This type of role play can be used to measure staff management skills in giving instructions or delegating tasks, agreeing and setting objectives, reviewing and providing feedback on performance. Typical examples include coaching sessions and dealing with substandard performance.

Analysis–presentation exercises This type of exercise usually comes in two parts. The first part consists of individual analysis of a problem which is usually complex, detailed and open to several possible solutions. The participants need to:

- analyse and fully understand the problem;
- identify and evaluate possible solutions;
- complete preparation for a presentation on the problem (causes and symptoms) and the possible solutions.

Competences tested by this part of the exercise may include:

- analytical skills;
- numeracy;
- imagination;
- commercial skills, strategy and vision;
- planning and organizing and time management.

The second part usually consists of a presentation of the outputs from part one to an assessor or group of observers, who then ask questions to establish the depth of comprehension and practicalities of the proposed solution. This part of the exercise may test the following competence areas:

- communications and social skills;
- listening skills;
- analysis (in face-to-face discussion);
- flexibility and self-control.

Planning exercises This is usually an individual exercise in which the participants analyse a problem and supporting information, together with plans for implementing a solution. This type of exercise is useful for identifying the extent to which participants are able to think around commercial problems and strategic issues, and to produce a plan of action which covers short-, medium- and long-term strategies.

Planning exercises usually provide evidence of abilities in the following areas:

- problem analysis;
- financial and numerical ability;
- strategy and vision;
- imagination;
- commercial awareness;
- planning and organizing.

In-tray exercises This is usually an individual exercise in which the participant analyses a problem which is pieced together from a number of in-tray items. The participant identifies degrees of relevance, importance and priorities for each in-tray item. This type of exercise is useful for testing abilities to identify causes and symptoms and to make deductions and inductions. It is also useful for testing ability at seeing commercial and strategic issues. Once the problem has been properly identified, participants are able to look for appropriate short-, medium- and long-term solutions, and to plan ways in which they can be successfully implemented. In-tray exercises can also be used to measure participants' abilities to assess priorities.

Competences which are typically tested by this type of exercise are:

- problem analysis;
- financial and numerical ability;
- strategy and vision;
- imagination;
- commercial awareness;
- planning and organizing.

Written exercises These exercises contain briefing materials which require participants to understand a problem or set of issues, and to demonstrate understanding by drafting a letter or written statement. Written exercises usually provide evidence of the following competency areas:

- problem analysis;
- commercial awareness;
- strategy and vision;
- written communications;
- social skills.

Summary There is no definitive list of exercise types, or of what an exercise type should be used to measure. It is quite possible to produce hybrid types of exercise which are a combination of some of the above. A general rule is that exercises which involve interactions with other people tend to provide evidence of social and communications skills, group process skills and the participant's own qualities such as flexibility and sense of purpose. Exercises which are individual problem-solving activities provide evidence of analytical, strategic and planning abilities. Applications and limitations of exercises are given in Table 3.2.

Biographical interview A well-planned and managed biographical interview can provide data about what participants have actually accomplished in a work-related setting, as opposed to the way in which they solve hypothetical exercises and simulations in a development centre. The interviewer should ask for specific examples of behaviour in each of the main areas of competence related to the individual's personal qualities. Typically, a good biographical interview can provide evidence of actual behaviour in the following areas:

- maturity;
- sense of purpose;
- self-control;
- interpersonal skills.

Biographical interviews can also be used to identify future intentions and career aspirations.

Table 3.2 *The applications and limitations of development centre exercises*

Uses	Strengths	Limitations
Group exercise Measures ability to interact with others	Can be used to test social, communications and personal qualities, also flexibility	Group dynamics may affect the performance of individuals
Can be used with group sizes of between four and six people		Observers may find some difficulty in recording the dialogue
Negotiation, selling or persuading exercise Measures ability to win commitment to a particular course of action or point of view	Can be used to test social and communications skills, selling and personal qualities such as sense of purpose. Some negotiations can be used to test assertiveness, problem analysis and planning	Preparation time can be lengthy The performance of an individual may be affected by the action of the other person in the exercise An outcome to the exercise may take longer than the allocated time
One-to-one exercise Measures ability to gain a shared understanding of a situation and to win commitment to a particular course of action	Can be used to test social and communications skills, empathy, persuasion and delegation	May require some preparation time The performance of a participant may be affected by the actions of a role player or other person in the discussion
Analysis–presentation (a) Analysis Measures problem-solving and decision-making ability. The participants are asked to analyse hard or soft data in order to under-stand a problem and then propose a means for resolving it	Can be used to test problem analysis, commercial skills, imagination, strategy and planning	May require complex problems and data Will require some preparation time, e.g. 1–2 hours Participants are often unwilling or unable to record in full their analysis of all problems and issues. This can make assessment difficult

Table 3.2 *(continued)*

Uses	Strengths	Limitations
(b) Presentation Measures ability to present complex ideas to other people in simple language and within a time limit	Can provide strong evidence of presentation skills, problem analysis, and responding to questions	Time-consuming and difficult to timetable if many participants Observers may need to role play as well as assess Participants' failure to analyse problems may adversely affect the presentation
Planning exercise Measures ability to plan a course of action to resolve problems	Can provide strong evidence of analysis, strategy and planning	Time-consuming to run Participants must be encouraged to draft detailed and legible plans
In-tray exercise Measures ability to understand complex problems, separate causes from symptoms, identify appropriate solutions and plan their implementation. Additionally, it provides evidence of prioritization and time management	Can provide strong evidence of analysis, strategy and planning	Time-consuming to run Participants must be encouraged to draft detailed and legible plans
Written exercise Measures written communications ability, and expression of complex data in simple written form	Can provide strong evidence of communications and social skills, analysis, strategy and commercial skills	Failure to understand the issues may mean that the written communication appears to be incomplete

Table 3.2   (continued)

Uses	Strengths	Limitations
Biographical interview Measures action and effectiveness in real situations rather than in simulations	Can provide strong evidence of the participant's sense of purpose, motivation and self-control in a pressured situation	This form of critical incident interview needs skilled observers who are able to encourage participants to talk about major workplace issues and how they have dealt with them
		Participants need to complete biographical inventories and observers need preparation time

Developing exercise themes

Having identified the types of exercise to use in order to gain adequate evidence against all competences and meet the objectives of the development centre, the next step is to acquire materials and themes for constructing exercises.

Acquiring materials

There are several ways in which ideas and materials for development centre exercises can be acquired.

Diagnostic interviewing

This can often be combined with the competency definition stage. It involves interviewing representatives of the target population of participants to find out what their jobs consist of. If the target population is going to be measured against the requirements of another job, the diagnostic interviews should be carried out with holders of benchmark jobs. The interviews can be of fairly short duration, usually lasting for about one hour. The purpose of each interview would be to:

- identify normal tasks completed by the job holder;
- prioritize tasks in terms of frequency;
- prioritize tasks in terms of complexity;
- obtain recent examples of the main tasks and
- how they were completed.

The key objective of the interview is to obtain examples of recent tasks, issues and problems which are associated with the job, together with a description of the way in which the job holder has managed them. A useful format for this type of interview is contained in Figure 3.1.

DIAGNOSTIC INTERVIEW

Date

INTERVIEWER	INTERVIEWEE
Name:	**Name:**
Work Address and Telephone Number	Work Address and Telephone Number

1. What are the objectives of your job?

1 _____

2 _____

3 _____

2. What are the main outputs of your job?

1 _____

2 _____

3 _____

4 _____

3. What are the main tasks you carry out in order to produce these outputs?

Output 1. [_____]

	Frequency	Rank
Task 1.		
Task 2.		
Task 3.		
Task 4.		

Recent Examples of Task Completion

Situation

Objectives in dealing with situation

Actual behaviours in dealing with situation

Results—what was the final outcome?

Figure 3.1   *Diagnostic interview sheet*

4. What are the main tasks you carry out in order to produce these outputs?

Output 2. [   ]

	Frequency	Rank
Task 1.		
Task 2.		
Task 3.		
Task 4.		

Recent Examples of Task Completion

Situation

Objectives in dealing with situation

Actual behaviours in dealing with situation

Results — what was the final outcome?

5. What are the main tasks you carry out in order to produce these outputs?

Output 3. [   ]

	Frequency	Rank
Task 1.		
Task 2.		
Task 3.		
Task 4.		

Recent Examples of Task Completion

Situation

Objectives in dealing with situation

Actual behaviours in dealing with situation

Results — what was the final outcome?

Figure 3.1 (continued)

6. What are the main tasks you carry out in order to produce these outputs?

Output 4.

	Frequency	Rank
Task 1.		
Task 2.		
Task 3.		
Task 4.		

Recent Examples of Task Completion

Situation

Objectives in dealing with situation

Actual behaviours in dealing with situation

Results — what was the final outcome?

Figure 3.1 *(continued)*

It is also helpful to obtain where possible any examples of in-tray material, correspondence or official documentation relating to the key tasks of the target job. There is no 'right number' of interviews to conduct in order to obtain materials for exercise design. The only criterion is to make sure that sufficient interviews have been carried out in order to cover any range of jobs.

Assessing a job holder

An alternative method for collecting exercise material is to follow a job holder for a day, making a record of the tasks and activities performed during the period of observation. The advantage of this approach over the interview is that the job assessor may emerge with a fuller picture of the job than the interviewer. The disadvantages of this approach are that it can be time-consuming and the tasks completed on the day of observation may not be typical. The job holder may also modify behaviours because of the observation.

The use of themes in exercise design

Having acquired exercise materials, it is often useful at this point to consider the use of themes. Every good exercise has a number of standard components:

1 **A role for the participant**. Participants are asked to assume that they are a manager, sales person, consultant, etc., or themselves for the purpose of the exercise.
2 **Organizational framework for the role**. Participants are told where or for whom they are working.

3 **Problem**. There is an explanation of the problem, issue or concern that participants need to resolve within the exercise.

4 **Task**. Participants are told of the required actions or outcomes on which their performance will be measured.

Development centre exercises can use a common theme throughout, in which case the role and organization will be the same for each exercise. The advantages of this approach are:

- enhanced realism;
- easier exercise construction;
- a developing problem across exercises.

Some disadvantages might be:

- a bad experience in one exercise may contaminate participant's performance in subsequent exercises;
- a developing theme may impede effective measurement of ability in all areas of competence;
- knowledge of the problem contained in one exercise may confuse participants in subsequent exercises.

Our experience in BT has shown that carefully developed themes can work well. Recent examples include a development centre for sales managers. An underlying theme of poor team performance due to previous inept sales team leadership was developed across three exercises:

1 **Analysis/presentation exercise**. Participants identified what was going wrong, what actions needed to be taken to redeem the situation, and which team members were under-performing against sales targets.

2 **Counselling exercise**. Participants undertook a one-to-one review and counselling interview with a poorly performing sales team member.

3 **Group exercise**. Participants discussed a joint approach as team leaders to resolving the skills deficit among their team members.

Thematic exercises are appropriate where the background of participants and the jobs which they will be doing in the future are both homogeneous. If these criteria are met, a common theme across all exercises will not give a consistent advantage to particular participants at the expense of other participants. An alternative approach to a common theme across all exercises is to make each exercise a discrete and separate activity, unrelated to all the others. This is useful for measuring effectiveness against a heterogeneous set of skills. Examples include high potential for the future, where participants come from a range of backgrounds and would probably work in different functional areas in the future.

Face validity

A third consideration in acquiring and using exercise materials is that of face validity. Face validity refers to the element of realism within exercises. Participants and observers need to feel that the situations, problems and tasks contained within the development centre have an element of realism, reflecting the actual tasks completed by participants now or in the future.

Development centres can be designed so that they have high predictive or criterion validity, but this will not necessarily convince those associated with the programme if there is no element of realism in what participants are being asked to do as well.

Language This is the fourth consideration in exercise design, and is closely related to face validity. It is important that appropriate language is used to describe situations, problems and tasks within the exercises. The language should reflect that which is used by the participants. Language becomes a particular problem in development centres used for functional specialists, where technical vocabularies are used. A pitfall that BT development centre designers fell into recently was with a development centre for the sales force. Jargon words had specific meanings for the sales force, and were in everyday use. These meanings were often radically different from *Oxford English Dictionary* definitions. Considerable confusion arose for participants when the designers used these words in a non-sales context. As a result, we always check our use of language with subject experts within the organization which will be using the development centre.

Exercise design

Effective development centre exercises can be designed quickly and efficiently by trainers and personnel managers, using easy-to-hand materials and problems which have high levels of face validity. A few basic rules need to be observed:

1 Identify which competences are to be tested by which exercise, and that key competences are adequately tested by the range of exercises.
2 Plan the exercise carefully using the planning pro forma (Figure 3.2) before working on the detail.
3 Have a clear set of objectives for each exercise.

Exercise planning pro forma Time invested in planning each exercise is well spent. A well-planned exercise tends to work effectively and will not need subsequent modifications and corrections. The BT development centre design team has evolved a simple planning pro forma which helps designers clarify key issues (Figure 3.2).

Designing written exercises Written exercises usually require participants to draft a written communication, expressing detailed, complex or technical information in a way that a non-expert can easily understand. Typical subjects for a written exercise include drafting a letter of reply to a customer or complainant, drafting an article for publication and providing written instructions. Participants are usually given background information about the problem or issue and a brief which explains what is expected of them. A good written exercise usually tests intellectual abilities such as problem analysis and commercial awareness as well as communications and social skills. Consequently, an effective written exercise will follow certain design conventions:

DEVELOPMENT CENTRE EXERCISE DESIGN PRO FORMA

DC Programme [_____]

DC Exercise Title [_____]

DC Designers [_____] **Date** [_____]

1. Competences Tested:
1. _____
2. _____
3. _____
4. _____
5. _____
6. _____

2. Exercise Objectives:
1. _____
2. _____
3. _____
4. _____

3. Time Allocation (Participants)
Preparation Time _____
Completion Time _____

4. Participant:
Role _____
Organization _____
Problem _____
Task _____

5. Exercise Outputs:
(Completed by Participant)
1. _____
2. _____
3. _____
4. _____

6. Observer's Role: _____

7. Observer's Activities:
1. _____
2. _____
3. _____
4. _____

8. Time allocation (Observers):
Preparation _____
Briefing _____
Other _____
Marking _____

Figure 3.2 DC design pro forma

9. Role Player: Role _____

Organization _____

Problem _____

Task _____

10. Role Player Activities: 1. _____

2. _____

3. _____

4. _____

11. Time Allocation (Role Players) Preparation Time _____

Completion Time _____

12. Documentation — Participants:

1. _____	9. _____
2. _____	10. _____
3. _____	11. _____
4. _____	12. _____
5. _____	13. _____
6. _____	14 _____
7. _____	15. _____
8. _____	16. _____

13. Documentation — Observers:

1. _____	6. _____
2. _____	7. _____
3. _____	8. _____
4. _____	9. _____
5. _____	10. _____

14. Documentation — Role Players:

1. _____	6. _____
2. _____	7. _____
3. _____	8. _____
4. _____	9. _____
5. _____	10. _____

Figure 3.2 (continued)

1 It will contain about five issues which the participant has to identify from the background materials and deal with in the written communication.
2 It will provide possible solutions to some problems, but these will be embedded in the support materials and the participant will have to identify them.
3 It will contain difficult and unpalatable problems with no easy solution which participants will have to face up to in the written communication.
4 It will require the participant to follow normal social conventions for presenting difficult information.

Written exercises usually last for between 50 and 75 minutes. They are easy to administer and observers use standard marking guidance to assess the drafts. They are particularly effective as a means for measuring participants' abilities at dealing with customers.

Assessors' guidance for this exercise would include all of the data which the participants use. Additionally, observers would have marking guidance which would list:

- items that must be included in a good written draft;
- additional items that would appear in a very good draft;
- items that should be excluded from a good draft.

These can be identified during the assessor training. Details are contained in Chapter 7.

Designing in-tray exercises

In-tray exercises typically contain a number of related items which collectively explain a problem. Participants sort through the in-tray paperwork, piecing together the information in order to understand the problem in its entirety. This usually includes causes and symptoms. Participants have to plan a course of action to deal with the problems. Most in-tray items also contain individual problems associated with each item. These also have to be dealt with. A typical in-tray exercise lasting for about an hour or an hour and a half would contain 12–15 items. The time limit would normally include planning a course of action. This enables observers to assess the participant's ability to set priorities and to plan action over short-, medium- and long-term planning horizons.

An in-tray exercise can be constructed by following a few simple rules.

1 Identify the main problems and issues on which the participants will need to be tested, e.g. staff management, interpretation of numerical or financial data, resolving conflicting demands on resources.
2 Identify a work-based situation that will encompass most of these problems and issues.
3 Plan a framework of interlinking in-tray items which require participants to cross-reference between various items in order fully to understand the problems.
4 Collect or design data such as memos, letters and statistics which will form the basis of each in-tray item.

A typical design framework for an in-tray exercise is illustrated below:

Role. The participant plays the part of a new project manager.
Organization. The participant is now working for a small subsidiary which designs and markets high technology communications equipment for personal and business use.
Problem. The participant has been seconded as a replacement for a former colleague who was project manager for a new 'videophone' project. The former manager was absent due to sick leave. This caused the project to fall behind budget and schedule. The six staff do not seem to be working efficiently.
Task. This is the participant's first day in the new job, and the accumulated in-tray has to be dealt with.

In-tray items

Item 1	Letter from equipment supplier threatening to cease today further supplies needed for production if outstanding invoice not paid. Linked to items 6 and 7.
Item 2	Letter of resignation from chief technician on the project— unhappy at lack of leadership. Linked to items 9, 10 and 11.
Item 3	Letter from potential customer requesting a demonstration on a date quoted by previous project manager. Linked to items 5 and 13.
Item 4	Budgetary data showing that the project is under-spending in some areas and over-spending in others, such as overtime.
Item 5	Memo from managing director asking for planning meeting, clashes with date on item 3.
Item 6	Memo about invoice from supplier, indicates problem with deliveries. Links to item 1.
Item 7	Solicitor's letter representing another supplier who has not been paid. Links to items 1 and 6.
Item 8	Newspaper article about video telephones, outlining Japanese entry into the market and the race for an industry standard.
Item 9	Time sheets to sign, showing high overtime. Linked to item 4.
Item 10	Monthly reports showing work behind schedule. Linked to items 4 and 9.
Item 11	Memo from chief technician complaining at laziness of some project members, that he was having to do their work as well as his. Linked to items 2 and 10.
Item 12	Complaint from customer about the way in which one technician had behaved during demonstration. Linked to items 2, 10 and 11.
Item 13	Details of an important trade fair, clashing with dates on items 3 and 5.
Item 14	Memo from finance director about delays and inaccuracies in financial data/payment due to computer error in previous month (does not explain item 1).
Item 15	Staff records, showing that some have a poor record of attendance, meeting objectives and excessive overtime claims. Linked to items 2, 10, 11 and 12.

Assessors' guidance for this exercise would include all of the data which the participants use. Additionally, observers would have marking guidance which would list:

- details of the links between each in-tray item;
- effective ways of dealing with individual items;
- underlying problems and issues that a good participant would identify by making links between items.

These can be identified during the assessor training. Details are contained in Chapter 7.

Designing analysis–presentation exercises

Analysis–presentation exercises require participants to analyse a situation and then present their findings. The analysis usually has two parts.

Problem analysis

Understand a current problem or situation   Typically, this is done by reading a number of documents in order to understand a problem or related problems. The documents usually contain a balance of 'hard' factual data and 'soft' data where participants make informed judgements. This usually leads participants to a fuller understanding of the current situation that they face.

Identify and plan action to resolve the problem or situation   This requires participants to identify the required state of efficiency or effectiveness for the future, and to identify the most efficient means of achieving this state. Good participants will identify various options, undertake some form of solution effect analysis, be aware of wider strategic issues, and undertake some form of implementation planning.

Presentation

This involves a presentation by the participants, showing their understanding of the problem and their suggestions for resolving it. The skill requirement for this activity is a combination of intellect and communication. Most presentations also include time for questioning participants. The sophistication of the presentation will depend on preparation time. Typically, they would include flipchart presentations lasting 10–15 minutes, followed by 15 minutes of questions. Analysis–presentation exercises are quite straightforward to design. The key stages are as follows:

1 Establish the main problems and issues with which the participant has to deal. These can be listed in terms of causes, symptoms and linked issues.
2 Collect or design documentation which explains these problems and issues.
3 Establish a context in which the participant will resolve the problems and issues, i.e. a role, organization, problem and task.

An example of an analysis–presentation design is listed below.

Role. The participant plays the part of a new project manager.
Organization. The participant is now working for a small subsidiary

which designs and markets high technology communications equipment for personal and business use.

Problem. The participant has been seconded as a replacement for a former colleague who was project manager for a new 'videophone' project. The former manager was absent due to sick leave. This caused the project to fall behind budget and schedule. The six staff do not seem to be working efficiently.

Task. This is the participant's first day in the new job, and the accumulated in-tray has to be dealt with.

Problems and issues

1 Under-performing team members, demonstrated by:
   (a) hard data on performance and output;
   (b) soft data including complaints, vague objectives, poor supervision, no training.
2 Lack of budgetary and financial control:
   (a) hard data on income and expenditure, impending bankruptcy;
   (b) soft data on unpaid bills, unpaid invoices.
3 Poor production control:
   (a) hard data on product lines and production which conflict with data from marketing;
   (b) soft data on specific customer requests and indications that production will cease due to lack of materials.
4 Poor staff morale:
   (a) hard data on staff turnover;
   (b) soft data including resignation letters and poor quality accommodation.

Participants use the data to identify underlying causes such as poor leadership, poor staff management and the absence of effective management information systems. They identify short-term actions to redress immediate problems and longer-term actions to deal with the fundamental problems of poor management. Ideas are then presented, using a format left to the participant's own choosing, or a format outlined in the exercise instructions.

Assessors' guidance for this exercise would include all of the data which the participants use. Additionally, assessors would have marking guidance listing:

- details of the links between each issue;
- effective ways of dealing with individual issues;
- underlying problems that a good participant would identify by making links between issues;
- a list of questions to ask after the presentation.

These can be identified during the assessor training. Details are contained in Chapter 7.

Designing planning exercises

These are a variant of the in-tray and analysis–presentation exercises. Participants are asked to assimilate a range of data and then to plan a course of action. As discussed earlier in this chapter, development centre exercises generally fall into one of three broad categories: dealing with crises, exploiting situations and creating new systems and opportunities. Planning exercises tend to fall into the creativity classification since they provide participants with the opportunity to develop new ways of working.

Planning exercises are straightforward to design if a few basic rules are followed.

1 Establish the main problems and issues with which the participant has to deal. These can be listed in terms of broad objectives, opportunities and desired outcomes.
2 Collect or design documentation which explains these problems and issues.
3 Establish a context in which the participant will resolve the problems, i.e. a role, organization, problem and task.

An example of a simple planning exercise design is listed below.

Role. The participant plays the part of a new project manager.
Organization. The participant is now working for a small subsidiary which designs and markets high technology communications equipment for personal and business use.
Problem. The participant has been seconded from his or her usual job in order to plan the production and marketing of a revolutionary new video conferencing product. A prototype has just been developed by the R&D team. This is the participant's first day in the new job.
Task. The managing director has asked for a detailed project plan for the production and marketing of this new product.

Supporting data

Item 1	The video conferencing system needs a special network, and data showing a breakdown of network installation costs is included on a geographical basis.
Item 2	A list of potential customers, together with their geographical locations in the United Kingdom. This can be used in conjunction with item 1 for calculating network installation costs. The demand from each potential customer can be used in conjunction with item 3 to calculate production costs.
Item 3	A breakdown of component volume supplies and costs, which can be used to calculate the most efficient production levels.
Item 4	Warning of interruptions to production capability in the fourth financial quarter due to machine installation and maintenance programmes. This is the period of greatest customer demand, as indicated by item 2.
Item 5	*Financial Times* cutting which illustrates the threat posed by the Japanese competition, together with the need for a European standard and the possibility of a big order for the EC Commission in Brussels.
Item 6	Staffing data, indicating difficulties in obtaining skilled production staff.
Item 7	Urgent request from marketing for advanced warning on sales and marketing strategy.

Item 8   Income and expenditure forecasts for the next year, indicating an urgent need for more short-term working capital.

Participants analyse the data and complete their plans for production and marketing, dealing with any other issues which are important. Observers often experience difficulty in marking a planning exercise because of the potentially different formats adopted by participants. It can be helpful to provide a standard 'planning form' for the participants' answers. These would normally be divided into columns which are headed up with titles such as short-, medium- and long-term actions, objectives and desired outcomes.

Assessors' guidance for this exercise would include all of the data which the participants use. Additionally, assessors would have marking guidance listing:

• details of the links between each issue, and the appropriate action to take;
• effective ways of dealing with individual issues;
• underlying problems that a good participant would identify by making links between issues.

These can be identified during the assessor training. Details are contained in Chapter 7.

Designing selling, influencing and negotiating exercises

These exercises are interactive and usually require role players. They can vary in complexity, and usually require some preparation time for participants to assimilate information and to develop objectives and strategies. Participants usually work alone during the preparation stage. It is often useful to design a preparation period which requires participants to list their objectives and strategies for the interaction so that a comparison can be made after the exercise between what the participant planned to do and what actually happened. Any differences between planning and implementation can be explored in a feedback or counselling session.

The qualities and abilities which are measured in this type of exercise are usually planning, process and communications skills. Consequently, it is often helpful to make the problem which forms the content of the interaction as straightforward as possible. A few basic design rules are listed below:

1 Identify which competences are to be tested by this exercise.
2 List the skills and behaviours associated with each competence which could be observed.
3 List the activities that the participant would complete during the exercise in order to demonstrate effectiveness in the required skills and behaviours.
4 Identify a problem or task that would enable the participant to demonstrate the behaviours.
5 Devise a context within which the participant could deal with this problem.

Table 3.3 *Measurement of competences in exercises (I)*

Competences	Behaviours	Activities and outcome
Selling skills	• Explain own position • Identify other's position • Explain benefit • Deal with objections • Gain commitment • Close sale	Sell video conferencing
Social skills	• Listen to other's point of view • Show understanding of other's point of view • Empathy	Maintain goodwill and effective working relationships with customer
Communications	• Speak clearly, concisely and fluently • Ask open and probing questions	Express own views clearly
Sense of purpose	• Complete task in spite of difficulties	Agree sale
Flexibility	• Adapt own style to meet needs of 'customer' • Remain calm and effective in the face of difficulties	Complete task

An example of this approach is illustrated in Table 3.3.

The problem or task would be to sell video conferencing services to the communications manager of a large multinational company based in the United Kingdom. The context would be:

Role. The participant plays the part of a member of the sales force.
Organization. The participant is working for a small professional sales force of an independent company which designs and produces high technology communications equipment for personal and business use.
Problem. The participant has been invited to meet the communications manager of a large UK-based multinational company seconded from his or her usual job in order to explain and sell a new state-of-the-art video conferencing system.
Task. The participant has to sell the product by explaining own position, identifying the position of the other person, explaining benefits, dealing with objections, gaining commitment and closing the sale.

Assessors' guidance for this exercise would include all of the data which the participants use. Additionally, assessors would have marking guidance listing:

- details of the six steps of a sale;
- effective ways of dealing with each stage.

These can be identified during the assessor training. Details are contained in Chapter 7.

The role player who plays the customer would have details about the customer's organization, requirements and possible objections. The role players would be told to treat all participants in the same way and to agree a sale if the participant met certain criteria.

Designing group exercises

Group exercises test the abilities of participants to work with others in order to achieve certain objectives. The competences best tested by this type of activity are team membership, team leadership, interpersonal and communications skills and personal qualities such as sense of purpose and self-control. Group exercises are comparatively easy to design but tend to be more difficult for observers to assess. There are a few simple design rules to follow:

1 Identify which competences are to be tested by this exercise.
2 List the skills and behaviours associated with each competence which could be observed.
3 List the activities that the participant would complete during the exercise in order to demonstrate effectiveness in the required skills and behaviours.
4 Identify a problem or task that would enable the participant to demonstrate the behaviours.
5 Devise a context within which the participant could deal with this problem.

An example of this approach is illustrated in Table 3.4.

The problem or task would be to gain group consensus for three candidates to be selected from a group of ten to be interviewed for a special project.

Role. The participant plays the part of a member of the project management team.
Organization. The participant is working for a small research and development team which is designing and producing a high technology communications video conferencing product for personal and business use.
Problem. The participant has been invited to meet with other project managers in order to select three job applicants for interview. The applicants each have strengths and weaknesses as potential project team members. The only available data are the applications forms, of which every participant has a copy.
Task. The participant has to identify own preferred candidates in pre-meeting preparation and list them on a form, together with a strategy

Table 3.4 *Measurement of competences by exercises (II)*

Competences	Behaviours	Activities and outcome
Team membership and leadership	• Clarifying group objectives • Suggesting or supporting a group process to achieve objectives • Monitoring group progress against objectives • Monitoring the success of the agreed process • Summarizing • Checking time • Bringing in others	Participate in defining objectives and process
Persuasion skills	• Explain own position • Identify other's position • Explain benefit • Deal with objections • Gain agreement	Persuade other group members that one particular candidate is best
Social skills	• Listen to other's point of view • Show understanding of other's point of view • Empathy • Checking understanding by summarizing and clarifying	Maintain goodwill and effective working relationships with other group members
Communications	• Speak clearly, concisely and fluently • Ask open and probing questions	Express own views clearly
Sense of purpose	• Complete task in spite of difficulties	Agree group consensus candidate
Flexibility	• Adapt own style to meet needs of group • Remain calm and effective in the face of difficulties	Complete task

for convincing the other team members. Participants then enter a group discussion to convince others of their own choice but ultimately to reach a group consensus decision on the short list of three.

Assessors would have the same information for this exercise as the participants. Additionally, observers would have marking guidance listing:

• examples of effective behaviour for each of the competences tested;
• a summary of the advantages and disadvantages of each candidate.

These can be identified during the assessor training. Details are contained in Chapter 7.

The role player who plays the customer would have details about the customer's organization, requirements and possible objections. The role players would be told to treat all participants in the same way and to agree a sale if the participant met certain criteria.

Designing a counselling or one-to-one exercise

This type of exercise can be used to test the participant's abilities to manage a discussion of a sensitive issue such as poor performance. The exercise is usually in two parts. The first part consists of individual preparation in which the participant reads the briefing papers, identifies objectives desired for the discussion and prepares a strategy. The role player can also use this time for familiarization with the problem and the desired responses. The participant's objectives and strategy can be written on to a standard form before the discussion and compared with the final outcome at the end of the exercise. Any differences between planned and actual action can be discussed with the participant during the feedback session. The second part of the exercise involves a discussion with the role player who works from standard notes.

Design of this type of exercise is straightforward and follows a few standard rules:

1 Identify which competences are to be tested by this exercise.
2 List the skills and behaviours associated with each competence which could be observed.
3 List the activities that the participant would complete during the exercise in order to demonstrate effectiveness in the required skills and behaviours.
4 Identify a problem or task that would enable the participant to demonstrate the behaviours.
5 Devise a context within which the participant could deal with this problem.

An example of this approach is illustrated in Table 3.5.

The problem or task would be to gain group consensus for three candidates to be selected from a group of ten to be interviewed for a special project:

Role. The participant plays the part of a manager.
Organization. The participant manages a small, specialist research and

Table 3.5   *Measurement of competences by exercises (III)*

Competences	Behaviours	Activities and outcome
Meetings Leadership	• Clarifying meeting objectives • Suggesting and agreeing an agenda • Monitoring progress against agenda and objectives • Summarizing • Checking time • Confirming agreement	Leadership in defining the objectives and agenda
Persuasion skills	• Explain own position • Identify other's position • Explain requirements • Deal with objections • Gain agreement	Explain current position, show required standard and current shortfall. Gain agreement to the way forward
Social skills	• Listen to other's point of view • Show understanding of other's point of view • Empathy • Check understanding by summarizing and clarifying	Maintain goodwill and effective working relationships with other person
Communications	• Speak clearly, concisely and fluently • Ask open and probing questions	Express own views clearly
Sense of purpose	• Complete task in spite of difficulties	Agree way to improve performance
Flexibility	• Adapt own style to meet needs of others where possible • Remain calm and effective in the face of difficulties	Complete task

development team which is designing and producing a high technology communications video conferencing product for personal and business use.

Problem. A member of the team is not working effectively, and is failing to meet crucial deadlines and objectives. This is causing hold-ups in the project, and is also badly affecting the morale of other team members.

Task. The participant has to meet the team member, explain what is happening, find out why, and agree a plan of action to raise performance to the required level.

Assessors would have the same information for this exercise as the participants. Additionally, observers would have marking guidance listing:

- examples of effective behaviour for each of the competences tested;
- a summary of the desired outcomes from the discussion.

These can be identified during the assessor training. Details are contained in Chapter 7.

The role player who plays the under-performing team member would have details about the role, together with some possible reasons why performance might be substandard. The role players would be told to treat all participants in the same way and to agree a plan for improvement as long as his or her issues are dealt with as well.

Biographical interviews
These have hitherto been discussed as part of the range of exercise instruments which are available to test participants' abilities against the development centre competences. The design of biographical interviews, and more particularly the skill with which observers manage them, is the subject of Chapter 4.

Implementation issues

Time limits for exercises
Experience provides a good basis for making judgements about the time allocation for each exercise. The precise time will be determined by a number of factors. These include:

- complexity of the exercises;
- available time slots within the timetable;
- the number of exercises contained within the development centre timetable;
- concentration levels of participants;
- the requirements for specific evidence of abilities.

Typical exercise durations are listed in Table 3.6.

Table 3.6 Typical exercise timings

Exercise	Time (minutes)
In-tray exercise	60–90
Analysis–presentation	
• Analysis	60–90
• Presentation	20–30
Planning	60–90
Written	50–60
Selling, negotiating	
• Preparation	30–45
• Meeting	20–30
One-to-one meeting	
• Preparation	30–45
• Meeting	20–30

The second, more detailed timetable is completed after the exercises have been designed and piloted. This usually consists of a participant's version which details the sequence of events which they complete for the duration of the development centre. A separate assessor's version contains the same timetable information that the participants receive. It also contains information about development centre introductions, briefings and marking of exercises, and providing final feedback. Further timetables are produced for workshop secretaries and role players.

The main components of a development centre timetable are shown in Table 3.7.

The main principles of timetable construction are as follows:

1 Ensure that the development centre is designed for an even number of participants (6–12 is the norm). The numbers affect dynamics of a group exercise, and six is the largest practical size for a group exercise. A participant number of more than six will require two group exercises.
2 Ensure a ratio of one assessor to two participants.
3 Give numbers to the participants (1,2,3,4 . . .) and letters to the observers (A,B,C,D . . .).
4 Ensure that participants have a continuous sequence of activity so that they are not left with nothing to do at any point (rest and reflection are useful but need to be balanced against perceptions of 'wasting time').

Table 3.7 *Example timetable*

---

1   Introduction
    objectives
    process
    ownership and use of data
    competences and exercises
    participants
    observers
    role player and secretary

2   Exercises: three or four are usually included

3   Biographical interview

4   Psychometric tests

5   Feedback and development planning interview

---

5   Ensure that observers use participants' preparation time to mark the previous exercise.
6   Ensure that every assessor sees every participant in at least one development centre activity.
7   Ensure that role players are used efficiently and have some recovery time between role plays (they can forget questions easily 'Have I asked you this . . . or did I ask the last participant . . .?').
8   Ensure that all exercises end during the middle of the afternoon of the final full day so that observers can get up to date with their marking and assessment and review the performance of each participant.
9   Ensure that adequate time is available for the feedback and development planning interviews on the final morning or final day.
10 Ensure that participants who are waiting for a final feedback interview with their personal assessor, or who have completed the final feedback interview and are waiting for the development close have some task to occupy them.

The example timetable illustrated in Table 3.8 is for a three-day development centre for 12 participants. It is run by six observers and a psychometric test expert. The timetable is in two parts, with a version for both participants and assessors.

Table 3.8 (a)   *Example timetable for participants at a development centre for sales managers*

Day 1

11.00   Introductions
  • Participants and observers
  • Objectives
  • Outcomes
  • Confidentiality

11.45   Principles of feedback
  • Johari window
  • Giving and receiving feedback

12.00   Occupational Personality Questionnaire (OPQ)

12.30   Lunch

1.30   Group exercise
  • Briefing
  • Individual preparation

1.50

Group A	Group B
Participants	Participants
1,2,3,4,5,6	7,8,9,10,11,12
Assessors	Assessors
A,B,C	D,E,F

2.30   Review with assessor

Assessor A:	1 then 2	Assessor D:	7 then 8
B:	3 then 4	E:	9 then 10
C:	5 then 6	F:	11 then 12

3.00   Tea

3.15   Biographical interviews

A interviews 12	D interviews 6
B interviews 10	E interviews 4
C interviews 8	F interviews 2

1,3,5,7,9,11 complete GMA–N tests

4.00   Biographical interviews

A interviews 11	D interviews 5
B interviews 9	E interviews 3
C interviews 7	F interviews 1

2,4,6,8,10,12 complete GMA–N tests

5.45   Close

Day 2

8.40   Assemble

8.45   Overview of the day

9.00   Analysis–presentation exercise
- Briefing
- Individual analysis

10.30   Coffee for 1,3,5,7,9,11

10.30   Analysis–presentation exercise

Presentations

2 presents to D	8 presents to A
4 presents to E	10 presents to B
6 presents to F	12 presents to C

11.00   Coffee for 2,4,6,8,10,12

Presentations

1 presents to D	8 presents to A
3 presents to E	9 presents to B
5 presents to F	11 presents to C

11.30   Stress seminar
- Causes
- Symptoms
- Coping mechanisms

12.30   Lunch

1.30   Written exercise
- Briefing
- Individual preparation and completion

2.30   Tea

2.45   One-to-one staff counselling exercise
- Briefing
- Individual preparation

	Role player A	Role player B
Assessor A	3	
Assessor B	5	
Assessor C	7	
Assessor D		9
Assessor E		11
Assessor F		1

2,4,6,8,10,12 complete GMA–V tests

4.00   Tea

4.15

	Role player A	Role player B
Assessor A	4	
Assessor B	6	
Assessor C	8	
Assessor D		10
Assessor E		12
Assessor F		2

1,3,5,7,9,11 complete GMA–V tests

5.30   Close

Day 3

8.40	Assemble
8.45	Overview of day
9.00	Psychometric test feedback
10.00	Feedback interviews

A interviews 12   D interviews 6
B interviews 10   E interviews 4
C interviews 8   F interviews 2

1,3,5,7,9,11 receive 30 minute individual psychometric feedback

11.30	Feedback interviews

A interviews 11   D interviews 5
B interviews 9   E interviews 3
C interviews 7   F interviews 1

2,4,6,8,10,12 receive 30 minute individual psychometric feedback

1.00	Lunch
2.00	Review and close

Table 3.8 (b)   *Example timetable for observers at a development centre for sales managers*

	Participants	Assessors
Day 1		
11.00	Introductions • Participants/observers • Objectives • Outcomes • Confidentiality	Introduction managed by assessor A. All other observers attend
11.45	Principles of feedback • Johari window • Giving and receiving feedback	Managed by psychometrician
12.00	Occupational Personality Questionnaire (OPQ)	Assessors prepare for biographical interviews
12.30	Lunch	Psychometrician scores/ interprets OPQ
1.30	Group exercise • Briefing • Individual preparation	Briefed by Assessor B

1.50   Group A discussion (50 minutes)

Participants	Assessors
1,2,3,4,5,6	A,B,C

	Participants	Assessors
	1.50 Group B discussion (50 minutes)	
	Participants 7,8,9,10,11,12	Assessors D,E,F
2.30	Group exercise review with assessor	
	Participants 1 then 2	Assessor A
	3 then 4	B
	5 then 6	C
	7 then 8	D
	9 then 10	E
	11 then 12	F
3.00	Tea	
3.15	Biographical interviews	
	A interviews 12	D interviews 6
	B interviews 10	E interviews 4
	C interviews 8	F interviews 2
	1,3,5,7,9,11 complete GMA–N tests	Managed by psychometrician
4.40	Biographical interviews	
	A interviews 11	D interviews 5
	B interviews 9	E interviews 3
	C interviews 7	F interviews 1
	2,4,6,8,10,12 complete GMA–N tests	Managed by psychometrician
5.45	Close	
Day 2		
8.40	Assemble	
8.45	Overview of the day	Managed by Assessor A
9.00	Analysis–presentation exercise	
	• Briefing	Briefed by Assessor C
	• Individual analysis	Assessors write reports on biographical interviews
10.30	Coffee for 1,3,5,7,9,11	
10.30	Analysis–presentation exercise	
	Presentations	
	2 presents to	Assessor D
	4 presents to	Assessor E
	6 presents to	Assessor F

	Participants	Assessors
	8 presents to	Assessor A
	10 presents to	Assessor B
	12 presents to	Assessor C
11.00	Coffee for 2,4,6,8,10,12	
11.00	Presentations	
	1 presents to	Assessor D
	3 presents to	Assessor E
	5 presents to	Assessor F
	7 presents to	Assessor A
	9 presents to	Assessor B
	11 presents to	Assessor C
11.30	Stress seminar	
	• Causes	Managed by
	• Symptoms	psychometric expert
	• Coping mechanisms	
		Assessors mark analysis presentation
12.30	Lunch	
1.30	Written exercise	Briefed by Assessor A
	• Briefing	Assessors mark
	• Individual preparation and completion	analysis presentation
2.30	Tea	Assessors mark written exercise
2.45	One-to-one staff counselling exercise	
	• Briefing	Briefed by Assessor A
	• Individual preparation	

3.15	Role player A		Role player B
	Assessor A	3	
	Assessor B	5	
	Assessor C	7	
	Assessor D		9
	Assessor E		11
	Assessor F		1

	2,4,6,8,10,12 complete GMA–V tests
4.00	Tea

	Participants	Assessors
	Role player A	Role player B

		Role player A	Role player B
4.15			
	Assessor A	4	
	Assessor B	6	
	Assessor C	8	
	Assessor D		10
	Assessor E		12
	Assessor F		2

1,3,5,7,9,11 complete GMA–V tests

	Participants	Assessors
5.30	Close	Assessors mark one-to-one exercise
7.30	Dinner	

Day 3

	Participants	Assessors
8.40	Assemble	
8.45	Overview of day	Managed by Assessor A
9.00	Psychometric test feedback (group)	Managed by psychometrics expert
		Assessors' conference preparation for final feedback interview
10.00	Coffee	
10.15	Feedback interviews	

A interviews 12		D interviews 6
B interviews 10		E interviews 4
C interviews 8		F interviews 2

1,3,5,7,9,11 receive 30 minute individual psychometric feedback

	Participants
11.30	Feedback interviews

A interviews 11		D interviews 5
B interviews 9		E interviews 3
C interviews 7		F interviews 1

2,4,6,8,10,12 receive 30 minute individual psychometric feedback

	Participants	Assessors
12.45	Lunch	
1.45	Review and close	Managed by Assessor A

Case study: Practical applications at Norwich Union Insurance Group

Background

In 1988, the Life Society of the Norwich Union commissioned a newly formed internal organization development team to help with the improvement of some of the existing personnel processes. This was felt necessary because of an awareness that some of these processes were no longer meeting actual needs and were not as effective as they could be. The areas needing the most urgent attention were in management selection and development, and manpower and succession planning. In addition, most of the training taking place tended to be prescriptive and not delivered on the basis of identified need. The brief was to investigate and analyse the current state, design and implement improved appropriate processes and evaluate the results. The recommendations acted upon included the introduction of assessment centres (to improve management selection), and proposals for development of managers involving needs-based management training and development.

The overall aim was to interlock the whole in order to create a pool of management talent available for future management jobs. Development centres played a key part through helping existing and future managers to identify their own learning needs relative to the needs of the current or future job, in conjunction with their own line manager. The key to maximizing effectiveness was felt to be centred around participants having some personal input into their own development to help stimulate a motivation to learn together, with active involvement from the line manager. The objective was to move the organization towards a learning culture.

Design and implementation

The centres were designed to help identify the learning needs of groups of people, usually numbering eight, who were at a peer group level in the same type of job. In designing the centre content, a competency-based approach was first used; the competences being identified by a critical incident process with the sponsoring line manager to elicit the specific knowledge, skills and attitudes needed to function well in the job.

Simulations were designed from other information supplied by the sponsoring line manager based on current 'live' major issues and problems of the day to create relevance to the work that participants actually did. This information was also gathered using critical incident methodology.

The centres were comprised of large and small group discussions, management exercises and simulations, presentations and a self-report, self-score development questionnaire. Between each simulation or exercise, candidates undertook some guided reflection from a set of written questions which focused them on their own performance in the exercises/ simulations and the learning needs that became evident. Feedback was available from the process facilitators and attending line managers who were trained in observation and feedback skills to ensure that feedback given was sensitively handled.

The process relied in part on the participants being open about their discovered learning needs and also being open to constructive feedback. In order to facilitate this, participants were taken through the principles behind the Johari window model as a way of illustrating the process they were about to undergo. Participants were invited to 'self-disclose' where they felt they needed to improve in the way of knowledge, skills and attributes and then to combine these data with 'feedback' made available to them by those observing their performance.

Practical learning points

What went well and has been maintained

- High involvement of participants in identifying their own learning needs (including use of a reflection process).
- Working in pairs 1:1 to help each other; excellent in inducing openness especially when at same peer level.
- Use of focused follow-up workshops to address learning needs shortly afterwards to ensure that developed motivation is not lost in delay.
- Exercises, discussions and simulations that mirror job tasks.
- Practical solutions to existing work problems are often uncovered in the focused group discussions and used by line managers in improving work processes.
- Involvement of the line manager in the design and delivery of the centre.

What we are now doing differently

- Participants given a full brief on the process well before the centre and competencies being observed are declared 'up front'. Greater initial openness to help allay participants' concerns and to foster reciprocation.
- One-to-one feedback immediately after each exercise; learning is reinforced before it is lost.
- Generic competencies now exist for all management jobs (as part of a recently introduced performance management system); competency identification before event design is now much less time-consuming.

The future

Work is currently ongoing in the following arenas:

- Further innovation and research into development centre design.
- Introduction of development centres to other parts of Norwich Union Insurance Group.
- Creation of 'career development centres' for those at a definable

career crossroads (e.g. project manager or information technology consultants) taking into account:
—individuals' preferences;
—line management views on individuals' capabilities.

This event is likely to consist of a more formalized area of assessment (with assessors observing behaviours) together with opportunities to identify participants' personal strengths and limitations to help towards a successful career 'fit'.

• Introduction of development committees for senior management career succession.

Further reading

Further information about the design of development centre materials is contained in the following publications.

Gill, R.W.T. (1979) 'The in-tray (in-basket) exercise as a measure of management potential', *Journal of Occupational Psychology*, 52, 185–97.
Goodge, P. (1988) 'Task-based assessment', *Journal of European Industrial Training* 12 June.
Stewart, A. and Stewart, V. (1981) *Tomorrow's Managers Today*, Institute of Personnel Management, London.

4 The use of interviews and biographical questionnaires

Tricia Marchbank and David Beard

Introduction

This chapter discusses the use of interview techniques and biographical questionnaires in a development centre programme. It looks specifically at the current debate about interviewing for selection and development, much of which focuses on the validity of interviews as the basis for predicting future job performance. The discussion moves on to applications of interview techniques within a development centre, particularly the use of interviews to collect data on participants' past performance and to identify career aspirations. There then follows a description of the main interview techniques which can be used as part of a development centre programme. The chapter ends with a reading list.

This chapter is divided into seven short sections:

- Introduction
- Current debate on the use of interviews
- Situational and simulation interviews
- Critical incident interviews
- Aspirations interviews
- Workplace questionnaires and biodata
- References and further reading

Current debate on the use of interviews

The widespread use of interviews as a tool in the selection and assessment of people, particularly in Britain, has prompted considerable debate about the effectiveness of the technique. Hunter and Hunter (1984) estimate that 99 per cent of British companies use interviews at some point in their selection and development processes, as opposed to less than 40 per cent which use ability tests, personality questionnaires or assessment centres.

Hunter and Hunter calculate that the predictive validity of unstructured interviews, their accuracy in predicting subsequent job performance, is very low, and quote correlation coefficients of 0.14. This would indicate that unstructured interviews produce decisions which turn out to be accurate in 14 per cent of cases. Herriot (1988), commenting on the widespread commitment to interviewing, suggests that this reflects both a general confusion over the purpose of interviews on the part of interviewers, and an expectation that interviews are a social process. He concludes that organizations 'do not adopt selection procedures primarily because they are valid'.

During the last decade, occupational psychologists have explored ways in which interviews could become more accurate predictors of subsequent workplace performance. Weisner and Cronshaw (1988) looked at the degree of structure on interview validity. They identified two elements that contribute towards a more accurate interview—reliability and criterion-related validity.

1 **Reliability**. An interview has to be a reliable process for collecting evidence and making a decision about an interviewee's abilities. Reliability means that two interviewers using the same process to interview the same person would produce the same overall assessment rating. Alternatively, one interviewer who interviewed the same interviewee, using the same process but at two different times, would produce the same rating on both occasions.

2 **Criterion-related validity**. An interviewer has to collect information about the interviewee's work-related abilities. Consequently, the questions which are asked during an interview need to be highly relevant to the requirements of the target job.

Weisner and Cronshaw conclude that an interview cannot be valid if it is not reliable. That is, interviewers need to be clear about the reasons for conducting the interview and the process for conducting the interview before it can produce data which will lead to accurate predictions about workplace performance. Problems of reliability occur when the interviewer is unclear about the purpose of the interview. This often leads to biases in assessment. Anderson and Shackleton (1990) investigated the impact of interviewer bias in selecting university graduates for managerial work. They discovered that interviewees' non-verbal behaviour contaminated the interviewer's decision-making processes, and led to decisions based on self-image perceptions (the interviewee was perceived as similar to the interviewer), personal bias and stereotyping. Smith *et al.* (1979) also discuss the problems of interviewer bias. They suggest that interviewers typically reach a decision after 4–5 minutes, and that they are unduly influenced by earlier or later discussions during the interview. These tend to focus on memorable topics, and so interviewers fall victim to the 'primacy-recency effect'.

Weisner and Cronshaw's work suggests that a highly structured interview, in which the interviewer asks specific work-related questions, results in more accurate decisions than unstructured interviews. They also found that predictive validity increases if the interview is conducted as a 'board', with two interviewers who discuss the evidence and reached a consensus decision at the end of the interview.

Wright *et al.* (1989) look at structured situational interviews, and conclude from meta-analysis studies (aggregated statistical data from a number of small sample studies) that this form of interview is a more accurate predictor of subsequent job performance than unstructured interviews. Wright *et al.* quote correlation coefficients of between 0.47 and 0.54.

Situational interviews consist of a 'series of job-related questions with pre-determined answers that are consistently applied across all interviews for a particular job' Wright *et al.* (1989). They produce four types of question which are commonly found in such interviews:

1 Job knowledge questions, which test specific knowledge that is needed to complete a particular task.
2 Situational questions, which test the interviewees response in a particular work situation.
3 Job simulation questions, which ask interviewees to discuss how they would complete a work-related task.
4 Work requirement questions, which cover more conventional interview topics such as mobility and availability for work.

The process for defining situational and simulation questions is described below on pages 102–5.

Structured situational interviews described by Wright *et al.* are useful techniques for identifying the way in which interviewees would resolve hypothetical problems. The limitations of this approach are discussed by Janz (1982) and Orpen (1985), who argue that this does not provide evidence of the way in which interviewees have resolved real workplace problems. Janz developed an alternative form of structured interview which he termed patterned behaviour description interviews (PBDI). These consist of a set of standard questions relating to specific work-related situations. Interviewees are asked to describe the way in which they have dealt with these situations in their recent work experience. Orpen tested the predictive validity of this approach in a study of insurance sales staff and found a correlation coefficient of 0.54 between interview rating and subsequent job performance.

Structured interviews tend to have higher predictive validity for the following reasons:

1 Interviewers have a clear idea about the purpose and process of the interview, and are consequently less subjective in their decision making. This makes the interviews more reliable.
2 Structured interviews (particularly situational interviews) are based on job needs. Consequently, candidates are asked to provide evidence of their abilities in work-related areas. Latham *et al.* (1980) suggest that even with hypothetical questions there is a strong relationship between interviewees' intentions in the interview and actual behaviour in the workplace.

In the development centre context, interviews can provide useful data about a participant's abilities. In particular, interviews have value in identifying skills and abilities for future work at a different level or in a different function. Situational interviews, in the hypothetical form discussed by Wright *et al.*, or in the biographical format identified by Janz, can prove to be very useful. Additionally, the critical incident interview format can be used. This is based on the work of Flanagan (1954), and requires that interviewees identify specific and significant workplace situations from the recent past, and then describe how they behaved within those situations. This type of interview is less structured than that described by Janz, but operates on the same assumption that previous relevant behaviour is a good predictor of future behaviour in similar work situations.

Situational and simulation interviews

Situational interviews ask candidates a standard set of questions in order to gain evidence of their abilities to resolve work-related problems. Consequently, some care is needed in the research and design of these interviews so that appropriate job-related questions are asked. There are five steps to the design of a set of situational interview questions. This will produce a bank of about 20 questions, and between 5 and 10 would be used in an interview of 60 minutes. The number and choice of questions would be determined by the participant's background and experience. The five steps are listed below.

Step 1 A careful job analysis is carried out by interviewing a range of job holders, all of whom are perceived as effective, in order to identify important tasks, situations and problems within the job. Flanagan's critical incident interview technique can be used in order to gain descriptive data (see Chapter 2). The number of interviews will be determined by the consistency of the jobs: if the jobs are similar, a smaller number of interviews will be needed. If 20 critical incident interviews are conducted, and each interviewee identifies three critical incidents, 60 job-related critical incidents will be identified. The incidents will undoubtedly include some overlap, and the 20 most frequently quoted cases can be retained for further design work.

Step 2 Having collected data on 20 typical and significant workplace issues, the information now needs to be checked for accuracy, and model answers need to be identified, ranging from very effective to ineffective responses. This is done by producing a written statement of each of the 20 critical incidents which includes:

• the job;
• the situation faced by the job holder.

The data are then sent to the group of job holders who provided the critical incidents. They are asked to check the accuracy of each of the 20 situations or items. They are then asked to produce a description of an effective response, an average response and an ineffective response to each situation. This information provides the raw data for designing a rating scale, against which the interviewee's responses will be assessed.

Step 3   The interviewees' responses are then grouped so that all of the good responses, average responses and ineffective responses are clustered for each situation. A standard rating scale of 1–10 (1 = low and 10 = high) is added to each of the effective, average and ineffective responses for each statement. The data are sent back to the job holders, who are asked to rate the responses using the 1–10 rating scale. Any response which has a difference of more than 3 on the rating scale can be eliminated.

Step 4   The situations, responses and rating scales can then be produced as assessors' guidance for conducting the situational interviews. It is more appropriate to ask questions about situations with which the interviewee has no direct experience so that problem-solving techniques can be identified. There will probably be some need for interviewer training in order to use the technique effectively.

An example of a question in a situational interview might be:

'A member of your team has been seconded to work on an important project team managed by one of your colleagues. Your colleague casually mentioned to you that the secondee was not playing a very active role in the new team and was withholding information from other project team members. What would you do?'

Step 5   The interviewer would then listen to the answer, relate it to the appropriate model answer listed under 'effective', 'average' or 'ineffective', and give it an appropriate rating. The rating scale which has been described is a behaviourally anchored rating scale (BARS). This is described in more detail in Chapter 2.

Critical incident interviews

Critical incident interviews   Critical incident interviewing techniques were pioneered by Flanagan. They are based on the principle that identification and discussion of a few 'critical incidents' in the life of an interviewee will provide accurate evidence about the way in which that person is motivated and behaves, and thus provide the basis for predicting future behaviour in similar situations. This approach is based on a number of assumptions:

1 That patterns of behaviour and motivation remain fairly constant over time.
2 That an individual's approach to one critical incident is not situation-specific, but is based on personal values, attitudes and behaviours.
3 That an individual's behaviour in a non-work situation may have

parallels with work performance, and provide the basis for predicting performance in the work arena.

Biographical interviews

Many development centres use critical incident techniques in order to identify the performance of interviewees during significant events in their work or careers. These interviews discuss past behaviours and are often referred to as biographical interviews. They are frequently used as part of the data-gathering process, and provide evidence of workplace performance which can supplement the evidence gained from performance measured by the development centre exercises. Trained interviewers question participants about their recent workplace performance in areas of critical incidence, and use the criteria rating scale to assess performance against the competences which are being used. This approach provides evidence of actual performance in a workplace setting which supplements evidence of performance in hypothetical, but realistic, simulations. The data from biographical interviews are particularly relevant to the subsequent discussions about the participants' career aspirations.

Objectives of biographical interviews

The biographical interview differs from the exercises on the development centre in so far as it is not a simulation. It complements the exercises and plays a crucial role in obtaining evidence on the participant's performance in key areas of competence.

Development centre simulations, such as the group exercises, are not always suitable for making reliable assessments of qualities such as energy, determination and self-control, the ability to set one's own goals, and adaptability. Evidence of personal qualities and traits such as these may not always be accurately assessed. Evidence which is gained through performance in exercises is often influenced by the attendance at the workshop. For example, a quiet participant may not contribute a great deal in a group discussion exercise because the situation and the participants are unfamiliar but the biographical interview may reveal considerable abilities in similar types of activity in the workplace.

Competences tested in the biographical interview

Biographical interviews can be a rich source of evidence of abilities in competences which reflect personal qualities such as motivation, ability to cope with stress and maturity. They can also be used to measure ability to form effective working relationships, reflected by competences such as social skills and leadership.

Competences which are typically assessed during the interview are:

- Social and communications skills
- Team leadership skills
- Sense of purpose
- Flexibility
- Self-control
- Maturity and realistic self-image
- Adaptability to change
- Learning ability

Preparation for a biographical interview

Before attending a development centre, participants are often asked to complete a biographical interview form. The instructions ask the participant to be as specific as possible about actual incidents that occurred and that are relevant to the competences. In particular, participants are asked to write details of their actions and the outcome. These are brought to the development centre, and used by the observer and the participants as the basis for discussion during the interview. A typical form is illustrated in Figure 4.1 and biographical interview forms are discussed later in this chapter.

GRADUATE
DEVELOPMENT CENTRE

PERSONAL INTERVIEW

YOUR NAME	DATE

INSTRUCTIONS

- Please answer all of the questions and, while doing so, bear the following points in mind:
- Keep to the point, do not go into fine detail and try to keep within the space provided.
- Complete the full set of questions, taking your time and using your own words.

YOUR PRESENT JOB

Tell us briefly about your present job.

What do you do and what are you meant to achieve in your work?

The questions that follow ask for relevant examples from your own experience.

- The examples you give must relate to things **YOU ACTUALLY DID** — be precise about **YOUR** contribution to the event you are describing.
- The examples mainly refer to work but you may, if necessary, give relevant examples from your experiences outside work. These could include social, family leisure or educational.
- If you put something on the form, however, you should be prepared to discuss it in more detail.

Remember, for each example, you must state:

- What you did.
- How you did it.
- What the outcome or result was.

Figure 4.1 Personal interview form

REMEMBER ● WHAT DID YOU DO? ● HOW DID YOU DO IT? ● WHAT WAS THE RESULT?

PLANNING & ORGANIZING

Planning & organizing is essential to ensure successful outcomes.

Please give an example that illustrates your skills in this area.

TEAM & LEADERSHIP

It is important that sales & marketing people are able to work as members of a team.

Please give an example of an occasion when you had to work with a group to achieve a significant group result.

COMMUNICATION SKILLS

Communication is a key skill in sales and marketing.

Please give an example of a time when you have had the responsibility of explaining a complex situation proposal to one or more people.

Figure 4.1 (continued)

REMEMBER ● WHAT DID YOU DO? ● HOW DID YOU DO IT? ● WHAT WAS THE RESULT?

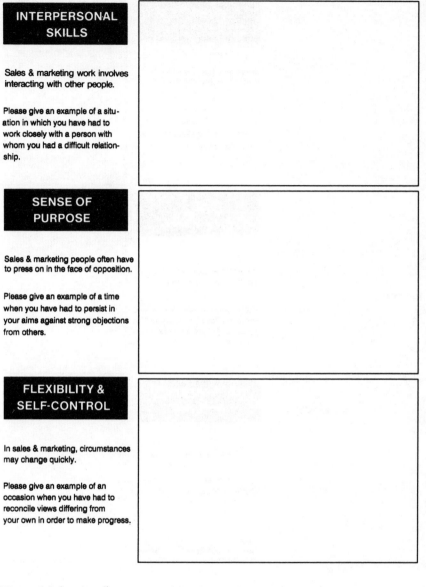

INTERPERSONAL SKILLS

Sales & marketing work involves interacting with other people.

Please give an example of a situation in which you have had to work closely with a person with whom you had a difficult relationship.

SENSE OF PURPOSE

Sales & marketing people often have to press on in the face of opposition.

Please give an example of a time when you have had to persist in your aims against strong objections from others.

FLEXIBILITY & SELF-CONTROL

In sales & marketing, circumstances may change quickly.

Please give an example of an occasion when you have had to reconcile views differing from your own in order to make progress.

Figure 4.1 (continued)

REMEMBER ● WHAT DID YOU DO? ● HOW DID YOU DO IT? ● WHAT WAS THE RESULT?

FLEXIBILITY & SELF-CONTROL

People have their own ways of handling disappointment.

Please give an example of an occasion when, after making some progress, you had to abandon your plans and start again.

TEAM & LEADERSHIP

Leadership is often demanded of those in sales & marketing.

Please give an example of a time when you have had to coordinate and/or control the work of a group of people.

YOUR FUTURE PLANS

Tell us about your plans for the future. What do you want to achieve and what are your plans? What have you done so far in pursuit of those plans?

Thank you for completing this Personal Interview Form. We will treat the contents as confidential.

Figure 4.1 (continued)

Opening the interview

The interview should be opened in the usual way using an ice-breaking question to relax the participant, ensuring that the atmosphere is friendly but business-like. The biographical interview can be an excellent opportunity to strike up a rapport with a participant with whom the observer will be later engaged in one-to-one feedback.

A few minutes should then be used to explain the purpose and format of the interview, and the way in which the biographical form will be used. It is also important to explain that the observer will be asking questions about actual workplace activities in order to obtain a clearer understanding of the participant's skills, abilities and work interests.

Specific points to explain in the introduction include:

- the need to discuss workplace activities;
- the ways in which the interview complements the exercises;
- the fact that the participant may not have come across the interviewing technique before, but that it is commonly used in many large companies in Europe, North America and Japan.

Criterion-referenced interviews

During a criterion-referenced interview (CRI) the interviewer asks a number of standard questions which are derived from careful job analysis. These are designed to identify the specific skills or experiences of an interviewee which are relevant to a particular job. If team leadership has been identified as an important element of the target job, the interviewer may ask the following question:

'Team leadership is an important element of this job. Tell me about a particular time when you had to lead a project team.'

This can be followed by probing questions to elicit details of the leadership role adopted by the interviewee.

'What were your objectives as team leader?'
'To what extent did you meet them?'
'What was the most difficult situation that you had to deal with as team leader?'
'How did you deal with this situation?'
'What was the outcome ?'

The answers can be rated against standard answers. This process is described under the section dealing with situational interviews.

There are two important differences between critical incidence biographical interviews and criterion-referenced interviews. These are as follows:

1 **Leading the interviewee**. Critical incident biographical interviews rely on the ability of interviewers to identify critical incidents without 'leading' the interviewee to a particular topic area or desired response. Consequently, biographical interviews often reveal rich sources of data because the interviewee may discuss significant events which would have been missed by a more directive approach.

However, biographical interviews may be more time consuming and require greater skills levels on the part of the interviewer.

2 **Controlling the interview**. Criterion-referenced interviews signal to the interviewee the relevant direction and topic areas. Consequently they are easy interviews to manage, and require less time in order to generate evidence of past behaviours in work-related settings. The skills required of interviewers may be less than for critical incident interviews.

Written reports   Observers need to obtain detailed evidence of abilities against each of the competences tested and then write an accurate summary report which lists the evidence and provides an assessment of the participant's effectiveness in each of the areas of competence tested by the interview.

Aspirations interviews

Development centres, unlike assessment centres, are designed to identify the training and development needs of existing employees for future work. The success of subsequent development activity will be dependent upon many factors, including the employees' motivation to develop in a particular direction. Consequently, a significant focus of development centre activity is to assess participants' abilities and future potential, and also to identify their aspirations and future career intentions. This can be done in three ways. Firstly, by measuring commitment and sense of purpose to the completion of tasks associated with a future role, Secondly, by using personality tests which measure flexibility, adaptability, tolerance of change and sense of purpose. Thirdly, by using aspirations interviews.

Aspirations interviews

These are a common feature of development centre programmes used by many organizations, for example the British Civil Service, American Express and ICI. The interviews would typically last for between 45 and 60 minutes and would usually consist of two parts; a career review and a discussion of career aspirations for the future. The career review is based on a biographical inventory which is completed by the participant in advance and sent to the programme managers before the development centre begins. This allows time for the assessors to complete interview preparation.

The biographical discussion would normally focus on the following issues:

1 Education—selection of courses and institutions, results, motivation, application in subsequent work.
2 Work—selection of jobs or career, main achievements, likes and dislikes, reasons for job changes.
3 Social—interests outside work, motivation, commitment, likes and dislikes.

The second part usually focuses on aspirations for the future, and the interviewer would normally ask questions about the following issues:

1 Participant's perceptions of the main elements of a 'good' job.
2 Elements of job tasks or work which the participant dislikes.
3 Participant's ambitions for work for the next two years, five years and ten years.
4 The realism of career aspirations, given current ability, experience, motivation or opportunity.
5 Participant's plans for realizing his or her career ambitions.

The data provide an opportunity for the organization to identify the participant's personal career ambitions and motivation. This will help the individual participant and the observer to plan personal development during the final feedback interview (see Chapter 6) which fits in with career or development opportunities that might exist within the organization.

Workplace questionnaires and biodata

Using a biographical interview form

Both the biographical and the aspirational interviews, as discussed in preceding sections of this chapter, rely on data derived from inventories and biographical forms. These are designed to enable observers to prepare for the interviews by planning discussion topics and questions which will quickly arrive at specific and relevant evidence for each competence.

Biographical inventories and questionnaires seek general, factual information about development centre participants, such as age, educational attainment and career history. They also invite participants to volunteer qualitative data, such as most preferred and least preferred job tasks, self-perceived strengths and development needs and career aspirations. A typical example of an inventory is illustrated in Figure 4.2.

The biographical inventory is usually completed by the participant in advance of the development centre and posted to the administrators who, in turn, distribute it to the assessor who will be conducting the interview. During the interview, the participant and the observer both have a copy of the form in front of them and work through the sections in sequential order. The written examples of achievements, aspirations, strengths, likes and dislikes enable the assessor to adopt the SOAR questioning technique to ascertain the:

• SITUATION faced by the participant;
• OBJECTIVES for dealing with the situation;
• ACTION that was actually taken to deal with the situation;
• RESULTS arising from the action which had been taken.

The interviewer should make detailed notes of the participant's responses in the usual way.

Application for Employment

BT is an equal opportunity employer. Suitability for the job is our only consideration when choosing people for employment. The information given below will help us
to assess this, and to check that no candidate receives less favourable treatment
because of race, gender, age, marital status or (subject to fitness for the job)
disability.

Please answer all questions using BLOCK CAPITALS and BLACK INK. A separate
sheet with your name on it may be used if you need more space for answers.

1   JOB

Please state the title of the job for which you are applying.

2 PERSONAL INFORMATION

Surname	Forenames
Title (Dr Mr Mrs Ms etc.)	
Permanent address	Address for further correspondence (if different)
Telephone Day	Evening

(please circle)

For BT applicants only. Are you registered with
the Management Redeployment and Rebalancing Unit?   Yes   No

For ALL applicants. Are you able to work in any
location within the UK?   Yes   No
(If NO please state where you are unable to work)

Are you able to work in: BT North America   Yes   No
　　　　　　　　　　　　BT Europe   Yes   No
　　　　　　　　　　　　BT Asia Pacific   Yes   No

Please list any future dates when you would not be available for interview.

Page 1 of 6

Figure 4.2   *Application for employment form*

3 EDUCATION/QUALIFICATIONS

Educational establishments attended

Name and address of school/college/university	From	To

Examinations/professional qualifications taken and results

Date	Subject	Qualification	Result/Grade

Page 2 of 6

Figure 4.2 (continued)

Development centres

4   EMPLOYMENT

Please provide details of employment during the last 5 years, and any service at any time with BT. Please include any periods of unemployment.

Dates From/To	Employer's name and address, description of job held, responsibilities and reason for leaving	Salary and other benefits

How much notice does your present employer require?

(1) Please indicate :

(a) Details of previous experience of managing customers and level of contact.

Page 3 of 6

Figure 4.2 (continued)

(b) Experience/Knowledge of BT products and services/other Telecom products and services.

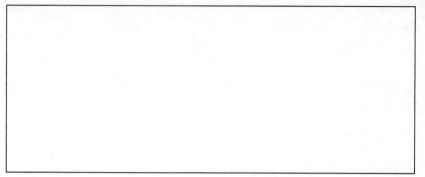

(c) Experience/Knowledge of computer systems and IT.

(2) Please indicate in the spaces provided any experience, skills, or work in the area suggested :

(a) Managing and leading teams.

Page 4 of 6

Figure 4.2 (continued)

(b) Project teams.

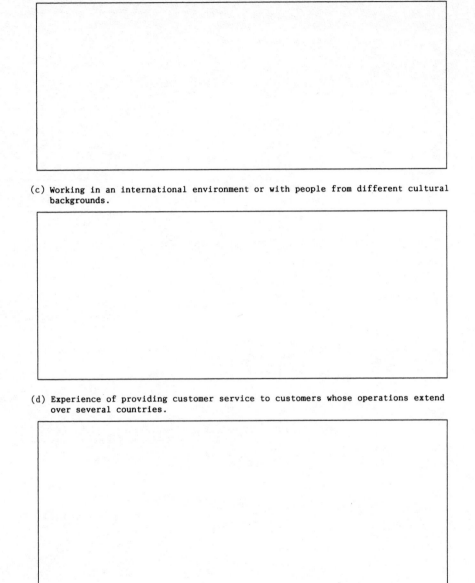

(c) Working in an international environment or with people from different cultural backgrounds.

(d) Experience of providing customer service to customers whose operations extend over several countries.

Figure 4.2 (continued)

ETHNIC ORIGINS   (Completion of this section is optional)

In order to help monitor the effectiveness of our equal opportunities policy, we ask applicants to provide the information requested below.
You should note that ethnic origin is not necessarily nationality or country of birth, it is the way in which you describe your ethnic identity and your racial origins.

I would best describe my ethnic origins as (show by a tick)

Asian ☐   Black ☐   Other (Please describe) ☐

Asian Oriental ☐   White ☐

ADDITIONAL INFORMATION

Please state your reasons for making this application.

Have you ever been found guilty by a court or court martial of any offence (under UK legislation not treated as spent under the Rehabilitation of Offenders legislation) or is there any case against you pending? If yes, please give particulars (unspent convictions will not necessarily bar you from employment).

Yes ☐   No ☐

Please include any additional information about yourself which could be relevant to this application.

I declare that to the best of my knowledge the information contained in this form is true, complete and accurate, and I understand that if any particulars I have given are found to be false, I may be regarded as ineligible for recruitment or dismissed after employment.

Signed :   Date :

Page 6 of 6

Figure 4.2 (continued)

How do others see me now?

- You have already assessed your own abilities against a number
  of qualities. As we all know, other people can sometimes have
  a totally different view of us. They may see different strengths
  or have a different image than the one which we wish to portray.
  Finding out what other people think of us is probably one of the
  most fruitful ways of learning about ourselves and hence
  developing in the future. The problem is how do we get that all-
  important feedback in an honest, helpful and constructive way?
  This section of the log is one way to do just that.

- The following questionnaires are similar to the one you have
  completed on yourself. Essentially you need to ask two
  colleagues and your line manager each to complete one of the
  questionnaires. Choose two colleagues who know you well and
  whose opinion you respect. If your present line manager does
  not know you well enough, then ask your previous line manager.
  When you ask them, stress that you need honest answers and
  really would value their views. The questionnaires are treated
  in confidence and should be sent off by your colleagues/manager
  in the addressed envelopes which are provided. At the
  development centre you will receive a summary of their replies
  which means that you will not be able to identify any individual's
  comments.

- Your colleagues'/manager's questionnaires need to be sent off in
  time to get to the development centre manager in time to allow
  three working days before the DC itself. Make a note of that
  date on the front page of each questionnaire before you give
  them to your colleague/manager.

Figure 4.3 *Tutor development centre workplace performance questionnaires*

<u>TUTOR DEVELOPMENT CENTRES QUESTIONNAIRE</u>

Dear

I will soon be attending a Tutor Development Centre. One of the objectives of the Centre is to help me gain a clearer picture of my strengths and development needs. To help me gain that picture I would like you to complete the following questionnaire about how you see me.

I would appreciate your views based on the times we have worked together. Your replies will be treated in strictest confidence. Once you have sent off the completed questionnaire in the addressed envelope, your replies will be re-written and joined with replies from other people. You do not need to put your name on the questionnaire.

Please return the questionnaire by ....

Yours

L43AAC

Figure 4.3 *(continued)*

<u>DEVELOPMENT QUESTIONNAIRE</u>

Name of the person who asked you to complete this questionnaire:

....

- The following questionnaire is in two parts. First you are asked
  to give your general impressions of the individual concerned (a
  kind of pen picture). Next you are asked to consider the
  individual's work performance against a number of qualities (group
  of skills/attitudes which are seen as important for the types of
  work in BTMCC).

L43AAC

Figure 4.3 *(continued)*

<u>PART 1</u>

A   What image or picture do you have of this individual at work? (A brief pen picture of how you see this person, but not just physical characteristics).

B   Complete the following sentences as if you were describing the individual to someone else (but not just physical characteristics).

He/she is ....

He/she is ....

He/she is ....

He/she is ....

L43AAC

Figure 4.3 (continued)

- Next there are a number of qualities defined. Think of the individual's abilities/performance with each quality. Also think of the abilities of other colleagues in the college and use them as a 'yardstick' to measure the individual. Finally, make a rating of the individual on the following scale:

  6 = Outstanding. He/she is very effective at the types of work requiring all aspects of this quality.

  5 = Good. He/she is effective, but not outstanding at all aspects of this quality.

  4 = Acceptable. He/she is only just effective on all aspects OR he/she is effective on most aspects, but not on others.

  3 = Marginal. He/she is not as effective as he/she could be on most aspects.

  2 = He/she is not as effective as he/she could be on all aspects of this quality.

  1 = He/she is ineffective at work which requires this quality.

  X = Don't know. I've not seen the individual working in areas which require this quality.

- Simply put a ring around the number which reflects your view of the individual.

- Under each scale there is space for you to make notes. Please note any particular strengths or development needs within each quality. If you can, put down some examples which might amplify your rating.

L43AAC

Figure 4.3 *(continued)*

A   <u>Analysis</u>

Assimilates large amount of information. Approaches questions in a systematic, logical way, analyses things very carefully. Is very bright, masters complex problems very quickly. His/her analyses are penetrating and has a very quick mind, grasps concepts rapidly. Critical thinker, can produce arguments and criticisms of both sides of a case.

1	2	3	4	5	6	X

<u>NOTES</u>

B   <u>Helicopter</u>

Uses knowledge about changing internal situations and pressures to identify potential problems and opportunities. Is able to rise up above the immediate problem or situation to see the broader issues and implications. Relates facts and problems to an extremely wide context, perceives all possible relationships.

1	2	3	4	5	6	X

<u>NOTES</u>

L43AAC

Figure 4.3 (continued)

C   Oral Communication

Verbally fluent, has an extensive vocabulary. Keeps to the point, does not waffle. Explains abstract concepts with clarity and accuracy, uses analogies effectively. Delivery has got sparkle, is responsive to an audience. Sounds interested in and in command of material, makes it relevant and come alive.

1	2	3	4	5	6	X

NOTES

D   Listening

Listens carefully and actively, assimilates the information imparted by others. Perceives and responds to both verbal and non-verbal signals. Listens intently, does not interrupt and cut across the other speaker.

1	2	3	4	5	6	X

NOTES

L43AAC

Figure 4.3 *(continued)*

E   Planning and Organizing

Collects information well in advance. Spends much time planning
and preparing activities and tries to predict all eventualities.
Sets reliable and realistic timescales, establishes clear
priorities, strikes a balance between various options. Sets
methodical, thorough milestones on the way, and works to specific
targets. Manages own time effectively. Coordinates activities
of others efficiently and systematically.

1	2	3	4	5	6	X

NOTES

F   Achievement Motivation

Has plenty of energy and drive, is highly active. Strives single-
mindedly to get results and meets deadlines whenever possible.
Can be relied upon to see an assignment through from start to
finish, is highly resilient. Relishes a challenging task that
will stretch him or her. Is a self-starter, gets things off the
ground, is entrepreneurial.

1	2	.3	4	5	6	X

NOTES

L43AAC

Figure 4.3 (continued)

G   Innovative and Proactive

Seeks and accepts change and new challenges, goes out and creates
new opportunities. Produces imaginative ideas and solutions to
problems, able to step outside the traditional boundaries and
constraints. Has vision — sees what are possible and desirable
goals for the future. Is politically aware of organizational
changes, and the people involved, well tuned into the power
structure. Tries out new ideas and ways of doing things. Is not
hidebound or risk-averse.

1	2	3	4	5	6	X

NOTES

H   Self-appraisal

Appraises own performance accurately, analyses the good and bad
points after an event. Remembers, and learns from the negatives,
adapts behaviour accordingly. Brings out only the positive skills
and behaviours in future work. Understands clearly his or her own
need for success, is not driven by it. Has an accurate conception
of own impact on others, and their perceptions of him or her.

1	2	3	4	5	6	X

NOTES

L43AAC

Figure 4.3 *(continued)*

I Coping with Uncertainty/Pressure

Remains calm, level-headed and unemotional, controls his or her feelings when facing a stressful or unexpected situation. Buys time by checking our comments, bringing in others, inviting help from them and sharing the problem. Thinks on his or her feet, is decisive, talks his or her way out of a corner while retaining credibility. Shows persistence and resilience in the face of adversity.

1	2	3	4	5	6	X

NOTES

J Team Worker

Works closely with colleagues, gets on well with them, and supports their efforts. Establishes group aims and objectives, and the best ways of working towards them. Is unselfish, subordinates personal ambitions to the group's, overcomes conflict, resentment or inertia. Bounces ideas off others, will disagree when appropriate but works constructively towards common goals. Is open, does not talk behind their backs.

1	2	3	4	5	6	X

NOTES

L43AAC

Figure 4.3 *(continued)*

K   Interpersonal Sensitivity

Establishes rapport quickly, makes people feel comfortable and
at ease. Is sensitive to the other person's position, needs
and feelings, and able to work with these. Overcomes any
negative views about others, informs them of his or her own
feelings and shares common experiences. Establishes a safe
environment and encourages others to talk. Is non-judgemental,
does not make personal criticisms, maintains their self-esteem.
Helps them come to terms with their own needs and problems, and
to reach a solution.

1	2	3	4	5	6	X

NOTES

L   Influencing Others

Persuades others to change their minds by manner and reasonable
arguments. Will be forceful and press personal views when he or
she believes in them but does not become overly assertive and
aggressive -- will admit when wrong or when the consensus is
strongly against. When negotiating, understands the other side's
needs and position, knows the exact strength of own case.
Establishes a range of outcomes acceptable to both sides and
presses for the one most acceptable to him or her.

1	2	3	4	5	6	X

NOTES

L43AAC

Figure 4.3 (continued)

M   Adaptability

Adapts behaviour and material to the changing requirements of different audiences and contacts. Maintains effectiveness in a wide range of different situations.

1	2	3	4	5	6	X

NOTES

Thank you for completing this questionnaire. Could you please send it off now in the addressed envelope.

L43AAC

Figure 4.3 *(continued)*

Working with incomplete forms

If a participant has not completed all questions on the form because he or she was unable to think of an example, then the observer may wish to clarify the question, ask open questions to identify analogous situations in other work-related areas or spend more time discussing activities which the participant has described. Additional approaches that could be tried include the following:

- Check understanding of the question.
- Rephrase the question.
- Ask a broader opening question, e.g. 'What sort of people do you work closely with?' 'What sort do you prefer?' 'What sort of people would you prefer not to work with?' to lead into the specific question. 'Give an example of a situation in which you have had to work closely with a person with whom you had a difficult relationship.' This may unblock the participant's thinking and provide leads for the interviewer to pick up.
- Allow time and reassurance.
- Use of silence.

A balanced approach is needed so that the participant is 'stretched' to think of relevant incidents but is not placed under stress.

Workplace questionnaires

An additional source of evidence about a participant, and one which is linked to job performance, is the workplace questionnaire. This is a common feature of development centres, and is linked to competences used in conjunction with the development centre exercises. The questionnaires are designed to be completed in advance of the development centre by people who know the participant in the workplace, preferably colleagues, line manager and the participants themselves. The completed questionnaires are posted to development centre administrators who aggregate the results to produce an average workplace score against each of the competences. These data are then integrated with the assessors' ratings and the psychometric test scores to produce a 'rounded' picture of the participant's abilities in the workplace, on the development centre, and from psychometric tests.

This full picture allows assessors to link data, identify consistent messages and establish patterns. An example of a workplace performance questionnaire is contained in Figure 4.3.

Biodata questionnaires

Biodata questionnaires are designed to collect information systematically about the skills, attainment levels, experience and abilities of development centre participants. In relation to development centre programmes, they can be used for two purposes. Firstly, as an initial sift mechanism to identify those people who should attend a programme. Secondly, as a data-gathering process on the programme to identify which participants should be placed into a particular job or role. Hunter and Hunter (1984), in discussing the uses and their limitations of biodata questionnaires, suggest that they are highly appropriate for making decisions but of limited value in deciding upon selection.

Table 4.1　*Summary of interviews and questionnaires*

Interview type	Purpose	Features	Preparation
Interviews			
1 Situational interviews	To identify how an interviewee would resolve a work-based problem which is related to a target job. The questions are hypothetical and ask 'How would you . . .?'	Standard questions are researched, and standard answers are produced, against which the interviewee's response is scored. There is an assumed correlation between how interviewees respond to the questions and how they would perform at work	Interviewers select 6–10 situational questions from a list of 20. Selection is based on the interviewee's experience
2 Critical incident interviews	To identify the past performance or behaviour of an interviewee in a workplace situation which is similar to that which the interviewee would face in a target job. The questions ask for actual behaviour 'How did you . . .?'	The skill of the interviewer determines the success of the interview. The interviewer identifies critical incidents and explores the way in which the interviewee dealt with the incident. There is an assumption that behaviours are a predictor of future behaviours	Interviewers analyse biographical data supplied in advance of the interview, and identify topic areas which will lead to appropriate critical incidents
3 Aspirational interviews	To identify career aspirations and plans for the future	Discussion of career history and future aspirations	Interivewers analyse a biographical inventory which the interviewee completes before the interview

Table 4.1   (*continued*)

Interview type	Purpose	Features	Preparation
Questionnaires			
1 Biographical inventories	These provide data for interviewers to prepare for interviews. They focus the minds of interviewees on past performance, career history and career plans	Biographical inventories contain open and closed questions to capture factual information and subjective data such as likes, dislikes and ambitions	Interviewees spend 30 minutes completing the inventory before attending a develop-ment centre. Interviewers spend 30 minutes reading the inventory and planning the interview
2 Workplace performance questionnaires	To identify the workplace performance of interviewees/ development centre participants against the relevant competences	The questionnaires are completed by the participant, the line manager, colleagues or staff and provide a range of percept-ions on workplace performance	Completed questionnaires have to be collated to produce an average performance rating (with ranges). The data are then integrated with those from other sources such as an observer's ratings and psychometric tests

Biodata questionnaires usually consist of two parts. Firstly, requests for factual data such as age, qualifications, work history and experience related to target jobs. This is 'hard' factual data. Secondly, requests for work preferences, attitudes and ambitions. This constitutes the 'soft' data. The answers are then scored using a standard scoring system, and questionnaire respondents whose scores fall within a certain range are identified as potentially capable of meeting certain job requirements.

Biodata questionnaires are designed using three simple stages. Firstly, a thorough job analysis is carried out in order to identify the skills which are necessary to complete a particular job to a high standard. This usually involves critical incident interviews among the manager population of the target job group. It may also involve interviews or direct observations of people who have been identified as effective job holders.

Secondly, items of behaviour which denote effective workplace per-formance are analysed (if they are mentioned frequently by the inter-viewees) and then pooled. They are sent back to the target population or their managers for confirmation, and for establishing a scoring system. Respondents are asked to rate the significance of the behaviour in terms of a contribution to the effective completion of the job.

Thirdly, the behaviours are written into a questionnaire and then trailed. This is carried out using a sample group which numbers at least four times the questionnaire items. The trail would normally be conducted using existing effective job holders. Items which result in bias can be removed. Once adopted, biodata questionnaires are usually updated every two years to ensure that items are relevant and reflect organizational needs.

The descriptive nature of this chapter does not lend itself to action points, or lists of 'do's and don'ts'. We trust the readers will draw what they need from it. A summary of interviews and questionnaires may be found in Table 4.1.

References and further reading

Anderson, N. and Shackleton, V. (1990) 'Decision making in the graduate selection interview: A field study', *Journal of Occupational Psychology*, 63, 63–76.

Flanagan, J.C. (1954) 'The critical incident technique', *Psychological Bulletin*, 51 (4).

Herriot, P. (1988) 'Selection at a crossroads', *Psychologist*, October, 388–92.

Hunter, J.E. and Hunter, R.F. (1984) 'Validity and utility of alternative predictors of job performance', *Psychologist Bulletin*, 96, 72–98.

Janz, T. (1982) 'Initial comparisons of patterned behaviour description interviews versus unstructured interviews', *Journal of Applied Psychology*, 67, 577–80.

Latham, G.P. *et al.* (1980) 'The situational interview', *Journal of Applied Psychology*, 65, 422–47.

Orpen, C. (1985) 'Patterned behaviour description interviews versus unstructured interviews: a comparative validity study', *Journal of Applied Psychology*, 70, 774–6.

Owens, W.A. (1976) 'Background data', in M.D. Dunnette (ed.) *Handbook of Industrial and Organizational Psychology*, Rand McNally, Chicago.

Smith, M., Gregg, M. and Andrews, D. (1979) *Selection and Assessment: A New Approach*, Pitman, London.

Weisner, W.H. and Cronshaw, S.P. (1988) 'A meta-analytic investigation of the impact of interview format and structure on the validity of the employment interview', *Journal of Occupational Psychology*, 61, 275–90.

Wright, P.M., Lichtenfels, P.A. and Pursell, E.D. (1989) 'The situational interview: additional studies and meta-analysis', *Journal of Occupational Psychology*, 62, 191–9.

5 The use of psychometric tests

Keith Coaley and Bridget Hogg

This chapter is divided into sections which cover issues relating to the selection and use of psychometric tests for development centre programmes:

- Introduction
- Tests and their uses
- Current debates about the use of tests
- Selecting tests
- The role of the psychometric test expert
- Integrating tests into development centre timetables
- Integration of test results with other data
- Case study: The BT sales force
- Psychometric tests in use
- Checklist
- Further reading
- Addresses of test publishers

Introduction

During the past decade there has been a substantial growth in the use of psychological assessment techniques for training and development purposes. Both the number of published tests and the number of people offering psychological assessment services have mushroomed. For development centres, both the quality of materials and the method of implementation are essential factors if psychometric tests are to be accepted by senior management and those who take part in the process. Poor quality methods and inadequate professionalism among practitioners will have serious consequences and a negative impact upon perceptions of the event.

On the other hand, appropriate psychometric test materials, carefully positioned and used, can make a major contribution to the effective design and outcomes of a development centre. Tests are most effectively used as one element in a range of assessment procedures, providing measures of personality and ability which offer important leads to follow up in feedback interviews. Tests can also give an indication of potential above that suggested by academic attainment.

Evidence suggests that tests which are professionally used and evaluated can provide objective, reliable and relevant information about the likelihood of job success and satisfaction of the job holder. Psychometric tests can:

- provide useful aggregate data for the purposes of performance review or for development centre validation;
- help participants to make personal decisions regarding career planning—self-awareness is a crucial basis for this process.

For these reasons it is important to make carefully considered decisions on:

- the objectives and desired outcomes of the use of psychometric assessment;
- the kinds and levels of psychometric materials to be used;
- who will have responsibility for the administration, scoring, interpretation, and provision of feedback and counselling of participants;
- how this process will be structured within the development centre timetable.

Many tests are marketed in ways designed to impress potential users, and publishers' brochures are frequently written in glowing, enthusiastic terms. However, it is important to remember that all of this may disguise what are inadequate test materials of both poor reliability and validity. For the newcomer to this complex area of work such a situation is not only bewildering and difficult to understand, but also poses a real danger to the successful design of development centres. Given that the lives and careers of people may be affected by test results, it is essential that organizations using tests do so in a responsible way.

The theoretical background to psychological testing is very extensive, but it is the intention to discuss here only those practical issues which are relevant and useful for the design and management of development centres. The aim of this chapter is to establish a basic practical understanding of psychometric tests and current issues, so that they may be used to make a valuable contribution to the outcomes of a programme of development centres.

Tests and their uses

A psychological test is a procedure for evaluating psychological functions. In general, there are three forms of tests, or questionnaires, which can contribute to the outcomes of the development centre. These are:

1 Tests of skills or aptitudes such as verbal or numerical reasoning.
2 Personality questionnaires such as the Occupational Personality Questionnaire (OPQ) or the Myers–Briggs Type Indicator.
3 Measures of work interests and preferences.

It is important that tests which are related to the occupational or organizational context are used as these are more relevant. There are many tests and questionnaires used by both clinical and educational psychologists but use of these would be mostly inappropriate and might raise complex or difficult issues. The most useful tests will have been designed and standardized for people at work, and are aimed to find out their abilities or preferences for behaviour in the work environment. In the case of aptitude tests, objective statistically based decisions can be made about people's capacities or potential to behave in certain ways, their potential for training, and their potential for success in different kinds of jobs.

To make best use of psychometric tests in a development centre, it is essential that quality materials are provided and that they are used in a professional and carefully managed fashion. A generally accepted view of the 'indicators of low quality' would include the following:

1 **Seemingly boundless enthusiasm for inadequate tests**. This is often a consequence of the organizational desire for the 'quick fix.' A test or computer-based test package which seems to offer a fast, comprehensive assessment of individuals for a relatively low price, and a minimum investment in training test users, is an approach adopted by many companies. It is a delusion to think that anything as complex or as subtle as human behaviour or personality can really be understood from the results of a few short tests.

2 **Inadequate feedback**. What the individual—and ultimately, the organization—gets out of tests will largely depend upon how well feedback is handled. This issue is considered later in Chapter 6. However, best practice would incorporate test usage within a collaborative or counselling framework, and this is particularly true in the context of the development centre. Making it clear that the test data will be shared on a one-to-one basis with participants increases their willingness to cooperate and to be honest in their responses. Validity, too, is improved.

In general, tests are designed to measure attributes or characteristics which have been identified by psychological research, and the results are related to well-defined 'populations'.

Aptitude tests and personality questionnaires will be considered in more detail as these are mostly used in development centres. However, interest inventories present a useful addition. They are designed to assess an individual's preferences for different types of work in a systematic way, and thus do not have right or wrong answers. Some inventories are based upon psychological theories about why people have preferences for certain kinds of job, while others are based upon a simple classification of work characteristics, such as social versus solitary or indoor versus outdoor work. These inventories may be useful in helping individuals to decide upon future career moves.

Factors to consider when deciding upon a particular psychological test include the following:

1 **Scope**. What range of attributes does the test cover and how specific or general is it?
2 **Reliability**. What is the degree of precision and do people tend to get the same score each time they take the test?
3 **Validity**. Does the test measure what it claims to measure? The most important evidence is information which shows that scores are related to a 'real' criterion measure, such as measure of job performance or training course outcome. The technical information provided with the test materials should give good information on the different aspects of validity.

The issue of validity is a difficult and complex area of study, and it is not intended here to discuss this in detail. Rather, it is intended to highlight the importance of both reliability and validity, and to direct the attention of the development centre designer to the need to check these out with experts in psychometrics or with the technical manuals for different test materials.

4 **Acceptability**. Usually people find tests acceptable when the reasons for taking them are carefully explained at the beginning of the development centre and when they know they will be given a confidential feedback of the results.

It is important to remember that any information you may obtain from testing belongs to the participant and his or her permission should be obtained to use this information. Experience shows that highlighting this issue encourages greater acceptability among participants.

5 **Practicality**. This involves the cost of the materials (which can vary widely), the time taken for presentation, administration and scoring, and the ease of use of the materials.

For every participant, the instructions given and the way the test is presented should be identical, or as close to this as possible. This is particularly important in ability testing.

One major cost to bear in mind is that only properly trained, qualified and registered people should be used for the administration, scoring and feedback of psychological tests. Such people are registered with the British Psychological Society (see addresses at the end of this chapter).

The BPS has sought to control access to psychological tests in order to protect the public from their abuse or misuse. Support is given by reputable test producers and publishers who provide training courses for non-psychologists and will sell tests only to individuals accredited with the BPS. Trained people possess either the Certificate or Statement of Competence in Occupational Testing.

Failure to use properly trained people for these purposes can result in wasted time, inaccurate advice, bias or unfairness, or unnecessary difficulties which require considerable expertise to resolve. Unfair or unwitting discriminatory use of psychometric tests could result in legal action.

6 **Fairness**. Are irrelevant issues likely to affect performance upon the test? If it can be shown that differences (e.g. between gender, ethnic groups, or age groups) reflect true differences between their suitability for a job, then the test bias is 'fair'. However, if the relationship between test scores and suitability differs from one group to another, then the test bias will be unfair. It is very important to check for evidence of bias, although this will not usually be a problem if tests are purchased from major test publishers.

More relevant issues for the context of the development centre are such things as fatigue, stress, boredom, anxiety or the influence of physical surroundings. These may cause participants to under-perform. It is important, therefore, to position the tests at a point in the timetable when participants are reasonably relaxed and are not too tired.

Abilities required to succeed on an aptitude test but which are not part of the construct being measured are called Beta abilities. These include all of the strategy elements involved in taking a test—use of time, skipping difficult questions, etc. Participants who are lacking in such abilities may also under-perform.

7 **Confidentiality of materials**. If unauthorized people gain access to test materials, this could have a damaging effect upon their reliability and validity. Standardization is also lost when participants have seen materials in advance and the testing procedure is devalued.

Where development centres are managed in either hotel or training accommodation, it is important to ensure facilities exist for the safe storage of materials and destruction of data which are no longer required for use.

Only trained administrators should have access to materials. Manuals can be kept on open shelves, but not administration sets which contain question booklets. A scoring key should never be left out where untrained people have access; someone who is distracted while scoring profiles should ensure that the scoring key is locked away.

Records need to be kept of psychometric booklets taken from storage, and materials should not be photocopied as this may break copyright laws.

Aptitude tests

Aptitude tests are usually designed to be work related and often have names which include job titles, such as a general clerical test or selling skills tests. A wide range of very specific tests are available for managerial and sub-managerial employees, and for this reason tests which are designed for the appropriate level should be selected.

Effective aptitude tests, such as those for verbal and numerical reasoning aptitude, can add real value to the development centre: they will provide participants with useful knowledge of themselves as a basis for developmental planning and will also enable the organization to accumulate data on an anonymous aggregate level about performance and skills. These data can then be used for performance review or for validation of the exercise materials and the related assessment procedure.

An individual's test score is only meaningful when considered against the spread of scores obtained by a relevant comparison group. The absolute score a person achieves is frequently referred to as the raw score. This is usually translated into a norm-referenced score which lies in relation to the scores obtained by other people, thus indicating whether the individual has performed at a level which is below average, average or above average. These scores are relative measures since they depend on the comparison group. This is an important issue to check out in deciding whether to use a particular test. Tests are available for the following levels:

- below-graduate educational attainment;
- graduate educational attainment;
- junior management level;
- senior management level.

Norm-referenced test scores are usually expressed in 'percentiles' (the percentage of the norm group which would be expected to achieve the same or a lower raw score) and this often needs to be carefully explained to those who use the test score. All good test manuals will provide information about the test's reliability and validity, and will contain information on norm groups for different populations which will help with the interpretation of results. They will also give practical advice on administration and scoring.

Development centre participants frequently ask if the aptitude tests being used are 'intelligence tests.' Such tests have been the subject of both public and academic controversy over many years. It is useful for the administrator to distinguish between intelligence tests and differential tests of aptitude. Development centre participants generally find aptitude tests to be acceptable and worth while.

Personality questionnaires

For individuals, personal awareness is a crucial factor in career management, and this requires some awareness of personality as well as the aptitudes one has to offer at work. It has been suggested that up to 70 per cent of the attributes which are associated with success at work are dimensions of personality rather than ability. However, positions of responsibility frequently depend upon qualifications and abilities. This dichotomy can often lead to conflict in the workplace.

The term 'personality' comes from the Latin word *persona*, which referred originally to a mask used by actors to portray different stage roles. The term later came to refer to the character being acted out rather than the mask itself. This raises the issue that personality and behaviour are changeable and are not fixed entities, but adapt to changing situations. Although this may be true to some extent, extensive research indicates that there is still an extensive degree of consistency in both.

Psychologists have taken widely differing views in attempting to define personality:

Self, a permanent subjective entity at the heart of our experiences.

(Carl Rogers)

[An entity which] enables us to predict what a person will do in real life situations.

(Professor Raymond B. Cattell)

Cattell's definition is particularly relevant to development centres, where the emphasis lies in assessment of the individual in order to predict future performance in the workplace, and to enhance performance and personal development.

There have also been a number of theories throughout history concerning the structure of personality, including psychoanalysis, although these have had little impact in the development of assessment techniques. The Myers–Briggs Type Indicator is an exception to this. More recently the theories of Hans Eysenck and Cattell have had more influence.

Eysenck suggested that there are three main personality factors: Extroversion–Introversion, Neuroticism–Stability and Tough versus Tender-Mindedness. The Extroversion and Stability dimensions are perceived as being independent of each other so that it is possible to classify adult personality into four principal types: Stable Extroverts, Unstable Extroverts, Unstable Introverts and Stable Introverts. This has led to the development of the Eysenck Personality Inventory (EPI).

Cattell's 16 Personality Factor Questionnaire, the 16PF, has been more widely used for occupational purposes. This is based upon Cattell's assumption that personality is described by 16 traits, including dimensions such as Outgoingness, Assertiveness, Conscientiousness, Tough-Mindedness, Shrewdness, Imagination.

Social precision and tension

There have also been a variety of approaches to the assessment of personality, including interviews, classification according to physical characteristics, projective techniques (such as the Rorschach inkblot technique), application forms, references, biodata, astrology, phrenology and graphology. The crucial issue for all of these techniques is validity—is there scientific data to prove that they accurately measure what they claim to measure? In many cases, the answer must be 'No'.

The most frequently used method of assessing personality, other than through the interview, is in the use of questionnaires or inventories, and this is the approach most easily applied to development centres. There are now a great many questionnaires on the market, and choosing an appropriate one needs some care. The development centre designer is advised to seek advice from a psychometrics expert who is registered with the British Psychological Society, or from the Society itself.

Questionnaires can be traced back to Francis Galton's studies of mental imagery in the late nineteenth century, although the credit for the first questionnaire to be constructed as a selection tool is often given to Woodworth's Personal Data Sheet which was designed for the assessment of neurotic behaviour among US soldiers in the First World War. Many other instruments have followed over the ensuing years—the 'prolific rabbits of the psychometric world', according to Cattell. Some were designed for use in clinical situations, such as the Minnesota Multiphasic Personality Inventory (MMPI), and are therefore not suitable for use on normal populations.

However, the California Personality Inventory (CPI), which was developed from the MMPI, may be used. This is a large general-purpose inventory intended for the prediction of behaviour of a wide range of normal people in a wide variety of settings. Intrusive clinical items were dropped from the 1987 version of the measure, although it is still less well known than other personality questionnaires.

The range of questionnaires suitable for use in a development centre is reasonably limited, although recent and continuing additions produced by psychological consultancies have extended the range. For the most well-known tests, such as the 16PF, the CPI, the MBTI, EPI, or Saville & Holdsworth's Occupational Personality Questionnaire (OPQ), details of norms calculated for particular populations, and reliability and validity studies are more available.

The OPQ consists of a battery of scales for measuring personality characteristics following research by SHL and sponsored by 53 UK organizations. The dimensions assessed are centred upon three suggested personality areas: the 'Relating Domain' concerned with social relationships; the Thinking Domain, including traits such as abstract thinking, practical and detail consciousness; and the Feeling Domain, concerned with emotions such as anxiety, tough-mindedness and emotional control.

It is important to request details of norms, reliability and validity when considering any questionnaire offered by a psychological consultancy for use in the development centre. Where the workshop is being designed for a specific group of managers, selection of a personality test which has norms available for such a group is preferred. If the event is being designed for an international organization, such as a company with centres in other countries, it may also be helpful to consider questionnaires available in different languages.

In using personality questionnaires as part of a development centre, it is useful to consider important issues. Firstly, do not be misled into thinking that a single type of personality predicts success in all jobs, or even a single attribute. Different attributes, and different combinations of them, are required for different jobs at different levels. A single trait might even predict success or failure in different aspects of the same occupation. In addition, personality characteristics are frequently best correlated with predictions of specific competences rather than overall working performance.

Recent Developments

Increasingly, computers are used to administer, score, and occasionally interpret tests. The reasons for this include the greater speed and efficiency of the approach, and the apparent ease with which the computer can be used to produce almost instantaneous reports. However, it should not be assumed that these assessments are equivalent to those generated by a person trained in the use of psychometric tests, who will have access to a wider range of information. Experience suggests that software may be useful for speeding up the process of scoring tests, but that interpretation and feedback in the development centre need to be carried out by another person. A participant who has been given simply an expert system print-out to take away is likely to feel neglected.

One benefit of the computer-based approach may be in improved collation and easier analysis of performance data for large groups of people attending development centres. A review of these needs is made elsewhere in this volume in considering validation and evaluation.

Test use has generally developed in an unsystematic way in many commercial organizations, and there has been recent evidence that some are now trying to put right that situation. There appears to be a movement towards developing a more structured and coherent framework for the use of psychometric measures in assessment and development with the aim of better integration of the different assessment needs and purposes including selection, promotion and management development. The outcome of this process will be the more appropriate use of questionnaires, etc., for the levels of the organization, and better links with longer-term career planning and development activities.

Current debates about the use of tests

There have been major arguments between experts in psychometric testing in recent years. These have been mostly of a very technical nature and conducted in journals concerned with personnel and management development. For those working in the management development field who seek practical applications of direct benefit to organizations and their managers, these arguments may have been confusing and have detracted from the use of personality tests. However, they should not deter development centre designers from making use of tests as part of a multiple assessment review. After all, it is virtually impossible to design a questionnaire that is free from all criticism.

The debate has centred primarily upon the relative merits of 'ipsative' and 'normative' personality questionnaires. Normative questionnaires use a rating scale, most often a three-point or five-point scale; while ipsative questionnaires force respondents to make a choice between two options. Examples of both types are illustrated in Table 5.1.

Criticisms can actually be made of both formats. For example, ipsative personality questionnaires produce some interdependence between the scales presented—it is not possible to be high on all the scales. On the other hand, the normative approach encourages people to go 'down the middle', using the unsure category more frequently; some people will

Table 5.1 *Typical scoring systems for ipsative and normative tests*

	Ipsative		Normative		
	Most true	Least true	False	Unsure	True
1 I enjoy being with people	0	0	0	0	0
2 I take part in energetic activities	0	0	0	0	0
3 I always adhere to strict deadlines	0	0	0	0	0

tend to agree with any question posed to them; while others might be mostly tempted to attempt to project a favourable image of themselves. This latter tendency is known as social desirability.

The nature of the arguments about ipsative and normative tests is predominantly technical and revolves around correlations, reliabilities and validities of ipsative scales. For example, it has been said that their validities against external criteria are overestimated and defy interpretation. Some experts have claimed that the authors of ipsative questionnaires are undertaking an exercise in futility 'like cheating at patience'. Some of the criticisms also appear to have become accepted by the Test Standards Committee of the British Psychological Society.

Conversely, other experts have argued strongly in favour of the use of the ipsative tests, and that there is nothing wrong about using them.

Ultimately, neither type of personality questionnaire is going to be perfect. Practitioners will need to remember that with ipsative tests the scales used are going to be interdependent to some extent; and that with normative tests there are going to be responses which involve tendency to agree, central tendency and social desirability. Those experts who appear to take a more balanced view of the arguments suggest that it might be best in practice to make use of both forms of questionnaire, but this would involve complex arrangements in timetabling for the development centre and problems of integrating feedback from different tests.

For the practitioner who simply aims to take advantage of the positive benefits of personality testing, as part of a multiple assessment, this argument is abstruse and unnecessary. The best advice is to continue with the use of tests which have been carefully considered and positioned within development centre programmes. Adequate and appropriate personality characteristics as well as test questions which appear to be relevant to the participant at the time are far more important than whether the scales are devised in an ipsative or normative fashion. These are more practical issues which the development centre designer can check out in purchasing materials.

Selecting tests

There are a number of practical considerations when selecting a test for use in a development centre:

- What you wish to gain from a test (personality preferences, ability assessments, measures of stress, etc.).
- Reliability, validity and fairness of a test.
- Cost of a test.
- Level the test is aimed at and its norm population.
- Length of time a test takes to administer, interpret and feedback.
- Availability of qualified psychometric experts to administer, score, interpret and feed back the tests chosen.

The use of psychometric tests always requires a fully qualified psychometric expert to be able to choose appropriate tests and utilize them to the best advantage.

The effective use of psychometric tests in a development centre programme requires a qualified psychometric test user to administer, score and interpret the test results. There is no mystique to this role, and anyone who has attended a training course in psychometric testing, which is recognized by the British Psychological Society, can register with the BPS as a competent psychometric test user. Table 5.3 (pages 152–3) illustrates the range of aptitude and personality tests which are currently available and which are relevant to development centres (see pages 152–3).

The role of the psychometric test expert

There are six key aspects to the psychometric expert's role prior to and during a development centre:

1 Advising on the use of suitable tests.
2 Integrating psychometric tests into the development centre timetable.
3 Introducing and explaining the purpose of the psychometric tests to observers and participants.
4 Administering, scoring, interpreting, and providing feedback on the results.
5 Ensuring confidential and secure storage of all psychometric test materials and results.
6 Collating psychometric results and exercise ratings for data analysis, such as performance reviews or validation studies.

Additionally, the role of the psychometric test expert can be expanded, on specialized development centres, to include, for example, running a stress seminar based on occupational stress questionnaires.

Integrating tests into development centre timetables

Once the decision has been made as to which psychometric tests are to be used, the only remaining problem is how to integrate these tests into the development centre timetable. Timetabling is one of the permanent nightmares of development centre implementation.

The diverse needs of development centre participants, observers and psychometric experts need to be taken into account in the development centre timetabling. Areas of prime concern are avoiding work overload on any of those involved and containing all activities within a practical timescale.

Integrating the administration and scoring of tests

Test administration typically takes about one hour for a personality profile and about three-quarters of an hour for an ability test. The actual length of time depends on the test used, the time needed to introduce the test and the time needed by participants to complete the example questions. The length of time needed for scoring of tests varies and should be checked in advance.

From the psychometric test expert's point of view, it is preferable to schedule the administration of tests near the commencement of the development centre, thus allowing greatest opportunity for scoring and interpretation of results. The needs of the test expert have to be balanced with the needs of observers who also wish to start their marking early and spread it evenly over the available time. More information about timetabling is contained in Chapter 3.

One useful technique is to include at an early point in the timetable an exercise which takes a long time to assess and psychometric tests. This gives both the psychometric test expert and the observers the opportunity to commence marking early, while providing variety, rather than overload, for the participants.

Integration of test results with other data

To aid the feedback process to participants it is often helpful to integrate, where possible, the psychometric results with data from the development centre exercises. This can be useful in instances where feedback covers styles of group interaction, preferred modes of thinking and preferred styles of influence.

This is usually done at observers' conferences. Some agreement may be needed with participants over the divulgence of confidential test results to development centre observers before an integration of psychometric test data and observers' exercise ratings can take place. Also, a similar agreement may be needed for psychometric test experts to provide observers with brief 'pen pictures' of participants' personality profiles in order for them to plan feedback interviews in a way that will be most helpful to the participants. Agreement is usually forthcoming if participants see a benefit to themselves.

Observers may not be trained in the use of psychometric tests, and psychometric test experts should check that:

- any information given to observers concerning participants' personality profiles is brief, accurate and explained clearly. Misinterpretation must be avoided and the observer should not provide feedback of test data to participants.
- all written information, including personality profiles, other than test data given to participants is destroyed after use.

While some aspects of participants' personality profiles can be usefully considered by observers in order to gain a fuller understanding in preparation for feedback interviews, this approach is more difficult with aptitude tests. The reasoning behind this is twofold. Firstly, the results tend to be expressed in a technical format, usually as comparative performance within a norm group. Frequently, some training is required to fully understand this information. Secondly, aptitude test results can be a delicate matter since within any group of development centre participants there is likely to be a range of test results, from high to low. Individual participants may need some careful feedback about the test, the results and the implications. This is often best carried out by a trained test user.

Integration of the results from personality profiles, aptitude tests and development centre exercises is most usefully carried out at an observers' conference. This process is explained in Chapter 6.

Seven questions about psychometric test feedback

There are many different styles of giving feedback but whichever style is used there are a number of principles that should be followed.

1 **Who gives feedback on psychometric test results?** Feedback should be given only by a qualified psychometric expert. The results of any psychometric instrument are confidential and should only be used for agreed purposes.
2 **For how long should the feedback last?** It is usual to indicate the amount of time allocated for any psychometric test feedback sessions. If the participant requests more time than is available, or further exploration of some issues, the psychometric expert could offer a follow-up meeting or refer the participant to a skilled counsellor. For practical reasons it is important to ensure that the timetable is adhered to. Care should also be taken to ensure that the feedback sessions do not become counselling sessions which are not part of the role of the psychometric test expert.
3 **What are the objectives of the feedback?** The psychometric expert can highlight the benefits of feedback at the start of any meeting, particularly: broader self-awareness of one's personality preferences, style and aptitudes; appreciation of the differences in style or ability of others; and appreciation of one's impact on others. An informal contract is also appropriate at this stage to help clarify the participant's expectations of the meeting. For example, the psychometric expert should make it clear that a feedback session is not an in-depth counselling session.

4 **What information should be fed back?** Good test manuals and train-ing highlight the important feedback issues. However, general points to include are that there are no good or bad personality profiles; that a personality questionnaire reflects preferences and styles of thinking and behaving, and these may or may not be appropriate in a given situation, but are not in themselves good or bad.

5 **What is the best style of feedback?** Feedback should be a two-way process, not a one-way information dump. The participant must be made aware that personal comments and discussion are a vital part of the feedback session.

6 **Should social desirability be discussed?** The psychometric expert needs to explain that the accuracy of the results depends on the level of honesty and self-awareness when respondents complete the ques-tionnaire. Personality profiles are not infallible as they are based upon self-report, neither are they 'cast in tablets of stone', there may be some degree of changeability over time.

7 **How do test results link in with personal development?** Finally, in the context of a development centre it is important to talk about a person's aims and hopes with respect to life and career goals. A development centre is a starting point for individual development. It is important to let the participant integrate feedback from observers and psychometric experts with personal work performance and future goals with the aim of producing a development plan.

Integrating test feedback

Feedback of aptitude tests is often relatively quick compared with feedback of personality questionnaires. Consequently, feedback sessions have to be properly planned, and the allocated time should be used efficiently.

In order to maximize the use of feedback time available, two psychometric test experts may be used to cover the feedback sessions. This may mean using an additional expert to feed back personality pro-files and test results. Alternatively, feedback may be spread over two days of the development centre, although this is more difficult to fit into a timetable.

All feedback generally happens on the last day of a development centre (psychometric profiles, test results, and observers' feedback sessions). Each participant will see an assigned observer for over one hour and a psychometric expert for about 40 minutes. Participants may see either their observer or the psychometric expert first. If the psychometric expert feeds back to a participant after the observer feedback has been received, the psychometric data can be more easily integrated with the other data. Personality preferences can be linked to performance on the development centre. For example, observed behaviour in a sales exer-cise can be linked to preferred styles of influence and interaction.

It is preferable to keep the observer–participant ratio high, about 2 : 1 or 3 : 1. An example timetable illustrating the integration of psychometric feedback into the observer feedback timetable is shown in Table 5.2. This is a timetable for 4 × observers, 2 × psychometric experts and 12 × participants.

Table 5.2   *Feedback timetable*

10.00	Observer A meets Participant 1 Observer B meets Participant 4 Observer C meets Participant 7 Observer D meets Participant 10	Participants 2,5,8,11 receive OPQ feedback
11.05	Observer A meets Participant 2 Observer B meets Participant 5 Observer C meets Participant 8 Observer D meets Participant 11	Participants 3,6,9,12 receive OPQ feedback
12.10	Observer A meets Participant 3 Observer B meets Participant 6 Observer C meets Participant 9 Observer D meets Participant 12	Participants 1,4,7,10 receive OPQ feedback

Case study: The BT sales force

The business background

BT's UK sales operation is a professional sales force of 3000 sales and support staff, together with 250 managers. In 1990 the General Manager was confronted by a number of key strategic decisions on how to manage change. To improve his organization he needed to:

- respond to a major company reorganization which transferred large business customers to another division, leaving him with a diminished customer base but identical sales targets;
- allocate existing staff into two new sales grades in order to service the new customer base more effectively;
- develop account management skills in the sales force, which had formerly worked from a basis of technical and product knowledge.

A project team from BT Training liaised with the General Manager and senior sales managers to identify the characteristics which staff would require in the new organization. Detailed job analysis was conducted including interviews, observations and critical incident analysis.

Areas of competence required among staff included analytical and strategic thinking skills; being able to plan and organize work; as well as being able to sell and influence others; product and commercial awareness; and being able to cooperate with and to lead others. Management abilities were classified into Behaviourally Anchored Rating Scales

(BARS) which were expressed as clearly recognizable skills, behaviours, knowledge and attitudes. Clear statements were required for acceptance in an organization which is task oriented and seeks to measure work performance against commercial criteria.

It was agreed that a programme of development centres should be set up as these could be 'customized' to meet business needs.

Selection and design
The objectives of the development centre were to provide the following:

1 Information that would highlight the development and training needs of the sales population and provide a basis for individual development planning involving line managers.
2 A wide-ranging skills audit that would provide aggregate data about skills and aptitudes in order to improve policy and decision making in the areas of manpower planning, succession planning, training and selection.
3 Information about the skills profiles of individual members of the sales force and personal counselling that would allow them to make decisions about their future roles in the new organization as account executives or account managers.

A three-day development centre was designed, using 45 senior sales managers as observers. They were selected on the basis of their commitment to developing sales people. These observers underwent detailed training and selection, including pass/fail training in objective interviewing techniques, as well as having their awareness heightened of interpersonal issues and the enhancement of self-esteem among staff. An observer training workshop was held for familiarization with exercises and to establish agreed rating standards.

During the design stage, exercise materials were subjected to validation by sales managers serving on the joint project team, and by a pilot event using staff with sales experience. The outcomes of both events led to amendments and improvements of the exercise materials.

Competences resulting from the job analysis were assessed by these exercises, which were designed so that they were based upon a 'storyboard' approach and so participants accumulated knowledge in a consistent fashion. This meant they did not have to absorb large quantities of new information at the beginning of each exercise. Participants also took the Graduate and Managerial Assessment (GMA) tests for both numerical and verbal reasoning ability, and the Occupational Personality Questionnaire (OPQ).

Arrangements were made so that each skill area was assessed by different observers to increase accuracy and observer reliability.

Line managers were drawn into the process by providing briefings before their people attended, and by arranging post-development centre review meetings to plan development activity when their people returned to work.

Design work was completed during autumn 1990, and the final content and process were signed off by the project team.

Implementation

A total of 635 participants took part in the development centre programme. The principles underpinning it were as follows:

1 Senior managers who acted as observers did not see their own people on an event.
2 Information obtained on each individual was treated in strict confidence.
3 Each participant owned and held the data collected on personal abilities. Only agreed action points for development were shared with line managers.
4 Only anonymous aggregate data were collected and maintained by the UK sales operations.

Effective use of resources was made through strict scheduling of exercises and psychometrics. The development centre was structured as:

Day 1 An introduction by a senior sales manager to explain the purpose of the event; administration of the Occupational Personality Questionnaire; written exercise; and the GMA verbal reasoning ability test.

Day 2 The GMA numerical reasoning test; planning, group and presentation exercises; and biographical interviews conducted by a personal observer.

Day 3 Feedback by the personal observer of the results of the exercises, and OPQ and GMA feedback by a registered psychometrics practitioner.

Evaluation

Evaluation of the benefits of the development centre programme was based upon interviews with 12 senior sales managers, using the critical incidents technique as well as scale and other available performance ratings. A total of 226 staff (35 per cent of participants) were managed by these managers. Both quantitative and qualitative data, linked to content and statistical procedures, were elicited during these interviews.

The managers provided accounts of 18 instances in which staff had experienced failures at work prior to the development centres. The costs involved were investigated in detail. These costs included payments by the sales person involved or the manager in order to rectify the situation, time wasted at both levels, and any lost customers through BT customers failing to complete negotiations.

Total costs for each individual amounted to £98 000 and the costs for the sample of 18 sales staff reached £1 764 000. Extended across the UK sales organization, the overall costs amounted to £67.2 million. The figure represents direct financial costs, time costs and lost business and is the estimated saving across the organization as a result of improved performance following the development centres.

Total costs expended for each event, including salary, travel and accommodation costs, and research, design and materials, amount to £11 223.

On this basis, the full opportunity cost of the programme of 15 development centres comes to £168 345. This is a one-off payment, while the savings calculated are established on a recurring basis.

Ratings given for staff performance both before and after the programme showed there had been a significant overall improvement in performance. There had been significant improvements in planning and organizing skills and in interpersonal skills. Improvements had also been found in competences relating to customer focus, planning and organizing, and job-related knowledge.

New business accounts had been opened and opportunities acquired through the development of new attitudes. Performance against sales targets showed a significant improvement, and there were six cases in which previously poor performers are now exceeding targets.

The managers said there is now a recognition by staff of the need for better ways of working. They had gained in confidence generally and this had resulted in higher levels of personal initiative and sense of purpose, sometimes through better use of prospect lists. There were significant gains in customer management, commercial awareness, planning and organizing, and sales skills.

More than 90 per cent of participants responded positively to the developmental counselling and feedback they had been given. A majority felt the exercises were valid and appropriate.

Conclusions The benefits of the development centres have enabled the UK sales organization to respond effectively to reorganization, including the allocation of staff into a new customer-oriented structure, and have developed account management skills in the sales force.

BT's sales force is now better positioned to respond positively to changing conditions in the telecommunications market in the 1990s. Emphasis upon the quality of service to BT's customers has been a major performance outcome.

Psychometric tests in use

Psychometric tests which are in common use are listed in Table 5.3, on pages 152–3.

Table 5.3 Psychometric tests that are commonly used on development centres

Target group of staff	Test name	Test supplier/ publisher	Type Aptitude = A Personality = P	Briefing time (min)*	Completion time (min)	Scoring time (min)	Feedback time (min)	BPS accreditation level for test interpreters
Graduates and Managers to Senior Managers	Graduate and Managerial Assessment Test • numerical • verbal • abstract	ASE/NFER NELSON	A	10–20	30	15	15	1
Junior, Middle & Senior Managers, Professional Staff, Sales Specialists, Skilled and Semi-Skilled, Unskilled Operatives and Clerks	Graduate and Management Item Bank • verbal • numerical • spatial • diagrammatic • mechanical • clerical • interest	SAVILLE & HOLDSWORTH Ltd	A	10	10–35	15	15	1
Clerical	General Clerical Test	PSYCHO-LOGICAL CORPORATION	A	10	45	15	15	1
Managers and Management Potential	Critical Reasoning Test • verbal • numerical	ASE/NFER NELSON	A	10	30	15	15	1
Managers, Sales Staff, Clerical and Technical Staff	Differential Aptitude Test • verbal • numerical • abstract	PSYCHO-LOGICAL CORPORATION	A	10	30	15	15	1

Target group of staff	Test name	Test supplier/ publisher	Type Aptitude = A Personality = P	Briefing time (min)*	Completion time (min)	Scoring time (min)	Feedback time (min)	BPS accreditation level for test interpreters
	• language • spelling • accuracy and speed • mechanical reasoning • space relations							
Managerial, Sales, Professional, Clerical and Technical Staff	Occupational Personality Questionnaire	SAVILLE & HOLDSWORTH Ltd	P	10	30–60	20	30	2
Managerial, Professional	Firo-B	OXFORD PSYCHOLOGY PRESS	P	10	20	10	15	2
Managerial/ Career Guidance	Myers Briggs Type Indicator	OXFORD PSYCHOLOGY PRESS	P	10	40	20	20	2
Managerial, Professional, Clerical	Occupational Stress Indicator	ASE/NFER NELSON	P	10	40	20	20	2
Managerial, Sales, Professional, Clerical and Technical Staff	16PF	ASE/NFER NELSON	P	10	30–60	20	30	2

* = Minimum time.

Checklist

Do's   1 Ensure you are clear as to why you want to use psychometric tests and what the outcomes will be.
2 Ensure that you choose tests that are relevant and applicable to the people doing them.
3 Ensure that quality administration and feedback are provided by properly trained, qualified and registered people.

Don'ts   1 Do not use inadequate tests with poor reliability and validity.
2 Do not disregard the importance of confidentiality.
3 Do not leave psychometric materials in places which are accessible to unqualified test users.

Further reading

BPS Books (1990) *Review of Psychometric Tests for Assessment in Vocational Training*, British Psychological Society

Holland, P.W. and Rubin, D.B. (1982) *Test Equating*, Academic Press, London.

Johnson, C.E., Wood, R. and Blinkhorn, S.F. (1988) 'Spyriouser and spuriouser: the use of ipsative personality tests', *Journal of Occupational Psychology*, 61 (2), 153–62.

Lumsden, J. (1979) 'Test theory', *Annual Review of Psychology*, 27, 154–80.

Smith, M., Gregg, M. and Adams, D. (1989) *Selection and Assessment—A New Appraisal*, Pitman, London.

Toplis, J., Dulewicz, V. and Fletcher, C. (1987) *Psychological Testing: A Practical Guide*, Institute of Personnel Management, London.

Addresses of test publishers

Assessment and Selection for Employment (NFER/Nelson)
Darville House
2 Oxford Road East
Windsor
Berkshire SL4 1DF
Great Britain
Tel: 0753 858961 (+44 753 858961)
Telex: 24966001
Fax: 0753 856830 (+44 753 856830)

British Psychological Society
St Andrew's House
48 Princess Road East
Leicester LE1 7DR
Great Britain
Tel: 0533 501203 (+44 533 501203)

Oxford Psychologists Press Ltd
Lambourne House
311–321 Banbury Road

Oxford OX2 7JH
Great Britain
Tel: 0865 510203 (+44 865 510203)

The Psychological Corporation
Foots Cray High Street
Sidcup
Kent DA14 5HP
Great Britain
Tel: 081 300 1149 (+44 81 300 1149)

Saville & Holdsworth Ltd
3 AC Court
High Street
Thames Ditton
Surrey KT7 0SR
Great Britain
Tel: 081 398 4170
Fax: 081 398 9544

6 Feedback techniques

Chris Latham and Tricia Marchbank

Introduction

This chapter focuses on the feedback process that can be used on development centres. The general characteristics of effective feedback are considered as well as specific applications, so that those who receive feedback at the end of a development centre can make best use of the information for personal development planning.

Specific guidance on planning a feedback interview and managing the process is given, along with some general points on feedback of psychometric test results. The use of the Johari window concept and its integration with learning models such as Kolb's learning cycle is considered. The chapter also includes case studies and practical examples to illustrate some feedback situations that can occur on a centre. The training implications for assessors are discussed, together with the need to integrate feedback data and incorporate it into development planning with the use of a development log.

The chapter consists of 10 sections:

- Introduction
- Objectives of feedback
- Creating conditions for effective feedback
- Training in feedback techniques
- Feedback case studies
- Development logs
- Case study: Ensuring high quality feedback and continuing development in ICI Pharmaceuticals
- Checklist
- References and further reading
- Useful addresses

Objectives of feedback

A fundamental characteristic of a development centre is the inclusion of feedback during the programme itself, in which the focus is on developmental action and planning. Other related characteristics include the creation of a climate in which it is possible to experiment, and where it is 'OK' to make mistakes. The development centre process also encourages participants to review their personal performance and analyse their own strengths and development needs.

The way in which feedback processes are designed and implemented is a key determinant of the success of a programme. Therefore, this chapter looks at the nature of feedback, and how it can be used to achieve the objectives of a development centre.

Feedback has been described as 'improved information which has more potential than anything I can think of for creating more competence in the day-to-day management of performance' (Gilbert, 1978).

The purpose of feedback on a development centre is to provide improved information. The whole process is designed around this objective. Two important success criteria are that the feedback should be given in a way that facilitates acceptance and appropriate developmental action planning.

Figure 6.1 illustrates a technique for managing feedback in a way that meets the criteria already discussed.

Contracting for feedback

People will attend a development centre for a variety of reasons and have different expectations. They may be expecting to 'be sorted out' or to receive in-depth counselling. As one line manager put it, 'A member of my staff will be attending next week and I think the course counsellor should know . . .'.

Participants need to know not only what they will be getting out of the feedback interview but also what the discussion boundaries are. This is best positioned at the beginning of the centre and again at the beginning of any feedback session by agreeing what will be discussed and how the discussion will take place.

Also relevant here is the question of who receives feedback from the development centre programme. It is likely that the sponsor of the programme will expect to get information about participants' perform-ance, and it is normal to produce aggregate data on overall performance of a population. However, it is not normal practice to provide feedback on individual performance beyond an agreed small circle of people— see Chapter 11 and the issue of ethics. The recipients of feedback will need to be clarified at an early stage as part of the contracting process. Any agreement with the sponsor of the development centre programme about the dissemination of information on skills and abilities of partici-pants needs to be shared with the participant at the beginning of the development centre.

Line managers will probably be expecting to receive information on the performance of their staff, and of course participants on the develop-ment centre will want to know how they are perceived by the assessors— what people think of them.

The detail of feedback provided to individual participants will depend on the aims and objectives of a particular development centre programme.

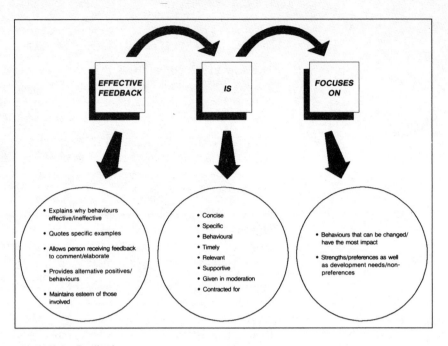

Figure 6.1   Feedback

However, the characteristics listed in Figure 6.1 for giving effective feed-back should apply, irrespective of the provider or recipient of the information.

Creating conditions for effective feedback

As with other interactions between people at work where performance is being discussed, it is important to provide appropriate conditions for conducting feedback meetings. Whatever the location of the development centre, an appropriate and confidential area should be allocated for feedback which ensures the following prerequisites:

- There are no visitors/telephone interruptions.
- Tables/chairs are arranged informally.
- There is adequate room size.
- There is appropriate heating, lighting and ventilation.
- Water jug and glasses are available.

A policy on smoking needs to be agreed. If assessors have requested no smoking in their feedback rooms then time may be needed for cigarette breaks.

Explanation of the feedback interview

Development centre feedback interviews are of central importance since they are the mechanism by which performance levels are discussed with participants. Feedback should help participants to understand their development needs and motivate them to act upon this information. Consequently, the purpose of feedback and the process by which it is carried out should be carefully explained. This can be done in pre-briefing literature and in line manager briefing before participants attend. It also needs to be explained in the introductory session of the development centre itself.

One useful way to explain feedback, which can be used in all of these channels of communication, is to describe the model detailed below, relating it to the development centre process and showing how participants can help make it work by being open about their skills, approaches to work and work preferences.

JOHARI WINDOW

The Johari window provides a useful method for demonstrating the benefits of feedback. It is a model developed by Joe Luft and Harry Ingham, 'Johari' being derived from their first names.

Figure 6.2 illustrates a way in which the model can be demonstrated. In development centre context the four 'panes' of the window can be explained as follows:

Open self This contains information about the participant which is public. The participant knows about himself or herself in this area, and so does the assessor. In the feedback interview there are likely to be many items of performance which are discussed, and about which the participant is aware and has a full understanding.

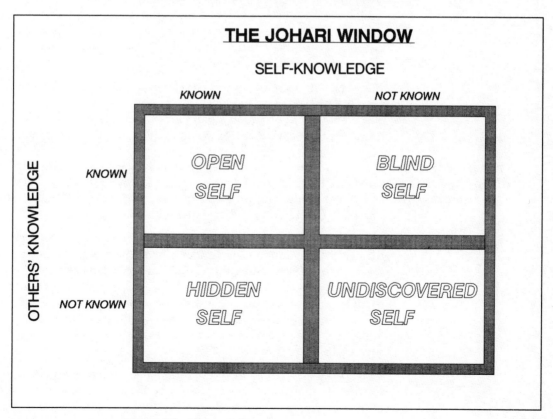

Figure 6.2 Johari window

Blind self   This 'pane' refers to information about the participant which he or she does not know, but which the assessor may know from personal observations or those made by colleagues.

Hidden self   This can also be referred to as the façade 'pane', and is sometimes described as a mask. It contains information that the participant knows about himself or herself but hides from the assessor. It may be some skill area that is relevant to the job but which the participant does not feel confident at, or the participant may have information about personal skills which he or she does not accept.

Undiscovered self   The last 'pane' contains things which neither the participant nor assessor knows about.

The 'size' of these windows can be different according to the situation. For example, an individual may be more open when interacting with a close friend than with a stranger. However, there will usually be a base size from which people operate. Some people are generally more open in all situations than others.

Using the Johari window in the feedback process

In terms of this model, feedback aims to reduce both the blind self and the hidden self by encouraging participants to accept feedback about their performance. Having accepted that their performance on the development centre demonstrated strengths in some areas and weaknesses in others, and that their performance on the development centre was indicative of workplace performance in similar activities, they can start to use this information to plan personal development in order to improve workplace performance.

The blind self decreases when participants receive feedback from other people. The hidden self reduces in size when participants provide observers with information about perceptions, feelings and opinions. Assessors then have a context within which to judge behaviour.

What goes wrong during feedback interviews?

The Johari window concept has proved very useful for planning and managing feedback interviews for the majority of development centre participants. However, problems may occur in a small number of cases. These are described below, together with coping strategies for assessors.

The assessor and participant may not be operating with any level of trust so that the hidden self is maintained. The assessor may promote this atmosphere by telling the participant the results but not allowing discussion or comment. Alternatively, the participant may choose not to share hopes and aspirations, and not commit himself or herself to developmental activity. This may be dealt with by social discussion to build trust or by reassurance from the assessor before discussing feedback issues.

Participants may refuse to accept information and instead either give spuriously rational reasons for their performance or talk disparagingly of the development centre content validity. As a consequence they block any attempt to examine their personal impact on other people or their work performance, and leave the feedback interview session with no alternative approaches to their present behaviour. This can be managed by offering subtle challenges. One approach is to identify the participant's own aspirations and then discuss the way in which his or her behaviour is perceived by others, and how others' perceptions may prevent the realization of aspirations.

Occasionally, participants have low levels of self-awareness and self-understanding and appear as silent members or low reactors with the rest of the group when completing the development centre's assessed exercises. Consequently, little is known about them at the end of the development centre, and the undiscovered self remains a comparatively large area. In this situation it is important to look at sources of evidence from individual work such as written exercises, and use this as the basis of discussion.

Once trust levels exist between an assessor and a participant the feedback interviews are always much more productive.

Explaining the Johari window

The concept of the Johari window is best introduced at the beginning of the development centre as part of the introduction. This tends to reinforce messages that the centre is developmental and not assessment orientated.

An alternative explanation of feedback may also be used.

COMPETENCY MODEL

This model is particularly relevant when dealing with competency-based development. It is concerned with self-awareness of one's own competence, and is illustrated in Figure 6.3.

The Johari model can be related to this in the following way. In order to move from unconscious incompetence (the blind self), or as Huntley (1990) puts it the 'don't know what they don't know' stage, to being conscious of incompetence so that something can be done about it the open self needs to be extended.

Feedback on the development centre is specifically aimed at doing just that. The conscious/unconscious model can be used to good effect with participants who are experienced in their work and cynical about the value of development centres.

In this situation the model can be presented by starting with the unconscious competence stage, explaining that it is normal to slip into the unconscious incompetence through complacency. The analogy of 'driving a car from A to B as an experienced driver and not being able to remember doing so!' is appropriate here. Then ask how many people drive according to the driving test rules. This offers an example of unconscious incompetence that can re-occur on a learned skill.

The development centre feedback can help to identify these areas. This point can be further reinforced by pointing out that the best athletes in the world still practise every day and have professional coaches.

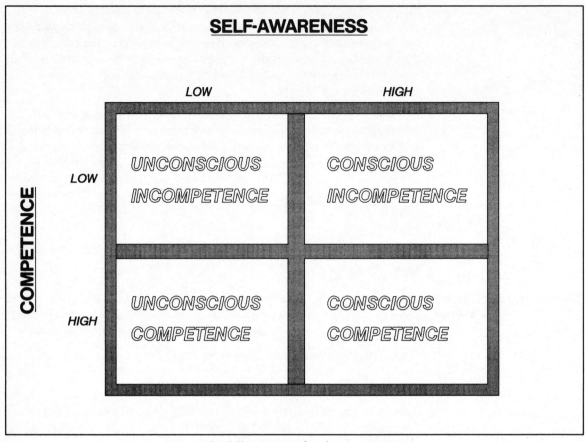

Figure 6.3 *Self-awareness of one's own competence*

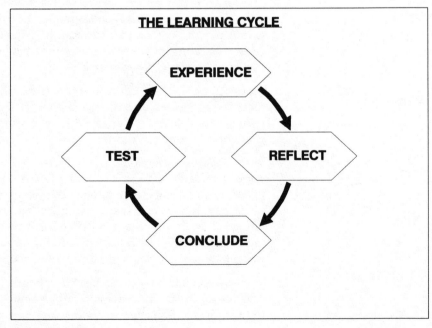

Figure 6.4 *The learning cycle*

Table 6.1 *Structure of feedback interview*

Sequence	Suggested content	Possible duration (min)
1	Introduction and purpose	10
2	Seek participant's view of the development centre and personal performance on the development centre	15
3	Go through each exercise	40
	• Ask participant to review what happened • Ask participant how they felt they tackled the problem • Provide observer's objective view • Explore differences • Identify one or two key points • Summarize overall performance	
4	Refer to development log/identify key development actions	15
5	Discuss next steps	10

Therefore, employees who adopt a similar approach are adopting best practice in skills maintenance.

LEARNING CYCLES

One other model that can also be used to explain the concept of feedback to participants is Kolb's learning cycle. Kolb argues that in order to learn, we need to go through four stages. These are illustrated in Figure 6.4.

Kolb calls these stages concrete experience/observations and reflections/ formations of abstract concepts and generalizations/ testing implications of concepts in new situations.

This model can be related to the development centre process in the following way. The development centre programme provides a structured experience, including time for individual reflection. The provision of specific feedback from assessors helps to complete the stage at which conclusions are drawn. Support from assessors at this stage facilitates the development of action plans and the testing of new behaviours which lead to beneficial change.

The feedback interview Feedback should take place at the end of the development centre before participants depart and while the experience is still fresh in their minds. At this stage participants are eager for feedback, reflective and willing to experiment with new approaches to work. Placing feedback interviews at this point in the timetable also meets the timely and relevant criteria for effectiveness which were mentioned at the beginning of this chapter.

Chapter 5 contains a timetable that shows how the assessor feedback can be integrated with the psychometric feedback. An example timetable for the one-to-one feedback interviews between assessors and participants is illustrated in Table 6.1.

Feedback interviews fully achieve their objectives when certain conditions are met:

- When trust levels exist between assessor and participant.
- When the feedback data are accurate, specific and concise.
- When assessors allow time and space for discussion.
- When the assessor is open and non-judgemental.
- When the participant is open, honest and enquiring.
- When confidentiality is respected.

Logistical issues   The timetable for one-to-one feedback typically allows 60–90 minutes per interview, and the logistics will be determined by factors such as the number of participants, the number of assessors and the assessor–participant ratio. The most common ratio of 2 : 1 would allow the completion of feedback interview during the course of half a day, with each assessor conducting two interviews.

Assessors can build trust with participants and increase the value of feedback by undertaking a 15-minute review on a one-to-one basis following the completion of each exercise. These short review meetings can focus on the participant's performance, learning points and possible future approaches to similar problems. The emphasis would be on the participant's perceptions of his or her performance and assessors would not give feedback until the end of the programme, by which time they would have produced a balanced and objective judgement of overall performance. The advantages of these short reviews are that they encourage participants to focus on personal performance and individual learning. They can encourage rapport building between assessors and participants in preparation for the final interview. They can also be used to enhance esteem and confidence if participants perceive that they performed badly in a particular exercise. The main disadvantages of this approach are that it requires extra work for assessors and uses up available time.

If this approach is adopted, it is helpful to include a personal review form for participants to complete before and after each exercise. This asks them to consider their objectives in completing the exercise, an assessment of performance in completing the exercise, and identification of personal learning points in completing this activity. Personal review forms can be used as the basis of discussion in the post-exercise meeting, and can provide a useful basis for comparing individual perceptions of performance and assessor's perceptions of performance in the final feedback interview. An example of such a form is illustrated in Figure 6.5.

PERSONAL PERFORMANCE REVIEW FORM

Participant's Name _____

Exercise _____   *Date* _____

SECTION 1. For completion before the exercise

1. What are my objectives in completing this exercise?

2. How will I achieve these objectives?

SECTION 2. For completion after the exercise

3. How successful was I in achieving the objectives?

   What did I do well?

   What did not work well?

4. What would I do differently next time?

SECTION 3. For completion after discussion with observer

5. What are my learning points from the discussion?

Figure 6.5   Personal performance review form

Psychometric test feedback

While detailed information about the use of psychometric tests is described in Chapter 5, guidance about the feedback of test results and the integration of test data with other performance results from development centre exercises is contained below. The technique for providing feedback on psychometric test data does not differ greatly from the general principles of feedback established at the beginning of this chapter. The main considerations involve:

• Explaining the purpose of tests.

- Providing an interpretation of the test results.
- Facilitating discussion on the implications.

A useful time-saving device is to provide an overview of the test to the entire group of participants, explaining the purpose, outcomes and general issues of interpretation. This obviates the need for explaining general issues to every participant during one-to-one feedback, and allows this time to be used for discussing individual results.

Key points to remember when giving psychometric feedback:

- There is ethical obligation to share psychometric test results' information with the test respondent, and in some cases a legal requirement to do so.
- Psychometric test results are often expressed in technical language, and respondents may need help with interpretation and understanding.
- The purpose of psychometric tests is not widely understood, and may lead to anxieties. Psychometricians need to spend time in allaying fears and countering misconceptions so that respondents can make best use of the information.

With ability tests it may not be appropriate to discuss strategies for improving the score during possible future attempts at the test, but instead look at changes in behaviour to cope with current ability.

Training in feedback techniques

The issue of feedback is constantly identified by assessors as a role which they have most concerns about. It is also a development centre skill area in which they feel least confident. Consequently, it is helpful to allocate some of the time during an assessor training workshop to feedback skills training. As with many skills training courses, one useful approach is behaviour modelling in which trainees are given a model, allowed the opportunity to practise using the model and offered feedback on their application of the model.

The provision of feedback by assessors is slightly different from other behavioural interactions in that there is an ethical dimension and a need for extremely good interpersonal skills. Consequently, before presenting a model for managing the feedback process it is often useful to include a discussion of ethical issues and social skills.

Ethics and skills of feedback

Assessors are not expected to be qualified counsellors but many counselling principles are relevant. These are illustrated in Figure 6.6.

A model for managing the feedback interview

Assessors may wish to use the following five-step process for managing the feedback interview, illustrated below. This contains a process that avoids the need for assessors to justify or to become defensive about assessment decisions.

Step 1   Explain objectives

It is useful to highlight that this interview is the most important element of the development centre, and that its purpose is to:

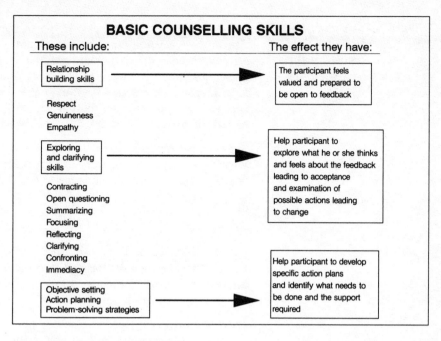

Figure 6.6 *Basic counselling skills*

(a) identify the participant's strengths and development needs;
(b) identify ways in which strengths can be used more extensively;
(c) look at the significance of weak areas, and how these might be overcome;
(d) look at approaches to development planning so that overall workplace planning might be improved.

Step 2   General views   Ask the participant for general views about the development centre, and discuss these if appropriate. This step allows participants to raise any matters that they see as important, and which may inhibit discussions of current performance and future development.

Step 3   Explain the feedback interview agenda   Suggest to the participant that one way of managing the feedback interview is to review each exercise in turn by:

(a) looking at its objectives;
(b) discussing the way in which the participant prepared for and completed the activity;
(c) identifying the participant's own perception of performance in that exercise;
(d) discussing the assessor's perceptions of the participant's performance;
(e) exploring differences between the individual's and the assessor's perceptions;
(f) identifying key learning points.

Step 4   Start with the first exercise that was completed by the participant

(a) Look at its objectives and ask the participant to describe the exercise, and what it required the participant to do. This is a useful activity because the participant may have completed several exercises subsequently, and in an intensive programme may by now have forgotten the detail of individual exercises.

(b) Discuss the way in which the participant prepared for and completed the activity.

Suggest that the participant refer to the personal assessment form, if these were used, and identify the approach adopted to complete the activity. This offers some insights to the participant's approach to workplace tasks.

(c) Identify the participant's own perception of performance in that exercise.

Ask the participant to identify aspects of the task which he or she perceived as being effective and those which were perceived as ineffective. Discuss the reasons for these perceptions.

(d) Discuss the assessor's perceptions of the participant's performance.

Provide an overview of the assessor's perceptions, offering the participant an opportunity to read any written reports completed by the assessor on his or her performance in that particular exercise.

(e) Explore differences between the individual's and the assessor's perceptions.

In most cases, participants view their performance in a way that is similar to the assessor's perception of the same event. In many cases, the participant exercises a harsher judgement than the assessor. Rarely does the participant reject the assessor's view.

If big differences in perception do emerge, the assessor who is managing the feedback interview should avoid justifying his or her assessment or that of a colleague, but instead should ask the participant questions such as:

'What do you think you did that caused the assessor to see you in that particular way?'

'How could you tackle a similar situation differently so that you are not seen in that way by other people?'

'How would you like to be viewed by others in this situation. What behaviours could you exhibit so that you are seen in the preferred way?'

(f) Identify key learning points.

Ask the participant to list key learning points from the discussion of performance in that exercise.

Step 5   Identify development priorities

Having completed a discussion of performance in all exercises, ask the participant to look at the list of key learning points that have been accumulated, and to select the three areas that would have most impact on his or her work.

Taking each of the three areas in turn, discuss ways in which the participant could:

(a) acquire skills in these areas through development action or training;
(b) apply and monitor the application of new skills in their current work;
(c) test that the new skills or modified behaviours were working and that workplace performance was better as a result.

Feedback case studies

Participant responses to feedback, and coping strategies for assessors

The assessor training workshop could also include some element of discussion on techniques for coping with different responses to feedback from participants. Common responses and assessor's coping strategies are illustrated in the case studies shown below. However, it is useful to remember that these examples of initial rejection of feedback are extreme responses seen in only a very small proportion of feedback interviews (maybe less than 5 per cent of all feedback interviews).

Situation 1
A participant was receiving feedback on a personality questionnaire. Prior to the development centre he had completed the same questionnaire and paid a consultancy firm to provide an interpretation. This suggested that the participant had no development needs and was highly competent.

During the development centre feedback interview the participant quoted the consultant's report in order to reinterpret or reject assessments made on the development centre. To help the participant focus on the present results the assessor challenged the participant in the following way:

Feedback: 'The results suggest you may have a relatively high anxiety level—how does this affect you?'

Response: 'I am very alive to what goes on around me.'

Feedback: 'Why do you take this result to mean what you have just said?'

The interpretation is then explained again.

The participant could not provide a reason at this point, apart from referring to the previous report. Consequently the assessor said, 'Restate in your own words the interpretation I have just given you.'

By offering him an alternative way to behave the assessor facilitated a move to looking at the present result and away from using the previous report as a defensive shield.

Situation 2

The participant had received feedback on performance from a trainee assessor during an assessor training workshop. He then asked for a second opinion from one of the tutors who was running the workshop. The tutor was aware that the trainee had found it difficult to provide feedback to this person. More specifically, that the recipient would accept positive feedback but reject feedback he saw as negative by saying 'In the real world I would do that differently.'

The tutor agreed to provide additional feedback as it was part of the contract with the 'mock' participants who were attending the assessor training workshop.

When the participant adopted the same approach with the tutor, dismissing development areas on the basis that they would not behave in that way in the real world the tutor asked 'What do you feel is the difference in terms of reality between those exercises in which you have done well and those in which you feel you have not done so well?

When the participant admitted there was no real difference, he then started to use the 'secret plan' argument to explain why material had been left out of his answer. When asked why he had not contributed in a group exercise he said that he had a strategy to observe the others, and deliberately did not explain his full plan for influencing the others so they would not be able to foil it.

The tutor then asked the broad question 'Do you have a skill if you don't display it?', which the participant was happy to discuss. This led to the more specific question 'How do you think the assessors could see what was going on in your mind?', to which the participant admitted they could not. The discussion then led on to actions which he could take to ensure that people saw him working effectively.

Situation 3

The person receiving feedback was a tense and passive individual, attending a centre where other participants were of a higher grade than he was. Reasons for his attendance were unclear. He had been nominated by his line managers and thought that he would be punished if he did not attend. During the feedback interview he expected to hear only about his faults and shortcomings.

The assessor giving the feedback decided that in this case it would be appropriate to feed back overall performance against each competence rather than focus on each exercise. In this way the participant could be helped to understand quickly general levels of ability rather than sticking with the detail of each exercise which might confirm the low esteem he had of himself.

The assessor noted that when he fed back specific rating scores the participant adopted a defensive posture. For exampe, arms held tight to the body and avoidance of eye contact. When the assessor changed the style of feedback to describing performance on the development in words, highlighting abilities and suggesting how these could be used, the participant relaxed his posture, opened his arms and looked more at the assessor. He also asked more questions and made more comments on the feedback.

Situation 4

A participant in his mid-forties received feedback on his performance after attending a specialist skills development centre. He had some specialist training and had held positions of responsibility in a sport at national level. He saw himself as worldly-wise and liked to use jargon where possible.

During the feedback session he learnt of an assessor's rating with which he was unhappy and would not accept. The rating referred to group exercise behaviour and he argued that the assessor was wrong and had not understood the strategy he was using.

In response to this, the assessor giving the feedback read out specifically what the participant had said at the group exercise and asked for his interpretation, and if that is what he had said.

The assessor then asked him why he thought another assessor who observed the incident had interpreted the behaviour in that way. When he said he didn't know the assessor asked 'What did you do that caused you to be perceived in this way?'

He still did not know so the assessor said 'Let us look at a different perspective. Imagine you are the other person in this interaction, if someone behaved in this way to you how would you feel? The response was 'I wouldn't like it.'

The assessor then asked 'What behaviours would you want to see in the other person in this situation?' The participant identified several and listed them when requested.

In this way the participant was helped to identify and accept that changes in his own behaviour would be beneficial.

Situation 5

In this situation the assessor was the same level as the person receiving feedback. The participant valued her status as a professional and did not want to receive feedback from someone she knew. She also thought that the centre focused too much on assessment.

The assessor discussed with the participant at the beginning of the feedback session what process to use for managing the feedback interview, and they agreed to explore the assessor's comments about performance in each exercise, taking each exercise in turn, then identify key learning points.

The participant indicated that she was interested in the comments of peers by saying 'I want to see what they think of me.'

She then rejected all assessments. For example when the assessors identified that some elements of an in-tray exercise had been disregarded the response was that the assessor had missed them in the post exercise assessment.

The assessor knew the participant was ambitious and dealt with this by moving away from the exercise to the job by asking the participant 'When planning in the work situation what sort of approach do senior managers value?'

The participant responded to this approach and between them they drew up a list, highlighting areas that the participant needed to develop in order to prove that she was ready for promotion. For each of these areas, a series of development activities was identified, and a development plan was drawn up.

Situation 6

The participant was highly rated and ambitious. At the beginning of the feedback session she said that she was there to learn, and wanted development points and guidance on how to use the data.

The process of feedback was agreed, and involved the assessor discussing performance for each exercise. Then possible development action was discussed. The participant liked this approach and asked for specific advice on how to deal with each agreed development point. She also asked how the psychometric feedback, which had already been explained during an earlier meeting, could be integrated with the performance data.

At the end of the feedback session she asked if she could contact the assessor for advice after she had returned to work, and a few weeks later she renewed the contact. An unofficial mentoring relationship was established.

Development logs

A big problem commonly faced by managers of development centre programmes is that the enthusiasm and motivation to develop, prompted by participation in a development centre, is often dissipated by inertia and activity after participants return to the workplace. The problem can be reduced by fostering a culture of independence among participants. This means that participants need to accept responsibility for their own development and they need an organizationally sanctioned process for planning and implementing developmental activity. This can be achieved through a development log.

Development logs are used to convert development needs identified by the development centre into work-based action which addresses these needs. They are a useful bridge between the development centre and the workplace. Owned by participants, they are used to store data about performance on a development centre, and contain the following information:

- A list of the competences that are used on the development centre.
- Space for recording data on development centre performance.
- Space to record priority development activities.
- A planning document to plan development activity for each priority development activity.
- Guidance on the training that an organization provides and which is relevant to each development centre competence.
- Guidance on workplace development activity, linked to each development centre competence.
- Reading lists.
- Useful names, addresses and sources of advice.

A good development log will be designed to encourage the collaboration of line managers in agreeing priority development areas, planning appropriate development activity and reviewing progress in implementing development plans. An example of a typical planning document contained in a development log is illustrated in Figure 6.7.

Designing a development log

Consideration should be given as to whether the log is loose-leaf, i.e. may be added to so that it can be used to file reports written by observers, or whether a bound volume is produced. A bound volume may lend itself to higher quality printing and can still contain pro formas to be completed by participants as a working document. However, it cannot be added to.

Cover designs

Ideally, the cover should allow for participants to identify their own log from other people's and should include their name.

Development Log

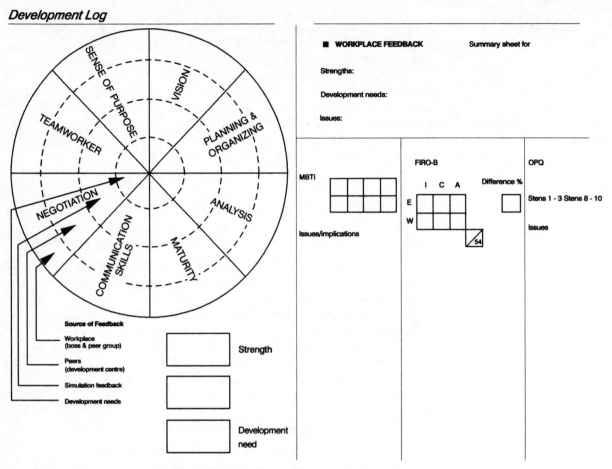

Figure 6.7   Development log

Summary of Contents
- Introduction
- Competences
- Personal evaluation of performance and feedback from observers
- Personal development planning
- Workplace development activities
- Suggested reading

Typical contents of a development log
- Introduction—this consists of an introduction to the development centre with details of the programme, objectives and the main outputs. It should emphasize confidentiality of data and also explain links with other development initiatives.
- Timetable—for the development centre.
- Competences—a full explanation of the competences and rating scales.
- Personal evaluation of performance—a questionnaire for participants to complete during and/or after each DC exercise. An example appears in Figure 6.5.

There can also be room to record results from psychometric tests undertaken during the event and to file written reports containing feedback from observers. An example is included in Figure 6.7.

Development planning

There are many different ways to design such a section but the basic ingredients are:

- an explanation of the process;
- a means to discuss assessor/participant ratings and to agree development areas;
- a means to agree priorities with the line manager;
- a means to translate development needs and action on to a personal development planner.

The identification of development areas can be assisted by focusing on the competences and behavioural anchors and on the priorities of the job. A pro forma personal development planner is shown in Figure 6.8.

Personal development planner

Some explanation of the development planning process should be included in the log. This should include the explanation of a process and the roles of participant, assessor and line manager in the development planning process.

Case study: Ensuring high quality feedback and continuing development in ICI Pharmaceuticals

The assessment and development centres run within the commercial function aim to provide data that will contribute to succession plans and that will help develop a broad base of talent. This demands that as much thought and effort go into the post-centre processes as to the planning, design and implementation of the centres themselves.

To achieve this we have introduced feedback training and processes designed to enable line managers to:

- keep the senior managers responsible for succession planning abreast of the individual's development and aspirations;
- use the centre reports to provide high-quality, usable feedback to the individual;
- build the agreed development actions into our normal performance management processes.

Following on from each centre an individual development report is prepared for each participant. This gives detailed feedback, in behavioural terms, on the individual's level of achievement against each element of the competency framework. Development needs are also noted, again in behavioural terms, although the report deliberately stops short of making recommendations about how the development need should be addressed. It is for the individual and his or her line manager to agree which are the priority needs, which strengths can be built upon and how these two elements might most effectively be addressed.

The draft report, which is derived from assessor reports, is tested with a small pool of assessors and managers before being finalized. This

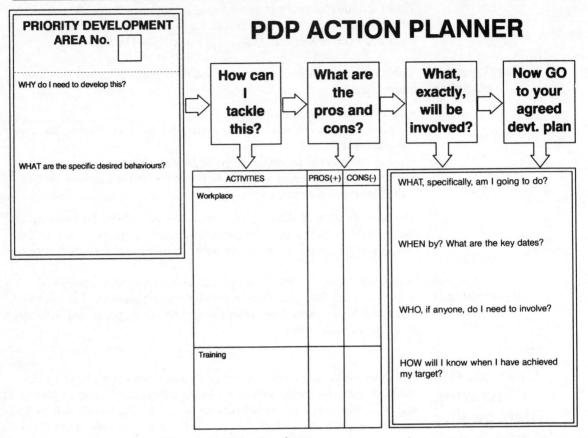

Figure 6.8   PDP action planner

provides an opportunity to check for sense and clarity. It also allows us to test whether the behavioural examples quoted substantiate the overall conclusion about an individual's competence and whether they will provide the basis of quality, usable feedback. They are tested against three key criteria:

- Specificity
- Relevance
- Observed behaviour rather than subjective judgements

Once the reports have been finalized, an executive summary is prepared for succession planning purposes. This highlights individuals' strengths and development needs and provides the career development group with a useful focus and summary of key information when considering individuals for particular vacancies and for future planning. These summaries have a maximum shelf life of two years. During that time, and subsequently, the individual's line manager is responsible for updating the representative on the career development group about the individual's progress against development goals in particular and competency framework in general.

The line manager can only do this effectively if the data from the centre are incorporated into normal management processes. All managers receive training, as part of our performance management processes, in the key skills of giving feedback and agreeing development goals and actions with individuals. Training for line managers of centre participants (who, although they may be trained assessors, will not have assessed their nominee), therefore, concentrates on:

- developing their understanding of the assessment/development centre process and how it fits into our overall management development scheme;
- familiarizing them with the general style and content of reports and, in particular, with the detail of their nominee's report;
- identifying key issues in feeding back the data to the individual (e.g. if the nominee's perception of his or her performance does not match the assessor's) and discussing how to handle these;
- deepening their understanding of and skills in giving feedback and in choosing appropriate development activities.

While much of the content is 'timeless', the training is deliberately held when the centre reports are available. Experience has shown that managers need time, space and availability of management developers to help them really understand the reports and the issues they raise.

Following on from the training, managers meet briefly with centre participants. At this meeting, they convey the 'headlines' of the report and suggest a process for handling feedback thereafter. The usual process is for the individual to read the report 'at leisure' and to meet with his or her manager some 7–10 days later.

At this meeting, the report—and its implications—are discussed in some detail. Typically, it will result in performance targets which will allow the individual to develop/demonstrate the competences in which he or she has performed less well, targets which will enable the individual to build on existing strengths, and a detailed development plan to enable achievement against these targets. This is reviewed at least once a quarter as part of the normal performance management process.

The majority of post-centre development is on the job through coaching and careful choice of work assignments. Where necessary, this is supplemented by off-job training.

As the individual develops, his or her 'sponsor' on the career development group is updated. Managers are required to do this formally at least once a year.

The feedback training and processes described above have contributed much to both the credibility and the value of our centres. We have moved from a position where development really only happened for the 'stars' to one where, by integrating feedback into our wider management processes, centres really are able to fulfil their twin aims of contributing to succession planning and developing a broad base of talent.

Both participants and managers recognize the value of and quality of post-centre development:

'I received positive and constructive feedback on my performance that set the scene for discussions on my development goals and subsequent action plans. The process of identifying development goals and then working up a plan to achieve these goals has been very beneficial. This, in my opinion, is probably the most important element of the centre, since I can now start addressing my needs to improve my performance.'

(Centre participant)

'My own view is that these [development reports] are a tremendous step forward in constructive, focused development.'

(Director of Marketing)

'The development needs at the end of each section are very valuable as a means of focusing on the relevance of centre feedback to real life.'

(Senior Product Manager)

The keys to our success in ensuring high quality feedback and continuing development are as follows:

- Review of draft reports by a small core of assessors.
- Building on the development processes/systems already in place.
- Making line managers responsible for handling centre feedback and for integrating actions arising from it into our normal management processes.
- Training them to fulfil these responsibilities.
- Limiting the 'shelf life' of centre reports and providing for regular updates.
- Asking participants for feedback on the 'de-brief' and subsequent development planning, in order to refine the training and support available to line managers.

Checklist

Do's
1 Include feedback of the results as part of the centre.
2 Explain the feedback process at the beginning of the centre.
3 Ensure assessors have the ability to feed back development centre results.
4 Provide a development centre log that participants can own and use for ongoing development.

Don'ts
1 Do not assume feedback will always be welcome.
2 Do not assume assessors are automatically comfortable giving feedback.

References and further reading

Beard, D. and Lee G. (1990) 'New connections in BT's development centres', *Personnel Management*, April, 61–3.
Egan, G. (1990) *The Skilled Helper*, 4th edn., Brooks Cole, Belmont, California.

Gilbert, J.F. (1978) *Human Competence: Engineering Worthy Performance*, McGraw-Hill, New York.

Huntley, S. (1990) 'Johari Window—How blind are we to its uses?', *Training and Development Journal*, June, 17–21.

Kolb, D.A. (1984) *Experiential Learning*, Prentice Hall, New Jersey.

Useful addresses

For feedback and counselling skills training:

Oxford Training
Bankside
Hanborough Business Park
Long Hanborough
Oxford OX7 2LJ
Great Britain
Tel: 0993 883338 (+44 993 883338)

Walpole Occupational Psychologists
61–63 St John Street
London WC1M 4AN
Great Britain
Tel: 071 253 2340 (+44 71 253 2340)

7 Implementation of development centre programmes

Tricia Marchbank and Anne Guymer

Introduction

This chapter discusses practical and logistical issues for consideration during the design and implementation stages of a development centre programme. It is divided into several sections and includes case studies, one of which shows how one organization has managed the design and implementation of development centre programmes. The sections are as follows:

- Introduction
- Project planning and management
- Assessor selection—criteria and issues regarding the selection of assessors to work on the events
- Assessor training—techniques to pass on the necessary skills and knowledge to assessors
- Line manager briefing—the role and the briefing for line managers
- Participant briefing
- Course secretaries—the role and the briefing for course secretaries.
- Role players—selecting and briefing role players
- Case Studies: 1. An Indian Government department
               2. Assessor training in ICI Pharmaceuticals
- Checklist
- References and further reading
- Useful addresses

Project planning and management

The design and implementation process of a development centre programme is a complex set of activities which leads to an outcome which meets the company's requirements for improving workplace performance of a target population. The design project cannot be carried out in isolation from implementation, and a project team is often needed to coordinate the work of design experts in order to produce something that meets the needs of the organization in a practical way.

Most development centre programmes are costly and need considerable commitment throughout an organization in order for them to work effectively. This needs effective coordination of concurrent activities. Additionally, development centre programmes tend to be highly visible and excite the interest of senior managers. Consequently, those who have responsibility for design and implementation often need to plan and manage the project in a highly efficient manner.

The key stages to effective project management are as follows:

1 Identify who is asking for the development centre programme
  (a) Do they have authority to commission it?
  (b) Do they have the budget to pay for it?
  (c) Do they have the power to implement it?
2 What are the objectives of the development centre programme?
  (a) What are the desired outcomes?
  (b) How will the owner know that it has met its objectives?
  (c) Who will attend?
  (d) What use will be made of the data on participants' skills?
  (e) What are the deadlines for implementation?
3 Who will design the development centre?
  (a) To what standards?
  (b) Who will agree to the design and to the finished product?
  (c) What are the limitations on cost and sophistication?
4 Who will run the development centres?
  (a) Who are the assessors?
  (b) How will they be selected, briefed and trained?
  (c) What is the role of the line managers, and who will brief them?
  (d) How will participants be selected and briefed?
5 Who will manage implementation?
  (a) Who will plan and manage the programme?
  (b) Where will the programme be implemented (office accommodation, hotel, training accommodation)?
  (c) Who will book accommodation?
  (d) Who will act as course secretary, how will he or she be briefed and trained?
  (e) How will role players (for exercises) be selected, briefed and trained?
  (f) How will assessors be programmed to run development centres?
6 How will the development centre be evaluated?
  (a) Who will design the evaluation process?
  (b) Who will carry out evaluation?
  (c) Who will receive the evaluation data, and in what form should the data be presented?

An effective method for managing design and implementation is to establish a project team which consists of the customer, designer and implementation manager. This will plan the entire project and organize appropriate resources. Specialist design and implementation teams can be set up to carry out specialist functions within this overall framework. The main design and implementation stages are illustrated in Figure 7.1. These can be incorporated into a computer-based project plan.

THE PROCESS OF DESIGN FOR DEVELOPMENT CENTRES

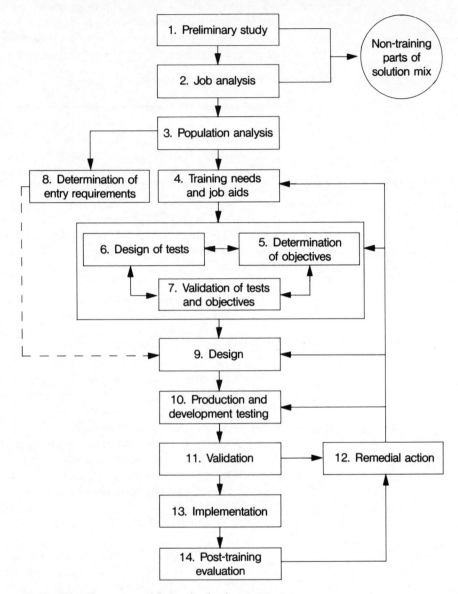

Figure 7.1   *The process of design for development centres*

Assessor selection

The assessor's role
Once the design team has completed work to an agreed specification on the content, timetable and materials of a development centre, responsibility for the success of the programme is effectively handed over to an implementation team and the assessors who will be running the programme. Assessment decisions about the performance of participants are based on observations and recorded evidence, so the accuracy of the data produced on a development centre is very heavily dependent upon the skills of assessors. The way in which participants perceive the development centre, and the value which they derive from taking part, are also affected by the behaviour and the skills of the assessor team.

The role of a development centre assessor can be summarized as follows:

1 To collect and record data on the performance and views of the participants during the development centre.
2 To collate and interpret during assessors' conferences information about the abilities of participants.
3 To provide individual participants with feedback from the development centre, and assistance in the formulation of realistic developmental action plans.
4 To discuss and agree with participants the way in which the development centre outputs can be used in the workplace, and how the line manager will be informed and involved.
5 To operate on the basis of confidentiality, not divulging information about participants to other people.

Selection criteria for assessors
In most cases, the assessors who run development centres are managers or supervisors who work within the organization. In many cases they will be known to the participants. Consequently, great care is needed in the selection and training of assessors. The precise criteria upon which assessors are selected will be influenced by organizational considerations. However, there are a number of generic qualities which are essential for effectively carrying out this role.

Assessment skills
The minimum skill which all assessors require is that of assessment. This is a 'hard' analytical skill and can be broken down into four elements:

1 **Observation**: the ability to observe the behaviours of participants as they complete activities within a development centre.
2 **Recording**: making written notes of behaviours as they occur, for later analysis. This constitutes the evidence of performance and ability.
3 **Classification**: classifying observed and recorded behaviour against the appropriate competences.
4 **Evaluation**: evaluating the performance of participants in each area of competence used on the development centre by evaluating the evidence and giving it a numerical rating, using the criteria rating scale (see Chapter 2).

Assessors acquire these skills through training in the use of critical incident interviewing techniques and assessment exercises. Many large companies such as ICI, Olivetti and BP have their own training programmes to provide managers with these skills. Specialist training companies such as Oxford Training and Saville & Holdsworth Ltd also offer good quality assessor training. Addresses for these organizations are given at the end of this chapter.

Additionally, assessors need to understand the specific details of exercises, timetable, feedback techniques and performance standards which are applicable to the development centre programme on which they will be working. This may require additional training in the form of familiarization workshops. Experience of training assessors indicates that they have concerns in two main areas. Firstly, in their ability to record evidence, particularly of activities such as group exercises. Secondly, in their ability to manage one-to-one feedback interviews. These are two areas of skills-building which can usefully be given detailed attention in any assessor training workshop. A third area of difficulty which often occurs on development centre programmes, and which can be pre-empted at the assessor training stage, is the quality of written reports. Assessors often have to give one-to-one feedback to participants using written reports which are produced by other assessors. In some instances this activity is made unnecessarily difficult by the poor quality of written reports. Assessor training should stress the need for concise, accurate and detailed reports.

Social and communication skills

In addition to the analytical skills of assessment, effective assessors also have good communications skills. Specifically:

- Listening skills
- Questioning skills
- Interpersonal skills
- Empathy

Personal qualities

A third dimension in which effective assessors score highly is that of personal qualities. These include:

- integrity, honesty and the ability to respect confidences;
- open mindedness and a non-judgemental approach;
- credibility based on experience and managerial professionalism.

Other considerations

The working relationship between assessors and participants also needs to be considered. If assessors are the line managers of the participant population then care is needed to avoid placing a line manager in the position of directly assessing a member of staff. This will avoid assessment errors arising from previous knowledge and perceptions of the participant, and will probably also alleviate extra pressure for the participant. An assessor–participant matrix drawn up in advance, indicating which assessor will observe which participants for each of the assessed exercises and feedback interviews, is a practical way to ensure the appropriate allocation of assessors to participants.

Number of assessors This will vary according to the number of participants, but an ideal assessor–participant ratio is 1 : 2. The main constraints to changing this ratio are related to resources and practical timetable issues.

Assessor population Responsibility for selection, briefing and training of assessors needs to be agreed at the initial contracting stage of the development programme. Experience indicates that two months may be needed in order to produce a skilled pool of assessors, particularly if busy line managers are used for this role.

Assessor selection and training is best carried out as an activity which runs concurrently with design.

Training assessors

In the section relating to assessor selection a distinction was made between training in generic assessment skills and familiarization training for running specific development centre programmes. The general assumption is made that skilled and experienced assessors can be used to run programmes with minimum additional training, although the BT Trainer Development Centre example in Chapter 1 should make one question this. This section provides guidance on both the provision of generic assessment skills and familiarization training for specific development centre programmes.

Assessment skills training One of the key prerequisites for assessor selection is that the potential assessor should be trained in assessment techniques. This is similar to the training that would be given to assessors from personnel departments who use the techniques for recruitment or promotion.

In large British and American organizations this form of training is often mandatory, and frequently of a pass/fail nature since employers need to ensure that assessors are competent to select the right people, and are aware of obligations under legislation to prevent discrimination in employment. In Britain, for example, the Sex Discrimination and Race Relations Acts outlaw unfair discrimination in selection, development and promotion. A number of professional training companies also provide this form of training.

Research has been carried out on assessor training, particularly by the British Civil Service and the United States Department of Labor. The findings, which have a major impact on training line managers in assessment skills, are summarized below.

1 **Leniency.** This is a tendency to over-mark across the whole spectrum of performance, often through failure to clarify performance standards. Trainee assessors who have positive views of people are often prone to leniency, and need training in accurately observing and recalling behaviour, and in recognizing differences in performance standards. Behaviour modelling videos are often useful ways of training people to apply a realistic assessment.

2 **Halo effect**. This occurs when assessors see one outstanding aspect of a person's performance and assume that other aspects must be equally good, to the extent that weaker areas are not recognized.

Jones advocates behaviour modelling videos to overcome this problem. However, he concludes that this may not increase rater reliability without also training in classification, performance standards, fairness and pooling evidence for overall evaluations. American psychologists have studied the effect of training as a way of reducing rating errors. Latham *et al.* (1980) found that two groups of managers who had been trained about errors of halo, contrast and similarity did not commit these errors six months later. A control group of managers who had received no training did so. The authors concede, however, that a limitation of their study is that the job applicants were only simulated on videotape.

Bernardin (1978) found that raters trained to be aware of rater error prior to assessing participants retained the methodology by keeping observational diaries. This group then demonstrated fewer leniency and halo errors.

In a major study in 1978, Bernardin set out to answer some of the remaining questions about training:

1 On the effect of time, he found a rapidly diminishing effect of training. The value of training disappeared after one rating period. This would seem to emphasize the need for careful timing of assessor training as close to the rating events as possible, and the need for continual refresher training.
2 On the internal and external criteria of training, he found that individuals who can identify errors in a test situation also avoid errors in live situations when rating on real development centres.
3 The length of training did not seem to be critical. The difference between sub-groups receiving 60 minute or 5–6 minute sessions was not apparent in the quality of ratings.

Contents of assessor training

Training in generic assessment skills is usually highly practical in nature, and normally consists of positive behaviour modelling followed by skills practices and feedback. The key model which underpins this training is Observe, Record, Classify and Evaluate (ORCE) model which is discussed in the section above. Course content will also include procedural aspects such as agreeing performance standards, the impact of anti-discrimination laws and assessment of effective performance among people from different cultural backgrounds.

Many development centres use interviews to acquire evidence of work performance. This relies on critical incidence techniques devised by Flanagan. Assessor training workshops should therefore provide a technique and skills practices for completing this activity. One useful technique is SOAR, which is a systematic approach to identifying what action a participant took in a specific situation at work, and how effective that action was in dealing with the situation. SOAR can be explained as follows:

- **Situation**. What was the situation? When, what and who was involved?
- **Objective**. What was the individual trying to achieve in dealing with the situation?
- **Action**. What exactly did the individual do or say in order to deal with the situation?
- **Result**. What was the outcome? How effective was the action? Did the individual learn anything?

The following set of guidelines provides a checklist of skills and abilities for assessors who have completed training in assessment techniques:

1 Only record participants' behaviour in actual exercises. The behaviours seen outside the exercises are not valid evidence.
2 Have a clear understanding of what you are looking for in each exercise by reading the assessors' and participants' briefs, and by checking the competences that are tested.
3 Record in detail what you see and hear. Do not make any assumptions about the participant's feelings or motives.
4 Record detailed, accurate and legible notes which can be used by other assessors for giving feedback. These notes will be returned to participants in the final feedback meeting and should be accurate descriptions of what the participant did, together with helpful development suggestions.
5 Only record evidence against the competences that are tested by the exercise. Do not cloud the issue with irrelevant data.
6 Remember that participants are probably under some pressure, make allowances for some minor changes in behaviour—this is a programme for development, not assessment.
7 Be open and friendly at all times—this is a learning situation and participants should be allowed to question their responses during exercises.
8 Maintain an objective approach. Assessors may be called upon to observe and comment upon someone who is known to them. They should base observations on observed performance in the exercises and not on knowledge of past behaviour.
9 Provide help and support in the final feedback interview by explaining the assessors' comments, focusing on strengths and development needs, and by encouraging the participant to take responsibility for development in the workplace with the involvement of his or her line manager.
10 Be positive in feedback. Encourage participants to select three areas for development and discuss with the participant how the line manager will be involved.

Once assessment skills training has been successfully completed, a solid base has been established effectively running development centres. Some additional training may be required for running specific programmes.

Training workshops to run specific development centres

Assessor training for specific development centres can build on the assessment centre skills base which has already been established. This training normally includes:

- an explanation of the target population and programme objectives;
- an overview of the exercises and timetables;
- an explanation of performance standards (see Chapter 2, pages 49–53);
- an explanation of feedback techniques (see Chapter 6).

Line manager briefing

Line managers arguably play the most crucial role in the development centre process. They are usually involved in the selection or nomination of participants, in briefing participants before they attend, and in managing development and training activity in the workplace once participants return from the development centre. Line managers can play three very significant functions in relation to the outcomes from a development centre programme:

1 To ensure that specific development needs which have been identified are effectively dealt with.
2 To check that participants' development plans are realistic and meet the needs of the organization, the individual's job and the individual's career path within the organization.
3 To ensure that agreed development plans are implemented.

The active involvement and participation of line managers will help to ensure that the development centre programme is integrated with other development activities, that it is linked to workplace needs, and is seen as a useful process rather than an imposition by personnel or senior managers. The cooperation of line managers also helps to ensure that improvements in workplace performance occur as a result of the programme. It also means that fewer monitoring and control systems need to be put in place.

As noted in Chapter 1, development centres can be seen as a threat by many line managers. It may appear that their staff are being taken away from them, that responsibility for developing their people is being taken over by others, or that their best people will be 'poached' by other managers. These problems can be overcome with some careful thought:

- A clear purpose for running a development centre programme.
- A communications strategy to inform line managers and participants.
- A clearly defined role, briefing and training for line managers.

Written briefing for line managers

The preparation of a written briefing document for line managers is a minimum requirement. This should be reinforced by a verbal briefing or presentation which includes an opportunity to ask questions.

Typically, written briefings contain the following information:

Development centre overview

- The programme
- What is a development centre?
- Objectives

- Location
- Timetable
- Competences
- Outputs (see Chapter 6, pages 158–62)
- Staff/assessors

The line manager's role

Summary of the line manager's role

The role of the line manager is crucial to the success of the development centre programme. The role involves the following:

1 Briefing participants before they attend so that they know what to expect and how to get the most from the development opportunity.
2 Before the participant attends the development centre, agreeing a review date to discuss the outcomes after the participant returns.
3 Supporting the participant in the planning and implementation of development activity in the key areas identified on the development centre.
4 Evaluating the development of participants as they implement their plans.

Pre-briefing

A 30 minute pre-briefing meeting would normally take place between the line manager and participant one week before the participant attends the development centre.

An agenda for this meeting might include:

1 Checking that participants know times and locations.
2 Explanation of objectives of development centres.
3 Description of content and timetable.
4 Explanation of assessors' role.
5 Explanation of confidentiality.
6 Explanation of outcomes.
7 Agreement of a diary date for post-development centre meetings to review outcomes and to plan development activity.
8 Answering participants' questions and concerns.
9 Explanation of a helpline for further information.

De-briefing

This meeting takes place after the participant's return from the development centre. The meeting should last for about one hour and include:

1 A review of the participant's performance on the development centre.
2 Clarification of the major development points identified.
3 Agreement over the relevance of the development points to the participant's job and future career plans.
4 Development planning: development activity
   (a) timescales
   (b) review dates
   (c) success criteria.

5 Any other issues.

The meeting on development planning could be structured in the following way:

- How did the participant feel about the development centre?
- Ask the participant to review his or her strengths. Where did they emerge? How work related are they? Are they being used now? How could they be used in the future?
- Ask the participant to review weaker areas: where did they emerge? How work related are they? What are the priorities? Given these weaker areas, how do they cope in the workplace? How could development needs be met? Plan development.

For this process, the development log or similar tool can be used. See Chapter 6 on development logs.

Line manager and assessor meetings

Depending on the objectives of a development centre programme and the culture of the organization where the programme is implemented, there are some issues surrounding the amount of information a line manager receives about the performance of a member of his or her staff on a development centre.

One alternative to the line manager automatically receiving written information about the performance of a participant is for the participant to own the data and to choose how to involve the line manager in follow-up activity. These issues are discussed in more detail in Chapter 11.

A second alternative is for the assessor who provided feedback to the participant to hold a briefing meeting with the line manager of the participant after the development centre, and to provide a verbal summary of performance.

Training for line managers

If line managers are asked to complete a pre-briefing and a development role for participants, they may require some training in order to carry out these activities. The training may include communications and presentation skills, coaching, career planning and counselling skills.

Participant briefing

Participants should be fully briefed by their line manager prior to attending the development centre. A suggested format for such a briefing session is discussed in the previous section which deals with line manager briefing.

Participant call-up

Each participant needs to receive a call-up letter prior to the event detailing the following:

- Location (with map)
- Times
- Overview of event
- Objectives of event

- List of other participants and assessors
- Biographical form and any other preparation to be completed for the start of the development centre.

Running a development centre: opening the workshop

Although participants should have been fully briefed by the line manager before attending, it is important to repeat and reinforce key information and messages at the opening of the event. This serves the purpose of ensuring quality and timeliness of briefing and also offers an ideal opportunity for introductions to take place between participants and assessors.

Suggested format for the introductory session

In some cases it may be appropriate to meet participants socially immediately before the event. An example might be an informal gathering during the evening before commencement of a residential development centre. This serves to break the ice. It also gives participants informal access to assessors, who are often senior managers. For many participants this may be a rare opportunity. Ice-breaking activities can make a significant difference to the successful opening of the event by dispelling any apprehension and saving time on the following day. However, assessors should be careful to reassure participants that a social meeting does not form part of the official observation of their behaviour for the purposes of assessment. If this is not clarified, the experience may be counter-productive.

Typically, development centres start in the following way:

1 **Coffee**. Assessors greet participants over coffee. There may be an element of tension and apprehension which can be dispelled by an informal start.

2 **Introductory session**. This is often managed by the senior assessor or centre manager.

Welcome participants to the development centre. Introduce self, other assessors and course secretary and explain the timetable for the first morning.

Ask participants, assessors and the course secretary to write an introductory flipchart and fix it to the wall. The flipchart could include the following points in words or pictures:

(a) preferred name;
(b) current job;
(c) past work;
(d) career ambitions;
(e) interests.

Ask everyone to introduce themselves briefly using the flipchart notes.

3 **Domestic arrangements**. Ask the course secretary to explain domestic arrangements. Points to cover:

(a) need to keep to schedule, busy week, be on time;
(b) menu, meal times and locations, teas, coffees;
(c) any dietary requirements;
(d) drinks and bar bills (payment of);
(e) phonecalls and messages (pagers on mute);
(f) settlement of accounts before leaving;
(g) fire instructions;
(h) room allocations for exercises and sessions.

4 **Aims and objectives**. Explain the aims and objectives of the development centre.

Aims:

(a) to provide a supportive climate;
(b) to identify current abilities;
(c) to plan development for greater effectiveness in the workplace.

Objectives:

(a) to identify specific strengths and development needs;
(b) to understand and use a process for development planning;
(c) to know how to plan personal development with the support of the line manager.

Remind participants that the development centre provides them with:

(a) detailed information about their strengths and development needs;
(b) a model for planning personal development in consultation and agreement with their line manager;
(c) guidance on how their line manager can be integrated into the development planning process.

5 **The role of the assessor**. Explain the role of the assessor in terms of:

(a) providing expert observation of participant skills;
(b) providing feedback and development planning;
(c) providing help with development planning;
(d) neutral and confidential;
(e) all written notes/comments to be returned to the participants;
(f) only anonymous, aggregate data to be retained for organizational purposes (manpower planning, training evaluation and budgets).

Explain that each assessor will see every participant in at least one activity, but that a personal assessor is assigned to each participant for the biographical interview and final feedback interview. Explain that the allocation of personal assessor to participants is on the basis of no previous contact.

6 **Development centre timetable and activities**. Explain the activities on the development centre. List the exercises to be undertaken, for example written exercise, analysis exercise, group exercise, biographical interview, psychometric tests, etc.

Explain timetable.

7 **Ask for any questions or concerns**. Deal with any questions or concerns. If this session looks as if it could go on for too long, note the issues and deal with them on a one-to-one basis or in the evening.

8 **Close introduction**. Finish on an upbeat note, saying that you hope the participants will find the event helpful and enjoyable, in the same way as previous development centre participants.

All sections of the introduction can be supported by visual aids. The section listing the assessed exercises can usefully be supported by a handout giving the participants background information on the theme or scenario that runs through them, together with explanations of the participants' assumed role. Such background information could include:

- participants' role in the fictitious organization;
- the timeframe in which the action takes place;
- the organization (basic facts and figures);
- main customers, products and services of the organization;
- an organization chart.

Opening endorsement by senior management

It can be valuable for a senior manager to attend the start of each development centre to reinforce and demonstrate his or her total commitment to the project by introducing the event and outlining the objectives. A briefing pack and slides can be produced for the senior manager's use.

Closing the event

At the formal close of the event, participants should be reminded of the need to review the outcomes of the development centres with their line managers as soon as possible. In an ongoing programme of development centres, it is also advisable to ask participants to keep the contents of the exercises confidential and not to reveal anything to future participants that might prevent them from gaining maximum benefit from attending the event.

Course secretaries

Most development centres require a course secretary to manage the participants and assessors, making sure that they attend the right activity at the right time, and have the relevant paperwork. Course secretaries need to be efficient, sensitive to the stress that people may be under, and aware of the confidential nature of the material to which they may have access. Care should be taken to select appropriately qualified people. Course secretaries also require a half-day training workshop in order to explain to them the purpose of the development centre and their role within it.

Typically, the role of the course secretary is to:

- organize accommodation;
- look after paperwork;
- ensure that reports are completed and securely stored;
- look after and prepare assessment materials for use;

- take messages and prevent interruptions to assessors and participants;
- ensure that complex and busy timetables are adhered to.

Role players' brief

Some development centre exercises measure the abilities of participants in managing one-to-one interactions. These simulations might include negotiations, counselling, interviews or sales calls. Such exercises often rely on role players who adopt the role of a customer, member of staff or senior manager.

Role players behave according to a script, and respond to behaviours which are exhibited by participants. Role players need to be selected and trained before the programme begins, and selection criteria would normally include the ability to:

- adopt the same approach with each participant;
- follow detailed guidance and not *ad lib*;
- maintain confidentiality.

Ideally, role players should not be known to participants. The number of role players used on a development centre programme should be kept to a minimum so that consistency of standards is maintained across development centres.

Case study 1: Design experiences of an Indian Government department

The following case study illustrates the way in which the Advanced Level Telecommunications Training Centre (ALTTC), a department of the Government of India, has collaborated with an international training organization to produce a standard process for design. The design process is used to produce competence-based tests and exercises which diagnose the training needs of engineers and technicians working for Indian Telecom, and which lead to appropriate training courses that meet workplace needs for effective performance. The design process works in different cultures and is based on systematic and scientific principles.

Background

For any learning to take place, it is essential that the development centre is structured and results oriented. In India we are developing modules based on the ITU (International Telecommunication Union) Training Development Guidelines (TDG).

These guidelines are within the framework of an inter-regional project called CODEVTEL (Course Development in the field of Telecommunications). The history of the CODEVTEL project goes back to the early 1970s when the ITU international cooperation in training development was initiated. This Task Force Committee submitted a draft project proposal in cooperation with ITU training division staff members, and this proposal was submitted to the Inter Regional Bureau of the UNDP for consideration. The UNDP agreed to finalize the major part of the project, and other telecommunications companies also contributed.

Preparatory work started in March 1995, in a few selected training centres before the work in this area was taken up more widely. The course development team received initial training by the CODEVTEL staff before starting design work.

The main features of the TDG project that distinguish it from other handbooks on training development and design are as follows:

- It is intended as a tool for *international* cooperation in training and development.
- This training development is *decentralized* which allows each participant to match the training to local needs while contributing to satisfying the common needs.
- It has been *tried out* in both *developing* and *industrialized* countries.
- It recognizes and emphasizes the fact the *basic values* and *reference frames* are *not* the same among all people.
- It encourages a *critical analysis* of *goals* at all levels of an organization.
- It recognizes and emphasizes the fact that *job amendments*, development of *job aids*, *job instructions*, etc., must go hand in hand with development of training courses.
- It encourages *active participation* in training and development of all concerned.
- It is *process* as well as *result* oriented.

Design model The various phases involved in development centre design are scientific, and a systems approach is adopted to analyse the training needs, design the programme, validate and revise the designed material, implement the programme and carry out evaluation or determine the total value of the training activity. Obviously, design philosophy has five distinct phases:

1 Needs analysis
2 Design
3 Production
4 Validation
5 Implementation and evaluation

Needs analysis This gives a description of the job, duties, tasks, etc., and the required skill, knowledge and attitude (S/K/A) for the target population. It is aimed to find the answer to the question of what to include in training? Analysis itself is carried out in four phases.

Preliminary study
The design procedure begins with preliminary study. It is the analysis of the work or business problem that may point to a solution mix, e.g. training and/or changes in organizational set-up may offer solution to the problem of performance in the field.

Job analysis
The job being performed is analysed, down to the minute details breaking

it into duties, tasks, sub-tasks and task elements. This affords identification of skills, knowledge and attitude (S/K/A), required to perform the job, and is referred to as 'should' level of S/K/A. Details are also discussed with the SME (Senior Management Executive).

Population analysis

Population or target population includes all the prospective trainees. The population analysis enables us to identify the 'is' level of the S/K/A of the target population. It also shows their learning preferences and styles.

Training needs

Training needs is the difference between S/K/A before and after the training, i.e. difference between 'should' and 'is' levels. It points to the quantum of training to be imparted to enable the trainees to perform at the specified standards.

Design

Design includes fixing objectives, designing test items that match objectives and selecting appropriate training strategy. It is aimed to find answers to the questions of how to train a trainee and how to know that the trainee has been trained. Design is carried out in five phases.

Determination of objectives

The objectives are determined taking into consideration the objectives of the organization and the standards of performance required, including the conditions under which the personnel perform in the field.

Design of tests

Tests are so designed as to match the objectives. For example, if the objective is to adjust a relay, the matching test item will be to adjust a maladjusted relay, according to the specifications within the prescribed time limit.

Production

Note that the tests are designed before the design of instructional material. The test items, designed by the course developer, are validated by SMEs and also by those who do not know the subject. Based on the feedback, these can be changed or revised, or the objectives themselves may be revised.

Determination of entry requirements

Depending on the availability of the prospective trainees and the educational level existing in the country, the entry level requirements are fixed, keeping in view the economic viability and socio-economic conditions in the country. An optimum solution is worked out such that duration of training is kept reasonably low, at a level that the organization or the department can afford.

Design

All the inputs required to design the development centre are put together. These include tests, exercises and answers. In addition to this material, plans, course timetable and a general brief is needed about the arrangements required to be made by the course administrator in order to conduct the development centre. The SMEs are consulted to check the accuracy of the contents of the material.

Validation   Validation includes production of the training material, determining the effectiveness and accuracy of the produced material, and carrying out revision, if necessary. It is carried out in three phases.

Production

Adequate number of copies of the materials are made available for validation in the training classes. The material is also checked for technical accuracy by the SME, as frequently as necessary.

Pilot

The course material is used with a group of prospective trainees, during a training session.

Revision

The feedback of the validation session is used for revising the training material, before it is sent for mass production.

Implementation and evaluation   Implementation and evaluation includes mass production of material and evaluating the efficacy of the programme in terms of improved workplace performance. It is carried out in two phases.

Implementation

The necessary equipment, material and manpower are made available at the training centres where the course is to be conducted. The people who will use the materials are given appropriate training.

Evaluation

Allowing 3–4 months after the trainees have been posted back in the field, feedback is collected from the trainees, as well as from their superiors, to identify improvements in workplace performance. These data are analysed and changes are incorporated if necessary.

Conclusions   The process of development centre design is shown in Figure 7.1, on page 182. As can be seen, the process keeps on evolving, until an equilibrium is achieved with the emergence of the best possible material. However, after some time it may again be necessary to incorporate further changes. In short, the process of course development is a dynamic one and continuous appraisal/modifications have to be carried out.

Case study 2: Assessor training in ICI Pharmaceuticals

The majority of assessors for running the programme come from within the commercial function and are senior managers. This core is supplemented by a small number of personnel and training professionals. All assessors must be trained in the function's competency framework and the elements of the centre that they are to assess.

While each centre differs slightly in overall design terms, there is sufficient similarity for training to be relevant to all four of our centres.

This case study describes the core assessor training. Briefings about the content and design of particular centres are held separately, outside the core training.

Competency framework familiarization

As the competency framework is used throughout the function as the basis for selection and for development planning, all managers undergo familiarization training. This aims to give a conceptual framework so that they can:

• understand what competences are (and what they are not);
• describe the benefits of using competences in selection, assessment, development and career planning;
• understand how competences link in with our management development processes and to give them a more detailed knowledge of the competency framework used so that they can:
  —assign behaviours to the appropriate competency;
  —give feedback in behavioural terms;
  —use the competency framework as a basis for development planning.

Group size varies from 6 to 20+. While there are economies of scale with larger groups, it is less easy to ensure real familiarity with the detail of the competency framework in groups of more than about 16.

The training design moves from the conceptual to the practical. Most managers readily grasp the conceptual framework. All are engaged in developing their people, and most are involved in recruitment and selection. The competency framework gives them a practical tool with the benefits of:

• a common language in a function where career moves between departments are the norm;
• targeting behaviours identified with success;
• providing clear, objective feedback.

Familiarity with the detail of the framework is achieved through practical exercises and quizzes. Most workshops include a half-day follow-up to consolidate the learning and to allow managers to practise using the framework in the interim.

While managers readily accept the concepts behind the use of competences and learn, relatively easily, the detail of our particular framework, they are less willing, initially, to accept the framework as a 'given'.

Acceptance of the validity of the detail of the framework is vital. We have achieved this through:

- developing the framework in-house, based on our own research rather than 'buying in';
- revalidating the framework after three years, and committing ourselves to regular revalidation;
- involving managers in developing job profiles.

Understanding the competency framework and using it in selection and development are the cornerstones on which assessor training is built.

Behavioural event interview (BEI) training

This is usually completed before assessors go on to be trained in group process observation skills. This is because:

- the skills taught are more easily and readily used in the workplace. Assessors have opportunities to consolidate their learning 'on the job';
- the skills taught are more closely linked with assessors' 'comfort zones'—interviewing is a familiar activity;
- interviewers work in pairs, so it is possible to link a newly trained assessor with someone who is more experienced.

The training aims to:

- provide the managers with an interview framework;
- differentiate between BEI and other interview techniques;
- develop the manager's questioning and listening skills;
- give managers the opportunity to practise their skills and the technique and, in particular, to gather data against the looked-for competences;
- reinforce their knowledge and understanding of the competency framework;
- lay the foundations of inter-assessor reliability.

Most of the training is dedicated to the managers interviewing 'candidates'. These interviews are observed, and managers receive feedback and are given opportunities to work on specific elements of their technique.

All 'candidates' are interviewed and rated independently by the interviewers. Their conclusions, and ratings, are shared towards the end of the training and this provides the basis for establishing inter-assessor reliability.

In developing this training, we have used both internal 'candidates' and volunteers from local colleges. The latter usually do not offer the breadth of experience and personal maturity required; MBA (or similar) students would be suitable. Internal 'candidates' need to be carefully chosen if their future career prospects or the integrity of the centres are not to be compromised.

Group process observation skills training

This workshop concentrates on enabling assessors to watch an individual, or individuals, engaged in a group activity and to record, classify, summarize and rate what they see. It looks, too, at the role of the assessor and how it differs, in this process, from the role when interviewing (passively recording data as opposed to actively seeking it in interviews).

In order to provide quality, usable feedback, assessors need to understand and accept the difference between 'conclusions' and 'evidence' and to accept the need to work from observed behaviours through to conclusions, rather than to start with judgements and then look for supporting evidence.

This understanding and acceptance is developed by:

- exploring, using their own experience, what hampers objective assessments;
- using a video clip and the assessments of it to reinforce this;
- comparing the quality and usability of data generated through the two approaches.

The workshop follows a pattern of using pen and paper exercises, derived from real centre data, to explore each of the five stages of the assessment process in turn, followed by practical application using a video clip of a management meeting. We have dropped our original plan to custom-make a video simulating a centre exercise in favour of using a commercially made management training video. This avoids the need to 'edit out' the periods of relative inactivity which exist in centres and real-life meetings.

Group size is kept small (8–10) to maximize the time available for individual coaching.

Evaluation and follow-up

Analysis of interview reports has shown relevant and less subjective data being recorded and a greater exposition of participants' development needs. Discussions with interviewers revealed, however, that they were reluctant to terminate unfruitful lines of enquiry. This has been addressed through a half-day refresher workshop.

Similarly, centre reports are analysed to reveal any additional training needs. The overall quality and usability of assessor summaries has improved markedly. Optional lunchtime refresher workshops are held from time to time to deal with specific issues as the need arises. These are particularly useful for new assessors and those who assess infrequently. Key to their success and popularity has been:

- timing—immediately before a centre;
- length—no more than 2 hours over lunchtime;
- relevance—as well as addressing any needs arising out of the analysis of centre reports, participants are asked what issues they would like to cover;
- updating—including input on recent development to our centres.

Subsequent evaluation of the effect of these refresher workshops has proved their worth. Training assessors is not a one-off activity, rather it should provide a model for continuous professional development.

Checklist

Do's   1 Select and train assessors carefully, giving regard to criteria for selection and the importance of their role.
2 Fully involve line managers and brief them for the vital role they will play after the events.
3 Cascade down development centre activity so that line managers have experienced what their people will go through.
4 Plan and organize rigorously as there are many logistical considerations in implementing such a programme.

Don'ts   1 Do not let line managers be the assessors of their own people, as this will reduce objectivity.
2 Do not compromise on the training standards for assessors in order to please/pacify the customer.
3 Do not pretend to be running a development centre when the hidden agenda is selection (see Chapters 1 and 11).
4 Do not skip understanding a review once the programme has been implemented. Capitalize on the learning.

References and further reading

Bernardin, H.J. (1978) 'Effects of rater training on leniency and halo errors in student ratings of instructors', *Journal of Applied Psychology*, 62, 422–7.

Jones, A. (1989) 'Assessment centres and measurement efficiency: evaluation of the need for change.' Paper presented at the Fourth West Congress on the Psychology of Work and Organisation, Cambridge, UK.

Landy, F.J. (1980) *Psychology of Work Behaviour* (Chapter 5), Dorsey Press, Homewood, Illinois.

Latham, G.P. *et al.* (1980) 'The situational interview', *Journal of Applied Psychology*, 65, 442–7.

Stewart, A. and Stewart, V. (1981) *Tomorrow's Managers Today*, Institute of Personnel Management, London.

Useful addresses

The following organizations provide assessment skills training:

Oxford Training
Bankside
Long Hanborough Business Park
Long Hanborough
Oxford OX7 2LJ
Great Britain
Tel: 0993 883338
  (+44 993 883338)

Saville & Holdsworth Ltd
3 AC Court
High Street
Thames Ditton
Surrey KT7 0SR
Great Britain
Tel: 081 398 4170
  (+44 81 398 4170)
Fax: 081 398 9544
  (+44 81 398 9544)

8 Development centre applications

Ray Knightley, Chris Latham and Geoff Lee

Introduction

This chapter looks at some of the current applications of development centre techniques, drawing on case studies from a number of organizations. The changes in applications have been dramatic during recent years, and development centres are now no longer confined to the identification of future potential. During the early stages of their use during the 1970s, most organizations used development centre programmes for members of their existing staff in order to identify those who could be developed for more senior or specialist roles in the future. Many of these programmes were prompted by labour market conditions which forced organizations to adopt staff development strategies in order to retain key groups of people in the face of 'poaching' activity by competitors.

A typical approach is illustrated by the experiences of one computer company based in the City of London. This organization experienced a 100 per cent turnover among programmers in a two-year period during the mid-1980s, as key staff were enticed into more lucrative jobs elsewhere. The company could not compete on compensation and benefits, but knew that programmers were interested in development towards a recognized professional status. It therefore introduced a development centre programme for computer programmers which used industry-wide competences to assess future professional development needs of its people. This was followed by a development package of training and work-based development leading to recognition by the British Computer Society. The development centre and two-year subsequent development programme reduced the turnover of staff to 20 per cent over a 24-month period, and enabled the company to retain key staff who would be the future senior managers.

Experimentation with different applications started during the late 1980s. Examples include the use of development centres to develop specialist and professional staff, to identify potential redeployees, and to complete skills audits for organizational development and change.

This chapter explores traditional and newer applications by looking at case studies which illustrate some recent uses of the development centre techniques. The chapter consists of short sections, each concentrating on a particular application which is then illustrated with a case study. The seven sections are listed below:

- Introduction
- Application 1: Identifying potential
  —Case study: Developing high performers in ICI Pharmaceuticals
- Application 2: Identifying redeployees
  —Case study: Helping to develop redeployees in BT
- Application 3: Developing specialists
  —Case Study 1: Developing sales managers in BT
  —Case Study 2: The National Educational Assessment Centre
- Application 4: Developing people in manufacturing
  —Case study: Developing technicians to national standards in the Rover Group
- Application 5: Developing people in financial services sector
  —Case study: American Express
- Further reading

Application 1: Identifying potential

The need to identify future leaders of an organization has long been a spur to the use of assessment centres. Senior managers would be failing in their duty if they did not seek out their successors and begin the process of educating, skilling and positioning them. Jargon about developing the 'bloodstock' of a company has become fashionable. That said, there are major problems with this seemingly obvious management development process, and 'high flyer' programmes have received a bad press.

- There is the difficulty of bringing the right people to any centre; if participants are identified by nomination, there is a good chance that either the line managers will not see the 'personnel memorandum' seeking nominations, that they will ignore this invitation to give up as a 'company asset' the key people who will help them achieve their objectives, or that they will send along their 'favourite' as a reward. All these problems surface at the 'development centre' workshop itself, when it becomes apparent that some of the wrong people have attended.
- The alternatives to nomination also bring complications; if appraisal or performance is the benchmark, what is the standard level? Do all line managers produce accurate reports? If, on the other hand, a selection process for entry is put in place, there has to be a careful choice about the most appropriate instrument, and if the entry is open to all, the work increases significantly. Screening entries can lead to abuse, and the setting of criteria such as grade or age can lead to indirect discrimination.
- The post-event difficulties are well known; 'crown princes' with expectations that their development will be managed for them. An inability to identify exactly where to place them, given that their previous unit has moved on. There is also a problem with the 'low flyers', i.e. the resentment among colleagues who did not attend a

centre and who do not carry an 'acceleration' label. This also impacts on the development centre, in giving it the appearance of an 'all or nothing' test, producing problems rather than results, in a secret and stressful event.

In case this list of possible woes seems fanciful, we have encountered them all during our work. Badly-thought-out high-flyer programmes do more harm than good, and bring odium on the designers as dissociation takes place.

The following steps or recommendations may help:

1 If you are working with external consultants, stay as close to them as possible. Where necessary, steer away from their off-the-shelf frameworks however well they are said to have worked in prestigious organizations. Other advice is offered in Chapter 11.

2 If you are walking in the steps of external consultants who have now departed because they were deemed to be 'not quite in touch with company strategy or values', or because they are too expensive, your options may be limited by your client's experiences.

It may not be possible to move away from unsuitable exercises, unmeasurable competences or psychometric tests with poor validity. In these circumstances, or when working in this field for the first time, it is essential to win the confidence of the senior managers while offering your best professional advice.

3 It is vital to 'sign-off' each phase of the project and exercise. Access to the senior managers who have the clearest perspective on the company's strategy should be sought at all costs. It is not unreasonable for them to devote some time to the vital subject of identifying their successors and securing the future of the organization. We have provided guidance in Chapter 2 on how to gather these data.

   (a) Resist pressures to compress the centres into fewer days if this would really damage the validity of findings or the usefulness of counselling.

   (b) Be clear on the standards that assessors are looking for. If the exercises are designed for very senior posts, but the participants are relatively junior, they will be dispirited at their inability to cope with the complexity of tasks. The assessors need to be aware of this in their assessment and feedback.

   (c) Ensure that the exercises are flexible, generic and varied, and that participants from different fields of work—operations, R&D, or finance—can cope if the centre is intended for use by all-comers with potential.

4 We have described the training of assessors. It is likely that the designers will have access to centres as psychometricians and sometimes to the final assessor's meeting to pool results and experiences. These opportunities should be taken. In the haste and excitement of assessing evidence, the procedures for classification of evidence and

rating of evidence may be overlooked. There can be some slippage into some sweeping, often subjective and negative statements. This can be tactfully dealt with by questions about process and evidence, plus some coaching.

5 It is also wise to reiterate the uses to which evidence of performance will be put, particularly by assessors, in their plenary discussions, and to the participant's line manager.

6 Seek validation data from participants and assessors by 'reactionnaires' at the end of development centres. Do so again after an appropriate time, and look for evaluation by checking the outcomes for each participant and their line manager[s]. We have described these processes in depth in Chapter 10.

7 Present the findings to the client in a positive way, and look for ways in which the programme could be changed, in the future in order to improve future programmes.

We offer the ICI Pharmaceuticals programme as an example of best practice in the case study below.

Case study: Developing high performers in ICI Pharmaceuticals

The context

Young managers within the commercial function typically spend their first 7–10 years in a variety of HQ and field posts, developing a broad base of sales and marketing expertise. Their careers are managed, through a career development group, on the basis of data derived from our performance management system.

While these data are important when considering managers for development towards more senior positions, it is not sufficient in itself. For example, it does not:

- indicate their ability to perform in increasingly complex situations;
- give data against some of the competences required in senior posts;
- indicate their ability to perform effectively in new environments.

For these reasons, young managers of potential are invited to participate in an extended assessment centre which aims to contribute to succession plans and help develop a broad base of talent.

The clear outcome of the centre for individuals is a view of how they are regarded, clearly articulated development needs if they are to be successful in senior positions and a commitment to helping them achieve these.

For the business, the benefits include better succession planning, better placement decisions, focused development and increased motivation and commitment.

Overall design considerations

Several themes predominate.

- Relevance to the individual and his or her experience to the business. This is crucial if the centre, and its outcomes, are to be supported by managers and participants alike.
- Recognizing past achievements and building these into the overall assessment.
- Testing against 'higher level' competences: particular relevance is placed on assessing competences which the individual may not have had opportunities to demonstrate in his or her career to date and on testing them against increasingly complex situations.
- '3D' testing: using a range of assessment techniques testing individuals in group and one-to-one situations; also testing individuals in prepared and *ad hoc* situations.
- Multiple assessments: each competency is assessed at least four times.
- Participants involved in managing the process: they are responsible for setting the timetable for three of the seven elements.

In addition, participants and managers are fully briefed about every aspect of the process.

Centre design

The centre comprises seven elements:

1 Nomination
2 Work-based project
3 Interviews
4 Psychometric tests
5 Residential business simulation
6 Self-assessment
7 Feedback and follow-up

Each is described below.

Nominations
These are made initially by the individual's line manager. He or she is responsible for supporting and coaching the individual through the centre and for agreeing and facilitating the implementation of subsequent development plans. The line manager's early involvement is therefore crucial to the overall success of the centre.

Nominations are restricted to people who are superior performers in their existing role and beginning to demonstrate the competences required at senior level. Nominations, which are made on the basis of information derived from our performance management systems, are ratified by the career development group. This is not merely 'rubber stamping', nominations will be deferred if it is felt that it is not in the individual's or the organization's best interests for someone to attend at a particular time. Individuals may also ask to have their nomination deferred. Reasons for deferral include, for example, a significant change in job or domestic circumstances, a major piece of work that would clash with centre dates, or doubts that the individual has demonstrated the breadth required.

This flexible approach to nominations has done much to establish the centre as a positive experience for all participants rather than an assessment hurdle to be gone through.

The work-based project
This comprises two elements: a written report and an oral presentation. Participants are given a broad brief within which they can choose their own remit; key elements of the brief are that:

- the outcome of the project must 'add value' within the time-scale of the centre;
- it must be clearly linked to business priorities—i.e. it is not an 'add on' but reflects real life;
- the project and its presentation should take no more than five working days over a period of three months;
- participants should, when choosing their remit, be mindful of the competences this element of the centre is designed to assess.

The first three elements of the brief clearly place the centre as central to, and part of, key business activities rather than something that has to be squeezed into an already full diary. It gains credibility with managers and participants who can see that they are being assessed against real-life situations.

Interviews
These are organized by the participant at a mutually convenient time over a three-month period and follow the behavioural event format, i.e. they focus on what individuals have actually achieved in their jobs. Again, the emphasis here is on linking the process into the individual's experience and demonstrated achievements.

A broader career-based interview, with an independent consultant, has been dropped. While this was valued by participants the 'status' of the information and its legitimate uses were unclear. Participants are now encouraged to engage in a post-centre career review with a senior manager.

Psychometric tests
These include a battery of critical reasoning tests, and personality profiling is also used.

Residential business simulation
This residential event uses a computer-based pharmaceutical case study and comprises a variety of group and individual work.

The computers are used to generate management information and to introduce constraints (e.g. cost or manpower constraints). Participants do not use the computers themselves—early experience showed that the technology is seductive and can detract from the main focus of the simulation. Instead, 'technical experts' are on hand to interrogate the computer and input data for participants.

The simulation deliberately uses an environment with which the participants are familiar. It goes beyond, however, the strict boundaries of the bulk of their experience (sales and marketing) since they are being tested against broader business roles.

Self-assessment
Throughout the centre, participants complete a learning log as part of their self-assessment. The purpose of this is twofold. Firstly, it encourages them to reflect on and learn from their experience and to incorporate improvements into subsequent stages of the centre. It also provides the manager responsible for feeding back the centre reports with a basis on which to approach feeding back sensitive data.

Feedback and follow-up
This is handled by the individual's line manager. Together, they are responsible for agreeing a development plan which is incorporated into our performance management system. The detail of this process and the training and support given to managers is described elsewhere (see Chapter 7).

Design review   The design is regularly reviewed against objectives, against the overall considerations outlined above and against the following questions:

1 Are the elements providing relevant data?
2 Are they distinguishing sufficiently between participants?
3 Are they distinguishing sufficiently between individual strengths and development needs?

A negative answer signals either a design issue and/or an assessor training need.

Application 2: Identifying redeployees

Case study: Helping to develop redeployees in BT

Introduction   Obviously, the highest type of efficiency is that which can utilise existing material to the best advantage.
                     Jawaharlal Nehru (1889–1964) in N.B. Sen, *Wit and Wisdom of India*

Obvious it may be, but too many senior managers overlook existing resources when changes in the operating environment lead to rationalization. The growth of global markets has forced instability on commercial enterprise. Given that change cannot be avoided, the only freedom for management is in how to deal with it. In future, the successful manager will be the one who can most effectively handle the effects of continuous change with minimum damage to the internal stability of his or her company. If change is well handled, organizations can cope with quite dramatic shifts in direction. Badly managed change will, on the other hand, inflict systemic damage at all levels.

It's very hard to work when you have no idea what will happen next. Frequently, 'final' changes are replaced by new ones every other week. So even when you're told you survived a 'final' round of cuts, you know you can still get another turn next month. No one can really know what's coming down to his level until they settle who's where on the top floors.

(Hirsch, 1987)

To redeploy or remove? A lack of fit (real or perceived) to the operating environment is normally the driving force behind rationalization. The need to 'do something quickly' will tend to allow symptomatic over-resourcing in some areas to obscure corresponding weakness in others. There may be a rushed decision on whether to go straight for removal of those spare resources rather than seek other areas where they could be effectively and economically redeployed. Redundancy is often the quickest and, on the face of it, the least expensive, despite redundancy payments and other costs. The excess people are simply amputated from the body commercial and that is that. Or is it ?

Martin and Nicholls (1987) identified three factors essential for the creation of a committed workforce:

1 A sense of belonging to the organization (through being informed, involved and sharing in success).
2 A sense of excitement in the job (possessing pride, trust and accountability for results).
3 Confidence in management leadership (perceived as having authority, dedication and competence).

Those senior managers making the decision to dismiss or redeploy might do well to consider which option is the most likely to effectively maintain those factors.

The possibility of a dilution of talent must also be considered. In a study for Coutts and Company, Smith (1981) found evidence that managers made redundant are often of a higher standard than those retained. It is easy to see, therefore, how a stand-alone voluntary redundancy procedure can remove some very good people while demoralizing and reducing the performance of those who stay.

A company faced with an essential downsizing may have to think carefully through the implications of the alternative courses of action.

The service arm of a major company felt itself to be under threat in the recession of the early 1980s. This group had traditionally provided a range of well-subscribed field advisory services to customers in support of high-value capital equipment distributed by the parent group.

Recently, however, head office decided to look at the possibilities of rationalizing the operation. Anticipating questions of cost being raised, senior managers in the service company decided to introduce a range of cost-cutting measures, at the core of which was a comparatively generous voluntary redundancy programme. This was particularly welcome to the best of the field staff who, with plenty of contacts in the industry, quickly opted for the package and departed to work for the company's larger customers who then promptly withdrew from their service contracts. The remaining field staff could not supply the quantity or quality of field support for even the diminished customer base.

The rationalization took longer than expected and the senior managers of the service company found themselves facing a continuing erosion of custom alongside growing levels of complaints about falling quality and availability of field service. Constrained by head office from increasing costs by recruiting, they had no choice but to sit it out. Business fell off to such an extent that, following completion of the rationalization, the parent group closed the operation completely and contracted out the service work.

Development centres in rationalization: South Midlands and Chilterns District

The methodology for the redeployment development centre differs in some key areas from that described elsewhere in this book. These differences arise mainly from the very specific circumstances in which the event is being designed to address.

Amalgamation and technological improvement led to a decrease in demand for skilled technicians who had maintained the previous generation of equipment. The outcome was that a total of 50 technical staff were surplus to projected needs. These people possessed extensive knowledge of the company's operations and, consequently, it was decided that they should be redeployed if possible.

There were current vacancies in marketing and computer operation and it was decided to put the technicians through a development centre programme which would allow both the participants and the managers with vacancies to make informed decisions on the way forward and to determine what training was needed to make any redeployees fully operational.

The outcome was that all of the technicians were placed in the marketing or DP functions.

Development centres and downsizing: logistics

A rather different situation arises where an entire function is being closed down and there are no 'local' vacancies. Staff might well have to move further afield to be redeployed.

A decision was made to close down an entire warehousing operation along with its administrative and other support services. The depot complex had been in existence for many years and most of the staff had lengthy service in a narrow range of work. As there were no vacancies in the immediate geographical area, the decisions on redeployment were very significant, from the point of view of the staff and the company.

The offer to all staff of attendance on a redeployment development centre programme was generally well received. Participants emerged with a skill set that they could sell to potential employers who would not be particularly interested in their specialized experience. The company was also able to negotiate redeployment with those whose skill profile matched specific needs elsewhere in the operation.

Designers must very carefully assess the situation and desired outcomes in order to arrive at a set of workable objectives specific to their company's needs.

Redeployment: general issues

Redeployment development centres can help employers in the following ways:

1 Identify those who possess competences important to the future survival of the company.
2 Provide a profile of the change-related training and development needs of those who will stay.
3 Provide those who will go with a profile of their key skills that they can use in the marketing of their labour.
4 Assist in the placing of the downsized workforce.

Competences

The basket of competences chosen for use in redeployment development centres must be subject to some special considerations. There will inevitably be some disconnection between the source and destination of the redeployees (whether inside or outside the company) and it is essential that the descriptive competences are meaningful to receiving managers and/or organizations. The competences, especially those with an intellectual base must be labelled in a clear and non-technical manner.

Consider the labels below:

Explication	Analysis
Adumbration	Planning
Ratiocination	Strategic thinking
Promethean ability	Creativity

The columns contain words of similar meaning but those on the left are obscure enough to create a certain (possibly tempting) mystique about the process, albeit at the cost of shared understanding. The rule for labelling redeployment competences is 'keep it simple'.

The competence labels in the right-hand column will be familiar to most managers, as will the personal competences relating to, for instance, social skills, determination and personal maturity. More uncertain, however, are competences related to management. These are often value laden and—if used at all—must be chosen with extreme care. It is easy to see that managerial behaviours valued in production departments may not be those prevailing in marketing.

The important thing is that the competences are descriptive and portable.

Design   One of the major freedoms in putting together a redeployment development centre is the generic nature of the exercises. In a normal convergent
development centre, the exercises are, in effect, close simulations of the
activities in specific jobs. In the redeployment development centre,
which looks at flexibility and adaptability, the exercises will be more
creative and generic. Similarly, the timetable may include batteries of
tests outside the normal run. The process should be like a scoop, picking
up on a wide range of abilities and skills.

Problems   To compensate for the enjoyability of designing lateral exercises, the
practitioner will have a number of significant problems to overcome.

Managerial disinterest
One major problem could arise from a lack of managerial commitment.
Managers feeling under threat may not respond well to an invitation to
take part in the development centre programme. As these are key people
in terms of success, the effort *must* be made to get them on board
through sensitive but firm briefing. If they still remain uninvolved, there
must be some question as to the wisdom of going ahead.

Lack of information
Arising from the same cause as the above, there may be problems in
getting sufficient information to make the development centre effective.
Designers must resist papering over cracks in their information base, if
necessary seeking support of top management.

Insecure people
These people are under stress. They may resist the idea of the develop-
ment centre in order to avoid possible exposure of their weaknesses.
Honesty is the answer here. Determine at the outset just what the
confidentiality contract is to be and stick to it no matter what the cost.
The specific ownership of data is important.

Short time-scales
These can be a real problem. Once a decision is made to rationalize an
operational area, management will not tolerate an extended wait while
the development centre programme gets under way. The time-scales
may even contract while the programme is running. There are no
answers to this problem. Practitioners should seek *exact* deadlines and
ensure that, as far as possible, there is enough time to complete
the programme.

No second chances
The development centre process must be right first time. There can be
no going back to revise the procedures. While effective planning and
tight administrative control will minimize the chances of error on any
development centre, it is especially important to get things tied down in
redeployment situations.

Constant changes

Be prepared for the development centre to be something of a drop-in (and drop-out) centre during the run of the programme. Participants, their line managers and observers may well give only patchy support at times. Try to get specific contracted support/attendance and arrange contingency cover if possible.

Process The process will be largely similar to that of a normal development centre. There is the same need for thorough introductory briefing and careful positioning by senior management, especially in terms of what follows the programme, data ownership and the level of confidentiality.

Special attention must be paid to the quality of feedback. As pointed out above, this is particularly important for insecure people who need support. Honey (1988) identifies four main problems in handling feedback.

1 Those receiving feedback may avoid or shorten sessions through worry about what they might hear.
2 Receivers of feedback may approach the sessions in a closed and defensive frame of mind through worry.
3 Those giving feedback may be over-concerned to avoid appearing condescending.
4 Feedback givers may be unskilled at providing non-judgemental and constructive feedback.

Feedback must be:

• *visionary* (look to the future);
• *thorough* (open and honest);
• *supportive* (non-judgemental and positive).

Outcomes If the development centre meets its objectives, the outcomes should be a valuable databank of skills and abilities present in the workforce. The employer will be able to use these skills contours to map the way ahead for those of the workforce who will remain.

Those who depart should be able to take with them a portfolio of identified skills which they can discuss with, and sell to, prospective employers instead of relying on experience that may be too specific to the previous employer. The possession of this information will, in any case, help to build the confidence of redundant staff who may have been out of the labour market for many years.

Like any other business decision, the design and implementation of a redeployment development centre must follow a careful comparison of costs and benefits.

Costs Like redundancy, redeployment development centres have a relatively heavy front-end cost. While this can be reduced by careful planning, there will be doubts expressed about 'going to all this trouble'. Modelling the development centre on a computer spreadsheet and careful project management are two major cost reduction activities.

Benefits   There are significant benefits to redeployment development centres:

1 They are an investment in people.
2 They may point the way to more effective use of resources when things pick up.
3 Redeployees often compare very favourably with new recruits.
4 Redeployment is often cheaper than redundancy.
5 A redeployment development centre may be re-tooled for general use.
6 They create a positive attitude towards the organization among those remaining as they observe the treatment accorded to colleagues.

Application 3: Developing specialists

Case study 1: Developing sales managers in BT (British Telecom)

The business problem   In 1990 the manager of a major sales unit was confronted by a number of strategic issues which needed to be resolved in a short period of time. These were:

1 A major reorganization which transferred all large customer accounts to a new sales unit but left the original unit with the same targets.
2 The need to reallocate existing staff from a range of product-based grades into two new functional grades in order to better serve customers' needs.
3 Developing account management skills in the sales force, which had formerly worked from a basis of technical and product knowledge characterized by a 'box-shifter' sales mentality.
4 Developing first-line managers to manage these changes, when they themselves were not managers but sales staff who had been promoted because of their good sales record.

The response   The sales organization responded to these needs in several ways. Firstly, line managers were given clear job descriptions and objectives which reflected their role as managers. Secondly, new management control systems were introduced which enabled them to monitor more effectively the performance of their teams and of individual team members. Thirdly, sales managers were given the responsibility for developing their teams, and were trained in the skills of leadership and coaching.

Armed with the new sales management skills and much clearer role definitions, sales managers dealt with the organizational changes that have been described, This provided a period of one year to consolidate and apply their new skills in a workplace environment. During this period, a development centre programme was implemented for their staff, the sales force. Many line managers were trained as assessors to run this programme, and all line managers had to supervise development activity for their staff in the workplace following their return from the development centre.

There then followed a development centre programme for sales managers, themselves, in which their management skills and abilities were measured, strengths and weaknesses were identified and personal development plans were produced.

The target population of sales managers had been identified as one that was likely to be under a lot of stress. A design criterion for the centre was the inclusion of opportunities for one-to-one discussions between participating sales managers and their personal assessor. Additionally, a stress management workshop was incorporated into the timetable.

After attending the development centre, sales managers use development logs to plan personal development activity which is undertaken by a combination of mandatory training programmes, self-selected distance learning packages and supervised workplace development activity. The development log is a recurrent theme throughout the diagnostic and developmental process. It is used to record strengths, development needs and agreed developmental action at the end of the development centre, and to record progress in closing skills gaps as the sales manager progresses through a series of competency-based training and development activities.

Outcomes The programme is still being validated and evaluated. However, initial results indicate the development centre programme was popular with the sales managers who attended. They particularly liked the integration of needs analysis on the centre and development activity which followed from it. Many participants had been assessors on the earlier programme which had been run for their staff, and consequently had a very positive view of the benefits of a development centre programme. The comparatively small number of senior sales managers meant that sales managers occasionally participated in a development centre where their own line manager was a member of the assessor team. This caused some concern.

Learning points Important lessons were learnt from the experience of designing and implementing this programme, and the main ones are summarized below:

• Participants who have been assessors on earlier, different programmes adopt a very positive attitude to development centres, and are keen to benefit from participation.
• Participants who had assessed on earlier, different development did not perform better than non-assessors.
• Line managers should not be used as observers on development centres attended by their staff.

Case study 2: The National Educational Assessment Centre

The National Educational Assessment Centre (NEAC) was set up in 1990 as a four-way partnership between the teaching profession (Secondary Heads Association), higher education (Oxford Polytechnic), industry (BT, Post Office, Rover and ICL) and the Government (Departments for Education and Employment). Its main purpose is to improve the preparation for headship by focusing on the development of management competences. The participants at an EAC are usually deputy heads or newly appointed heads; the assessors are heads and other senior educationalists who complete a four-day training course; other experienced heads are trained as mentors to support the participants once they have completed the EAC process.

A typical developmental EAC lasts five days. The participants attend for the first two days and undertake six exercises designed to simulate the tasks of headship. They are observed by the assessors who remain at the EAC for a further three days to discuss and agree performance ratings across the management competences and then write a final report for each participant. Care is taken to ensure that the assessor and participants are not known to each other before the EAC.

The participants and assessors work in teams of six with a 1:1 ratio. Each participant is observed on different exercises by five of the six assessors in a team. Within 15 working days of the end of the EAC, each participant meets with an EAC director to receive the report, discuss its contents and then agree a programme of personal development. Three copies of the report are produced: one for the participant, a second for the client who has paid for the participant to attend the EAC and a third copy is kept by NEAC for five years as a back-up.

During the EAC, participants complete a questionnaire about their current job including training and development that they have undertaken over the last two years and what they see as their main development needs. This information is set alongside the EAC evidence when assessors come to write the developmental sections of participants' reports. The main thrust of the suggestions for further development is always on action that the participant can take on the job, with the support of a mentor. Assessors will only occasionally refer to particular courses or training opportunities off the job.

The pilot phase of the NEAC Project (1990–92) has involved about 30 clients including 25 Local Educational Authorities (LEAs), the grant-maintained and the independent school sectors. Common standards and codes of practice with respect to issues like the selection of participants, assessors and mentors and the confidentiality of the EAC reports have been established by working together with the clients. Representatives from each client group meet regularly at the NEAC Users' Group to agree and implement the standards and practices. In the case of LEAs the client link-person who attends the Users' Group is typically a senior inspector with responsibility for professional development. Although NEAC's direct control over these aspects of the process is inevitably limited, the Project has based its work on two central principles: partnership and professional trust.

There have, in fact, been real benefits for the participants in going through a demanding developmental experience 'off-site' and on neutral territory where they are not known by the other participants or the assessors. The important complement to this dimension of the EAC experience is, of course, the successful integration of the developmental outcomes back in the workplace. This is achieved in several ways: by the participant questionnaire referred to earlier; by the active support of the participant's line manager when attending an EAC; and by the link with a mentor, who will usually work in the participant's own LEA. The key person in facilitating the link between EAC experience 'off-site' and further professional development 'on-site' is the client link-person.

A major challenge for the NEAC Project has been the introduction of a relatively expensive process to the public sector which has very limited resources for in-service training and development. Fortunately, the pilot phase was generously supported by the main partners referred to in the first paragraph. Clients purchased a subsidized 'unit' (or 'units') which trained one assessor (who then assessed at two EACs), took two partici- pants through the EAC process and trained two mentors. An independent evaluation of the pilot phase gave the EAC process a 'gold star' and des- pite shifting to fully allocated costs for NEAC services in the extension phase (from 1992 onwards), the number of clients has doubled. The basic message of the Project has been that quality schools need quality leadership and, therefore, that proper investment in the professional development of heads cannot be a waste of scarce resources. This message seems to have been received and accepted. It should, of course, be added that the EAC process is not only helpful for the participants in preparing for headship but also excellent professional development for the experienced heads who train as assessors and mentors.

Under pressure from clients, NEAC has produced a quite separate version of the EAC process for the selection of head teachers. This has now been used successfully by several school governing bodies during appointment procedures.

During the extension phase, a number of regional EACs will be estab- lished around the United Kingdom. They will operate on a franchise basis with NEAC being responsible for assessor training, the develop- ment of new exercises, evaluation and overall quality assurance. It seems that a fruitful use of assessment centres in the public sector is here to stay.

Application 4: Developing people in manufacturing

Case study: Developing technicians to national standards in the Rover Group

Along with the development of a system of national vocational qualifications (S/NVQs) and a set of national standards of competence, has come the need to implement standards of competence and assess individuals against these standards. The standards of competence that have been developed have focused on outcomes and outputs, whereas in the past the focus has been on the task or process.

Given the current debate between lead bodies and companies, it is no surprise to find that organizations question the relevance and applicability of National Standards of Competence. This short case study looks at one such organization who faced the problem and describes what they did. The company is involved in vehicle manufacture, and had to decide if adopting National Standards of Competence for its employed staff would aid them in achieving business goals.

This sector of the market is open to fierce competition both on price and quality of finish, so that any consideration about introducing standards of competence for staff which were developed externally to the organization created a potentially high risk factor. Agreeing to take up such standards of competence could put the organization into a market lead or could slow it down to the point where it was no longer able to compete effectively.

The pressures were very real but the board realized that in order for it to continue to compete effectively it had to rise to the challenge of change. It had to improve existing practices and raise staff competence just to maintain its existing market share. It also realized that introducing any change in working practices to focus on competences would have to be introduced rapidly so as not to disrupt the flow of production and quality quotas.

A further complication was that a variety of competences already existed which had been built up over a long period of time, based on custom and practice. The choice of change was to move from existing practice towards adopting the market competitors' standards of competence, to adapt to the industry lead body's specific standards of competence or to identify some other range of standards of competence.

On examination of the National Standards of Competence it soon became clear that they were not specific enough to meet the business and organizational needs. To a certain extent this was not surprising as the National Standards of Competence were originally developed to be applicable to all organizations within an industry lead body focus. They were generic in nature. The danger was that even though these competences reflected best practice, the competences themselves fell short of those required to meet the particular business and organizational needs.

In the debate that followed it was important to reinforce the position that competences could not be viewed in isolation from the business and organizational needs. The main question became whether or not the competences, if introduced, would be of sufficient value to enable the business to move forward towards achieving its business goals of becoming the new market leader in its chosen market niche. Once the business and organizational needs were put forward, it was seen that the National Standards of Competence in this leading industry sector would not be sufficient to meet the needs of this business. They were at a lower level than those required.

Once this conclusion was reached, the remaining options needed to be re-examined. The question now was whether to adopt these standards of competence exhibited by the market leader and main competitors or to adopt some other standard of competence.

After much reflection it was realized that the answer lay within the organization itself. Staff currently employed in the design, production, manufacture and assembly sites already knew what best practice was, and what the standards of competence should be for themselves within the industry. They did not have to take into account other or different parts of the industry sector to compromise on their levels of their standards. The problem lay with methodology to identify performance standards.

At this point, the idea of adopting the same methodology as used to create the National Standards of Competence was thought to be an effective way to define this organization's standards of competence. The methodology would allow them to focus on the outcomes and outputs which could be used to define competences for a number of functional and occupational groups. Functional analysis was chosen to begin the development of the organization-specific range of standards of competence.

The place to start was with those very individuals within the organization who were responsible in each of the chosen key occupational and functional groupings. In other words, the individuals doing the jobs themselves had to define for the business best practice and standards of competence, remembering that it was more than standard operating procedures or average performance levels, but not something so idealistic that no one could achieve it. Standards of competence had to be something you had to work for to achieve, and yet be achievable.

The next problem for this organization was how to enable this group of practitioners to identify and describe what they meant by standards of competence needed by the business. This in itself created a training and development need. In order for these groupings to approach development of standards of competence, they all had to be trained to a level of understanding within a fixed period of time before they could embark on their task of developing competences for their unique occupational and functional groupings.

They would all need a clear idea of what they were trying to achieve and they would all need to use the same common language and terms to express the competences they were about to develop and describe.

Time and resources for training this large group of key occupational and functional practitioners were agreed, and the groups were formed around strategic processes within the business. Each group was set the task of defining its own operational key purpose. Functional analysis was then applied to break down the key purpose statements into their own key roles, units, elements and performance criteria. In order to keep control over the processes, a central core team was created to monitor development and to compare each grouping's model so as to identify overlaps, gaps and those core competences that the business needed at this level for its skilled hourly paid grades.

This process is currently nearing completion. It has evolved with practitioners defining the future standards of performance for the business. The next phase will be to continue the process up the organization to include various technical, managerial and business function areas. Core teams link the standardized competence to the overall business objectives.

The first stage of this process will link standards of competence with a pay reward scheme. People will be rewarded for exhibiting and achieving their published levels of competence in the work area. This process will enable a competence matrix to be developed for employees, which is made explicit throughout the organization. The message is that the organization wishes its employees to develop the competences which it deems necessary for its business success.

There are a number of lessons to learn from this case study.

1 Standards of competence should be linked wherever possible to overall business needs and objectives.
2 Probably the richest source of information to identify best practice and standards of performance comes from the people actually involved in that occupation or function.
3 Support and training is needed for those practitioners who will be involved in defining best practice so that they describe competence and best practice in a common language.
4 Functional analysis, when applied consistently to a business, can help define individual standards of competence.
5 A strong sense of ownership and acceptance is achieved when practitioners are involved in setting standards for their occupational or functional groupings. This is especially valuable on the implementation of standards.
6 Businesses need to consider carefully their industry-specific National

Standards of Competence in the light of their business needs before
deciding whether or not to adopt part or all of them.

7 Some organizations will have business needs which will require them
to develop tailor-made sets of standard competences for staff which
are at a higher level than those published in their industry sector.

Application 5: Developing people in the financial services sector

Case study: American Express

The business imperative

American Express Travel Related Services is a global subsidiary of the
American Express Company with over 50 000 employees spanning 20
countries. Travel Related Services (TRS) is a diverse business which
includes the familiar green, gold and platinum consumer cards, travel
agencies, travel management services, publishing, banking and
financial services.

TRS made significant changes in 1992 in how business was conducted
and plans to approach it in the future. A changing, more competitive
business environment necessitated a new long-range vision and long-
term business strategy. This new strategy emphasizes a heightened
focus on quality, innovation and the customer—traditionally strong
points of the company. In support of this new business approach, we
adopted a set of values to 'live by' which are intended to provide guidance for employees' day-to-day activities. Our new strategy also called
for renewed focus on our three principal constituencies—employees,
customers and shareholders.

Very early on it became clear that to bring the new strategies to life
would require employees to demonstrate new skills and behaviours.
Sensing a change in the offing that would impact on virtually every
aspect of their working lives, employees were eager to know the behaviours and skills to be successful in this new business environment.
Essentially, they wanted to know what the company expected of them.

Recognition of employees' need to have a clear picture to help them
understand how they would look, what they would need to do, and
how they should behave when exceeding constituent expectations,
drove TRS to the creation of a new competency model. In designing
this new competency model, the authors set out to develop a

behavioural profile of the successful executive in TRS which would serve as a foundation for selection, assessment, development, and performance appraisal systems.

The process identifying the 'right' competencies

The first step in the five-month design process involved interviewing 12 well-respected, successful, visionary senior executives in TRS. These executives were asked to sort over 100 potential competencies into one of three categories: critically important to the business, moderately important, not as important.

More specifically, these executives were asked to think about the critical skills required to run the business effectively in the next one to three years (short term) and three to five years (medium/long term). Based on these interviews, the competency list was shortened to the 70 most critical dimensions.

In order to refine further and validate this list of critical dimensions, a questionnaire was developed to be distributed to the entire executive population worldwide. The questionnaire had three objectives:

1 To get input, and hopefully buy-in, on the competencies from a broad population.
2 To get the number of competencies down to a manageable size.
3 To understand the differences between functions, business units, levels, etc.

The 'Leadership Dimension Questionnaire' once again asked executives to rate the dimensions in terms of their importance for doing their jobs well and for successfully running the business in the short and long term. The 65 per cent response rate was considered excellent for a mail-back questionnaire.

Even with this large and diverse group, the questionnaire results were tremendously consistent. That consistency enabled the authors to reduce the number of competencies from 70 to 24. Statistical analyses were conducted to confirm the internal consistency of factors and allowed the competencies to be grouped into five clusters. Naming the clusters became the next challenge. It was understood that the names of the clusters would send a strong signal to employees about what was considered important. Therefore, the names of the clusters took on added importance. Fortunately, there was a strong relationship between the competency clusters and the TRS values. Consequently, the TRS values were chosen to name the competency clusters to reinforce the values as living, breathing guidelines for day-to-day life.

Keeping in mind the need to paint a vivid picture for employees, the next step of the process was the one deemed most critical. That is, the description of behaviours which would breathe life into leadership dimensions (competencies). Focus groups were conducted throughout the company involving employees at all levels to help better describe these dimensions for employees. The groups were asked, for example, what a successful executive would actually do to 'exceed customer expectations'. In the end, six descriptive behaviours were developed for each dimension.

At this point in the process, a competency model with 24 leadership dimensions was clustered into six categories. Each dimension was further described by six behaviour statements. The last step of the process was to gain senior management approval for implementation. The final competency model was distributed to the 15 top executives for their final thoughts and was very favourably received. With minor modifications, the new competency model was incorporated into a new performance appraisal instrument, which was introduced in October 1992.

Evaluation of the model and learning

Preliminary evaluation of the model will take place as part of the performance appraisal process. Attached to each performance appraisal is a brief survey which asks each executive to evaluate the competency model and its efficacy for appraising performance. Those surveys will be returned and analysed early in 1993. Evaluation in terms of its other uses, i.e. assessment, selection, development, will be in 1993.

The process used to generate the model worked very smoothly and effectively. By utilizing an approach that maximized employee involvement, employee buy-in, enthusiasm and support of the authors' efforts were obtained. In addition, ability to tie the competencies directly to pre-existing TRS values proved to be a huge advantage in terms of acceptance and face validity. Finally, the competency model was perceived as instrumental in meeting employees' needs to understand better 'how to live the TRS values' and be successful. With employees' assistance, the authors feel that they were successful in defining effective leadership more clearly.

References and further reading

Hirsch, P. (1987) *Pack Your Own Parachute*, Addison-Wesley, Wokingham.
Honey, P. (1988) *Improve Your People Skills*, Institute of Personnel Management, London.
Martin, P. and Nichols, J. (1987) *Creating a Committed Work Force*, Institute of Personnel Management, London.
Smith, J.M. (1981) 'The Paradox of Talent', Occasional research paper. Coutts Career Consultants, London.

9 Cultural issues and development centres

Sandy Schofield, Bridget Hogg and David Beard

Introduction

Development centres are predominantly Anglo-American assessment processes. As we saw in Chapter 1, they have evolved as instruments of development from the assessment centres used in selecting people to military or managerial posts in large organizations. The use of development centres has spread beyond the original cultural base of Anglo-American empiricism, and they are now widely used by companies that operate in other Western industrial countries. Development centres are common throughout Europe, and successfully operate in cultures as diverse as France (Moulinex and Rhone-Poulenc) and Sweden (Televerket).

Development centre programmes have also been successfully implemented in the non-Western cultures of Asia, an early example being British Telecom's programme for local sales staff in Hong Kong, Singapore, Australia and Japan. Competency-based management development programmes are widely used in India, for example by the National Productivity Council of India. The American training company, DDI, has used assessment centres for selection and development in a number of Japanese-based client organizations, and at the Toyota factory in Britain.

This chapter discusses some of the issues surrounding the use of development centres in different cultural environments. It looks specifically at the problems of designing development centres which will be used by participants from diverse cultural backgrounds; at the training needs of assessors from one culture who assess participants from a different culture; and at feedback techniques which are appropriate for participants from different cultures. It also includes some practical examples of development centres which have been used by companies that operate on a cross-cultural basis.

This chapter consists of eight sections:

- Introduction
- General cultural differences
- Design and implementation issues
- Implications for assessment and feedback

- Case study: Development centres in BT Asia-Pacific
- Checklist
- Further reading
- Useful addresses

General cultural differences

While it is possible for development centre programmes to be implemented across a wide spectrum of cultures, industries and nationalities, there are some limitations. Some Asian cultures, particularly the Japanese, emphasize communal activity and conformity more than the concepts of individual development which underpin development centre philosophy. In Japan, good management and effective workplace behaviour emphasize group cohesion, group consensus and conformity. Individual abilities in these areas are not easy to measure in a development centre.

In circumstances where development centre assessors are from the same cultural background as the participants, the programmes can operate very effectively without additional assessor training. However, problems often occur when the assessors are from a cultural background which is different to that of the participants. Assessors often fail to understand what constitutes effective behaviour among the participant population, or are unable to recognize it when it does appear. A solution to this problem involves cultural awareness training for assessors.

The impact of cultural differences on management style has generated a lot of discussion and research during the recent past. Much of this has been prompted by economic development, particularly by the advent of global markets and multinational corporations managed by 'international managers'.

Garratt (1981) writes that management styles are conditioned by cultural values. He sees attitudes influencing managerial behaviour. There are two views on the relationship between attitude and behaviour.

1 'Channelling': behaviour is a direct response to attitude.
2 'Perceptual screening': values influence perceptions of reality, which then determine behaviour.

The value system of a society underpins managerial behaviour and managerial behaviour reflects the value system of senior managers within the organization.

Specific examples of management differences across cultures were documented by Hofstede (1980). He compared management style and management work values, and produced a framework for comparative analysis based on four key dimensions:

1 Power-distance: the perceived distance between those who make policy decisions and manage, and those who implement decisions and who are managed.
2 Uncertainty avoidance: the extent to which managers tolerate ambiguity.
3 Individualism–collectivism: preferences for individual or collective action.

4 Masculinity–femininity: the extent to which management style is assertive and task centred (masculine) or role centred and nurturing (feminine).

Hofstede identified considerable differences even between comparatively homogeneous groups. For example, in Western Europe there were considerable differences between management styles (Table 9.1).

Managerial styles differ dramatically when comparisons are made between very different cultures. The biggest differences occur between the management styles which are on the one hand rooted in Judeo-Christian and Greek antecedence, including European, North American and Australasian culture, and those management styles which are based on Asian philosophies and religions, and include Japanese, Chinese and Indian management styles.

Redding (1980) looks at cognition processes in Western and Asian management styles, and identifies five major differences between the two approaches.

Causation

Causation is the form of explanations between events or phenomena.

Western

This is based on Greek philosophy:

• to refine explanations of the causation in such a way that one ended up with a mechanical explanation of the universe (Democritus); or
• to codify systematically and relate all aspects of the universe into a structural pattern which shows the mutual influences on its different parts (Aristotle).

When a Western manager tries to understand a problem he or she looks for causes and symptoms, and may use abstract concepts such as 'leadership', 'productivity' and 'morale' to explain the problem as a logical and sequential set of circumstances.

Asian

This is based on Confucism and Taoism:

• emphasizes the perception of concrete issues;
• does not rely on abstract thought;
• emphasizes the particular rather than universal;
• takes practicality as a central focus;
• is concerned with reconciliation, harmony and balance.

When an Asian manager tries to explain a problem, he or she looks at the circumstances in which the problem occurred, and will concentrate on the practical details, the total system and contingencies.

Probability

Probability is the extension of principles of causation into the future.

Western managers project the current situation into the future by a process of extrapolation. They use an abstract theory to make predictions, and spend a lot of time on the development of strategies.

Table 9.1 *Hofstede's four dimensions for measuring cultural differences*

	Britain	Germany	Italy
Power-distance	Low	Low	Med.
Uncertainty avoidance	Low	Med.	Med.
Masculinity–femininity	Masc.	Fem.	Masc.
Individualism	High	Med.	High

Asian managers are more fatalistic (the current situation is more important and the future will be determined by events beyond our control). Consequently, activities such as long-term planning and forecasting are less important or a waste of time.

Time   Western managers have a monochronic approach to time, and time is calibrated and linear. This encourages scheduling, deadlines and planning.

Asian managers have a polychronic approach to time: they start from nothing and return to nothing. Time is of little importance. This places an emphasis on end results, not time limits and deadlines.

Self   The Western value system (Greek/Judeo-Christian) places an emphasis on the individual. This is reflected in Western managers' concerns with 'self-realization', 'self-actualization' and 'self-development'. The individual has an existence which is separate from the community, society or group.

The Asian value system only sees people in relation to the society or community in which they live. There is no separate individual existence. The role of the individual is determined by society. There is little conception of individual privacy.

Morality   In Western thought there is an absolute moral code. All individuals are measured against the same code, which is rooted in Judeo-Christian thought. People who contravene the moral code often experience feelings of guilt.

Asian managers have no absolute moral benchmark. They are affected by the norms and conventions of the society in which they live. Asian managers suffer loss of face and shame if they contravene the social norms.

Design and implementation issues

Issues of cultural difference should be recognized in the design of a development centre. The cultural norms and conventions of the target population should be incorporated into the design of the assessment exercises and into processes of interaction between assessors and participants, and between the participants themselves. The discussion of

Table 9.2   *Impact of cultural differences on development centre design*

Exercise type	Western approach to a solution	Asian approach to a solution
In-tray and analysis	Identify symptoms of a problem and deduce the causes. Establish basic principles on which to generate a solution, and plan action to prevent a recurrence.	Adopt a contingency approach to problem definition, seeing any problem as situation-specific, and not necessarily linked to other wider issues.
	Answer may emphasize cause–effect and be linked to underlying principle or theory.	Answer may emphasize conditions which created the specific problem, and provide action-orientated solution.
Planning	Identify required action and plan activity by various deadlines.	Identify the main issues to be resolved.
	Answer may emphasize short, medium and long term, and look at the strategic implications.	Answer may concentrate on concrete action with detailed contingencies for each issue. Good solutions are more important than planning within artificial deadlines.
Group	Objectives are agreed, together with a process for achieving objectives. Within the exercise, some form of egalitarianism exists, even if roles are assigned. Informal roles emerge and are accepted. Individual identity is not determined by the group, and most people participate.	Group members take their identity from the group, and will be reluctant to contribute until the hierarchy of group members has become established. Pre-group discussion role assignment is important. There is little heated debate and group members defer to the 'chairman'.
One-to-one	Participants are often assertive in explaining their position, and will be able to disagree with the view of an adversary, while still accepting the validity of opposing views.	Participants maintain 'face' and harmony by avoiding the clear expression of opposing views, by not fully explaining their own position, and by seeking compromise.

exercise design in Chapter 3 highlighted a need for development centre exercises to reflect as realistically as possible the actual work activities of the target population. This principle can be extended to include the incorporation of management and cultural styles of the participant group.

Some guidance on the cultural impact for designers is provided in Table 9.2. It focuses on the major differences that exist between Western cultures and Asian cultures and which were discussed in the previous section of this chapter.

The main design issues relating to cultural differences are that:

- problem-solving exercises, such as the in-tray and analysis, should be designed to allow the problem-solving approach which is associated with a particular cultural style, and to measure abilities in the use of that approach;
- planning exercises should reflect cultural styles and impact on concepts such as time, strategy and prediction;
- exercises which measure the abilities of participants to manage social interaction should be designed to allow them to interact with others in a way which is appropriate to the cultural environment in which they work.

The usual design sequence for development centre exercises, as discussed in Chapter 3, is followed. However, more care is needed in researching performance criteria and the influence of cultural styles on the completion of work tasks.

Implications for assessment and feedback

Assessment and feedback are complex procedures carried out by development centre assessors. These people require an understanding of the performance standards attained by participants, and the ability to create rapport with participants to provide meaningful and helpful feedback.

Where differences exist between the cultural backgrounds of development centre participants and assessors, assessment becomes more complex. The real difficulty in cross-cultural assessment can be the identification, interpretation and evaluation of observed behaviours, and in the approach to feeding back this information. What is expected and acceptable in one culture may be alien in another. Consequently, it is often dangerous to attempt an assessment without an understanding of the cultural norms of the participant population.

Cultural awareness training

In order to reduce cultural misunderstandings it is important to understand three things:

1 Ethics, values and thinking styles of the cultural grouping of which the target population is a part.
2 Social norms, conventions and behaviours of the target population.
3 Effective workplace and managerial behaviours.

Methods for identifying levels of effectiveness in areas associated with item 3 have been described in Chapter 2. In addition, it is important to design development centre exercises and processes so that they are compatible with the cultural environment of the participant population as well as being valid predictors of workplace performance.

It is often vital to provide an in-depth cultural briefing for everyone involved in a development centre (assessors, psychometricians and designers), to introduce them to the thinking style, work patterns and behavioural norms of the participant population. It is also important that those involved in both design and implementation are aware of the cultural differences that may exist.

Cultural awareness briefing may also include documentation and reference material which contains the following information:

- Background to the country (geography, politics, weather).
- Practical hints (protocol, body contact, meals, gifts).
- Description of the culture of the country (values, ethics, thinking styles, emotional expression).
- Description of business and management styles (meetings, status and authority, decision-making styles).
- Assessment and feedback (styles to adopt and avoid, behavioural norms, creating rapport, non-verbal communication, attitudes to personal development).

Guidance on producing a cultural briefing pack

This section describes a practical method for producing a cultural briefing pack for use by assessors from the United Kingdom who had to run a development centre in South East Asia.

Key steps to a cultural briefing

1 **Identify countries or regions**. Identify the country, region or nationality that you wish to target. This may not be as easy as it seems. Recent work in preparing British managers for running a development centre in Singapore resulted in a number of cultural awareness briefings since the Singapore participant population included Chinese, Malay and Indian managers.

2 **Identify areas of focus**. Identify the aspects of attitude, thinking style and behaviour which assessors need to be aware of in order to complete their work effectively, for example, work-related behaviour of managers. Undertake a literature search for relevant information, using key words and phrases such as country name, management styles, cultural differences and training. This should provide a list of titles and abstracts for further investigation.

3 **Undertake research**. Read relevant articles and books (this may be an extensive operation since initial articles provide more references to follow up).

4 **Collate key information**. Collate the key points on a flipchart under titles such as:

(a) practical hints;
(b) management style;
(c) cultural norms.

5 **Contact cultural experts**. Interview experts who are knowledgeable about the relevant countries and nationalities. Embassies, cultural organizations, country nationals and expatriates are all useful sources of information.

6 **Review and organize data**. This can be done by several people, and can be organized under titles such as:

(a) topographical, climatic, economic and social data;
(b) practical hints on protocol, body contact, meals and gifts;
(c) description of the culture of the country, including important concepts and beliefs, thinking styles and emotional expression;
(d) description of business and management styles such as meetings status, authority and decision-making styles;
(e) assessment and feedback, including styles to adopt and to avoid, behavioural norms, creating rapport, non-verbal communication and attitudes to personal development.

7 **Produce culture briefings materials**. Decide on appropriate channels of communication for transmitting this information. The type of data will probably fall into one of two categories:

(a) reference material, which is usually factual, and the development centre assessors, participants or managers might need to refer to it on a regular basis—it is best presented in a written format;
(b) behaviour models for development centre staff which they may need to apply, practise and receive feedback on during the assessor training workshop.

It is also helpful to invite expert speakers to attend culture awareness training sessions.

Cultural differences, assessment and feedback

Knowledge of cultural differences will help assessors and psychometricians to make accurate assessments and provide helpful feedback. Firstly, the trained assessors will be better able to interpret observed behaviours. For example, Asian managers attending a meetings exercise tend not to contribute until they are asked to, and then never disagree in public because it would cause someone to lose face. In observing managers from such a culture during a group exercise, an assessor would be better able to interpret the actions of group members, understanding why someone behaved in such a way, and how effective the behaviour was in the circumstances in which it occurred.

Cultural differences affect the feedback process

An awareness of cultural differences is also vital to aid the provision of feedback to development centre participants. Before the feedback process starts, it is important that observers and psychometricians are aware of cultural differences which may affect the feedback process. Such differences include:

- level of formality expected by participant;
- participants' attitudes to personal development;
- sources of motivation (praise vs highlighting development needs, group vs individual focus);
- cultural norms regarding one-to-one meetings and feedback on performance;
- participants' willingness to discuss feedback;
- time management in meetings.

These differences must be highlighted to assessors and psychometricians in the cultural awareness briefings. They may affect the style of feedback and the means by which assessors and psychometricians build rapport. Assessors should adjust their methods of building rapport by adhering to the correct levels of formality, including forms of address and use of humour, so that the participant will feel as comfortable as possible during the feedback interview.

In some business cultures, such as the Japanese, it is uncommon for private one-to-one meetings to occur between boss and subordinate, especially with respect to feedback on performance. If such meetings occur they often have negative overtones—hence a development centre participant may approach the feedback interview with some severe reservations. An assessor should be aware of how participants may view the feedback interview.

As discussed, in many Asian cultures, such as Japan, an individual's identity is group-referenced rather than personal. An individual has no identity outside the group to which he or she belongs. Development centre feedback, with an emphasis on personal development, often appears irrelevant or incomprehensible. Psychometricians and assessors may find it more useful to focus feedback on the individual's contribution to the group. In cultures where Lockean individualism prevails, such as the United States and United Kingdom, motivation may be maximized by directing feedback towards individual development.

Another common cultural misunderstanding, which may cause some difficulties during the feedback process, arises from different perceptions of time. The feedback process during a development centre is limited by time constraints. Typically, the assessor's feedback may last for one or two hours. Where assessors and participants have different perceptions of time—polychronic and monochronic—misunderstandings over time management can lead to frustrations and distrust which will affect harmony within the feedback interview. The potential for misunderstandings can be anticipated in advance of the meeting, and agreement reached over the use of time within the feedback interview.

However much care is taken to become familiar with the culture of a country, there are often surprises during the first visit. The same often applies to the implementation of development centres, despite efforts to produce a sophisticated and relevant cultural pre-briefing. However, careful preparation and heightened awareness will reduce the number of misunderstandings, and make people more aware of them when they do occur.

Case study: Development centres in BT Asia-Pacific

Background   BT Asia-Pacific was created in 1991 from an amalgamation of the company's separate and isolated sales offices in Japan, Australia, Singapore and Hong Kong. The new region was identified as an important growth area, and the Regional Sales Director was keen to improve the already effective performance of his sales team by completing a skills audit and a skills development programme. He adopted a development centre approach, using a system which had already been successfully adopted in the United Kingdom.

There were two additional objectives in running a development centre programme. Firstly, it was designed to promote a common regional identity by providing a common experience for the sales force. This was important since BT Asia-Pacific had been created from a number of smaller country-based offices, each with its own product lines, management styles and sales culture. Secondly, it was designed to promote the account management skills needed for selling a new range of telecommunications services to global customers.

This project posed a major challenge for the designers since they had to produce one development centre programme for sales people who came from four very diverse cultural backgrounds. The main design criterion was that the development centre should be fair, appropriate and applicable to all sales people from across the region. A second major design problem was that senior sales managers from the United Kingdom (a fifth cultural grouping on the programme) would have to act as assessors since there were insufficient senior sales staff within the region to train as local assessors.

Cultural issues in relation to design   The project manager of the design team visited Hong Kong and Singapore to obtain background information and documentation of 'critical incidents' which denoted effective performance in order to ensure face validity of materials and predictive validity of processes. Meanwhile, the remainder of the team researched Chinese and Japanese culture. This included a half-day briefing from a Japanese consultancy: The Europe–Japan Centre.

The main points drawn from the research were that the Chinese populations in Singapore and Hong Kong were very Westernized, since the two cities were international trading centres and had both experienced

British administration. The authors were conscious that Chinese values and behaviours were still important in determining the business behaviour and management styles of the local members of the BT sales force. The biggest cultural differences were seen in Japan, where a high proportion of BT sales people were Western educated, but where there were very considerable cultural differences when compared with the rest of the region and with BT's UK-based sales force.

The overall conclusion was that the development centre exercises and processes would work in Asia-Pacific, but with some minor adaptations to fit local needs. The main focus needed to be on providing the assessors from the United Kingdom with a cultural understanding, particularly in relation to behaviours associated with effective performance.

A cultural awareness workshop was held for the UK-based assessors to prepare them for running the development centre programmes in a different cultural environment. They were provided with a briefing on each country, together with specific information on feedback issues and behaviours likely to be observed in group interactions. A booklet, *Observers' Cultural Briefing Handbook*, was produced as a reference manual to supplement the workshop.

The components of the development centre are listed below, with some of the features which were included to allow for cultural differences.

1 **Occupational Personality Questionnaire**. Japanese and Chinese versions of Saville & Holdsworth's OPQ (see Chapter 5) were made available. The main focus of assessor training and briefing was on feedback techniques and awareness of dimensions which might have cultural implications, e.g.'traditionally' orientated as opposed to 'change' oriented.
2 **Graduate and Managerial Assessment test—numerical**. The full GMA test battery was not used, as in earlier UK programmes, since English language verbal reasoning tests were seen as inappropriate for people whose first language was not English. However, the numerical test was used in order to provide direct comparisons with the British sales population.
3 **Written exercise**. This measured the ability of participants to convey complex technical data in a simple written format to non-experts.
4 **Group exercise**. This was designed to assess participants' abilities when working as team members to achieve group goals, a major activity in Chinese and Japanese work practice. The group task was designed to overcome initial Asian reticence in a group activity where roles and hierarchies are unclear.
5 **Sales presentation**. The sales presentation simulated typical conditions encountered by the sales people when dealing with a major influencer or decision-maker in a customer account. Clear role briefing was provided so that participants knew their own status within the interaction.
6 **Planning exercise**. The planning activity involved analysis of problems

relating to a particular customer, and planning a course of action to redeem the situation.

7 **One-to-one staff review meeting exercise**. This exercise was used with sales managers and enabled an assessment of their ability to deal with under-performing sales team members.

8 **Biographical interview**. This was based on a questionnaire completed by participants before attending the development centre. The interview concentrated on past successes, current work and career plans. Care was taken in designing the data-gathering form and in conducting the interview to use non-threatening language and to avoid discussions that could lead to 'loss of face'.

Experiences and learning points

Thirty sales people attended the development centres, which were run in Singapore, Hong Kong and Australia. Participant feedback was very positive, as were comments from the participants' line managers. Listed below is a collated account of several of the observers' and psychometricians' experiences, specifically relating to cultural differences which they identified between the Asia-Pacific and the UK development centre programmes.

The group exercise

Chairing of the group discussion in Singapore and Hong Kong was undertaken in a very formal fashion. Other group members tended to defer to the chairman, making minimal contributions to the discussion, and only participating when invited by the chairman. There was often no response to direct questions, and assessors were aware that this was often associated with the need to avoid 'loss of face'.

The Asian participants seemed to have a preference for receiving instructions, and rarely took initiatives. The Singapore development centre was also attended by two American sales account managers, and there were strikingly different approaches between the American and Chinese participants in behaviours associated with group activity. An interesting view was put forward by one of the Chinese on the American style of getting things done:

'They see what they want and they talk and talk while they are telling you. They make their decisions very quickly, whereas the Chinese are slower . . . they don't listen to our way of doing business here.'

This seems to be borne out by the opposing frustrations that the Americans expressed privately:

'They would all just sit there and say nothing if we left it to them.'

This could imply that the Chinese way of expressing ideas and making decisions is sufficiently different or that they may be overpowered by a Western approach. No response, therefore, may be due to politeness or to 'loss of face'.

Three Chinese women sales managers participated in the Hong Kong development centre, and they were far less assertive in expressing their views than their Chinese male colleagues. This was despite the fact that the women participants were better qualified and, in many cases, had a better sales record.

One-to-one situations: biographical interview, manager exercise, feedback

The biographical interviews ran contrary to expectations. The Asian participants were extremely open and willing to talk about their current work and about their career ambitions. This was in contrast to their British counterparts who attended development centres in the United Kingdom.

Observers were also surprised at how closely some participants sat with assessors during one-to-one feedback interviews. These experiences tended to conflict with research which indicated that Chinese people prefer minimal body contact. However, the assessors often found that they received little guidance from the participants, verbally or non-verbally, as to how the feedback was being received. This was despite a briefing session in the classroom beforehand explaining the process of feedback, and the need for the participants' involvement. Most were reluctant to discuss or challenge the outcomes. Therefore, assessors had to ask questions such as 'Do you understand?' or 'Would you like me to explain in more detail for you?' in order to check understanding. Discussions often did develop, but only slowly after careful rapport building by the assessors.

All assessors found they had to work very hard with their listening skills, particularly in Hong Kong, where the Chinese accents were very strong. While many of the candidates were Western educated (in one case a double degree from Nottingham), their accents were very pronounced, causing a few misunderstandings. As one assessor commented, 'it would have been useful to have had more opportunity to "tune in to" the accents before the development centre began'. The general feeling was that more time could have been usefully spent socializing before the development centre started.

Occupational Personality Questionnaire

The observers were advised by Saville & Holdsworth that there would be no need for any major changes in approach to feedback, but that certain dimensions may be emphasized as part of cultural values. This was found to be true, on the whole, while taking account of feedback issues already mentioned. In comparison to the UK sales force there was a tendency among Chinese managers to show preferences in the following way:

Traditional—High	Change—Low
Achievement—High	Competitive—Low
Independence—Low	

Written exercise

A common approach to this exercise was as one assessor put it 'flowery and old fashioned . . .'. The exercise is based on a customer's complaint. This may reflect the local education system and teaching of English.

Planning exercise A key feature of Chinese managers' approach to this exercise was accuracy and attention to detail. This was in dramatic contrast to the approach adopted by the UK sales force.

Checklist

1 The project manager should ensure that all people, i.e. designers, observers, course secretaries, involved in a multicultural development centre are provided with cultural awareness training.
2 As far as possible, check any theoretical cultural research with people who have already visited the country, or are residents of the country.
3 When designing the exercises, ensure they fit as far as possible the managerial and cultural norm of the participants.
4 Prior to a development centre it is extremely useful to spend time with the participants, to help break down potential barriers between the assessors and the participants. When working with participants from other countries this time period also helps with the understanding of each others' accents.
5 When providing feedback, particularly to Asian participants, throughout the process 'check understanding' and offer to clarify points further. They are less likely to ask for further clarity than their English counterparts.

References and further reading

Garratt, B. (1981) 'Contrasts in Chinese and Western management thinking', *Leadership and Organisation Development Journal*, 2 (1), 17–22.

Hofstede, G. (1980) *Culture's Consequences*, Sage, London.

Mant, A. (1977) *The Rise and Fall of the British Manager*, Macmillan, London.

Menthe, B. de (1987) *Japanese Etiquette and Ethics in Business*, Phoenix Publishing Associates, Canaan, New Hampshire, USA.

Nevis, E.C. (1983) 'Cultural assumptions and productivity: the United States and China', *Sloan Management Review*, Spring, 17–29.

Redding, S.G. (1980) 'Definition as an aspect of culture: exploratory view of the Chinese case', *Journal of Management Studies*, May, 127–49.

Yih-Heng Jou, J. and Kai Sung (1990) 'Chinese value systems and managerial behaviour', *International Journal of Psychology*, 25, 619–27.

Useful addresses

The following organizations provide cultural awareness briefings and training:

Consulnet
Nash House
St George Street
London W1R 9DE
Great Britain
Tel: 071 491 1791
    (+44 71 491 1791)
Fax: 071 491 4055
    (+44 71 491 4045)
Telex: 8952 8030 GCLDN-G

Centre for International Briefing
The Castle
Farnham
Surrey GU9 OAG
Great Britain
Tel: 0252 721194
    (+44 252 721194)

10 Development centre evaluations

Keith Coaley

Introduction

The aim of this chapter is to look at ways in which development centres may be evaluated. The emphasis is on practical techniques, based on extensive experience of evaluating development centre programmes in large organizations. The case study gives an example of practical application of evaluation techniques. It is hoped that this will enable training or personnel managers to devise their evaluation processes since there is no single 'right' approach, and this chapter does not set out to present a definitive statement on the complex issues involved in evaluation and validation.

A wide variety of approaches has been adopted in recent years, and success is dependent upon a number of factors, including the particular needs of the organization involved. Methodological problems do frequently occur, although in general the major problem in the commercial context has been that of the translation of training and development effectiveness into financial terms which will satisfy the requirements of management accountants. For the designer of development centres in the business environment this may provide the major aid to in-company justification.

There are many processes available for evaluating the effectiveness of development centres and designers will evolve techniques which fit their own needs and the requirements of their company. However, as with development centre design itself, there are three key principles which will promote success:

1 Be clear of the objectives and desired outcomes of the development centre programme.
2 Be clear of the objectives and desired outcomes of the evaluation process.
3 Plan the evaluation carefully in a logical and systematic manner during the stage of development centre design.

This chapter is divided into eight sections:

- Introduction
- Objectives of validation and evaluation—an explanation of how these terms may be defined in a practical and useful way

- Validating development centres—a practical guide to the construction of a validation process
- Evaluating development centres—a practical guide to evaluation and how the results may be translated into financial terms
- Case study: The BT Sales Force
- Checklist
- Further reading
- Useful addresses

Objectives of validation and evaluation

Demand for effective validation and evaluation techniques has grown substantially in recent years. This may be because training and personnel managers have a strong interest in being able to demonstrate the monetary or utility benefits of training events in terms of an increase in workplace and business performance. They also seek guidance on ways to demonstrate to their senior management the value of investing in training or development centres when the opportunity cost may be reduced investment in other areas.

There is both disagreement and confusion among practitioners over the terms 'validation' and 'evaluation', and the processes most often used to achieve these ends. It is useful to start with a definition of the terms in ways which will have practical application and benefits for the workplace. It is also important to distinguish validation and evaluation from participant questionnaire measures which are often distributed at the conclusion of training events. These questionnaires, sometimes referred to as 'happy sheets', are substantially influenced by the feelings, attitudes or perceptions of participants and are thus really measures of the course 'climate' at the time. They do not provide participants with the scope for an objective consideration of the training experienced, and it is not possible at this time for them to consider any benefits the training or development centre may have for their workplace performance. As a result analyses of these questionnaires may lead to very misleading results.

Validation

The Department of Trade and Industry has defined training as: 'The systematic development of the attitude, knowledge, skill and/or behaviour pattern required by an individual to perform adequately a given task or job.' This means that different forms of training or development need to be designed to specific, objectively-defined, job-oriented criteria.

Thus, validation concerns the assessment of the content and processes of development centres in order to confirm that they meet the required design criteria.

In training terms, the DTI defines validation as: 'A series of tests and assessments designed to ascertain whether a training programme or course has achieved the behavioural objectives specified.' In literal terms, this means: Does the training do what it was designed to do? Translated to development centres, the question becomes: 'Do the assessments made by observers really measure what we say they are measuring?' This takes us into the realm of the concept of validity.

Face validity This is a subjectively defined and evaluated form of validity which indicates popular perceptions about the extent to which the content of the development centre reflects actual job tasks for the target population. Simply put again, this answers the question: 'Do the measures constructed appear, at least superficially, to be appropriate for assessing the stated competences?' Face validity can be determined to some extent by asking senior managers to look at material designed for exercises and asking them whether it appears to be appropriate. Suggested amendments could then be carried out.

It is also useful to pilot exercise materials and the associated rating procedures using individuals who are knowledgeable about the target jobs but who are unlikely to take part in the development centres. Lastly, a post-DC questionnaire, which enables participants to reflect upon their experiences, can also be employed to assess the face validity of the exercises.

Content validity Content-related validity is the demonstration of a direct relationship between what is being measured by the development centre and the requirements of the target job or jobs. Technically, it is defined as the degree to which scores on the exercises may be accepted as representative of performance within a strictly defined job domain of which the test is a sample.

Content validity links the ratings given by observers to the performance of participants at work. This may be assessed by measures of association such as correlation coefficients which link the ratings with other ratings provided by line managers, or other available measures of performance. This latter group could, for example, consist of performance appraisal ratings.

Other measures may be available within the development centre itself, such as measures of work-related cognitive skills. For example, a high association between competences relating to analysis or analytical thinking with scores on a numerical reasoning test will provide a good indication of validity.

An indication of content validity may be given when line managers agree with the outcomes of the development centre for individual participants they know well. When the ratings indicate that a participant has the potential for future management development, the line manager may agree with this outcome based upon knowledge of that individual's performance in the workplace, and this provides a good indication of content validity. If there is disagreement, then this may suggest the need for a re-evaluation of the exercise involved.

Criterion validity Criterion-related validity is a statistical statement demonstrating the probable existence of a true relationship between performance at the development centre and subsequent success in the workplace. The emphasis should be upon the word 'probable' since there are no absolutes in the field of statistics. Findings are normally given in terms of the likelihood that the results obtained are not due to chance processes alone. The words 'statistical significance' are frequently used, based upon a less than 1 in 20 chance that the results are artificial, i.e. there is less than a 5 per cent probability that the results are due to chance.

Criterion validity can be assessed some three to six months after a programme of development centres, although in practice an assessment of content validity frequently appears adequate in the commercial context.

Evaluation

Evaluation is defined by the DTI as: 'The assessment of the total value of the training programme or course. Evaluation differs from validation in that it attempts to measure the overall worth and benefit of the course, and not just the achievement of the laid-down objectives.' In plain words again, this means: Was it worth doing the training? The terms 'worth', 'benefit' and 'value' are not defined by the DTI, although they would include costs and financial benefits when applied in a commercial environment.

Evaluation provides measurable outcomes from training courses or development centres which can be used to assess the impact on the workplace performance of the participants, and the subsequent impact of this on overall organizational performance.

Evaluation tends to present a more difficult process which takes place at some predetermined interval after attendance at the training event. It tries to measure the impact on workplace and business performance, and the extent to which skills or modified behaviours are successfully applied in the workplace.

Validating development centres

A simple process for validating development centres is described below.

- Materials for exercises need to be considered in detail and at length by senior managers working within the organization. This may take some time but is well worth doing for it enables the early identification of misleading or erroneous details. Such a validation stage needs to be built into the overall design process.
- Pilot the exercises by asking a group of people who have the requisite expertise and job-related knowledge to complete the activities in standard development centre conditions. They may find this to be a rather taxing task, particularly for such items as written and planning exercises, but are often cooperative and supportive if the purposes of the event are presented and explained carefully.

Following the pilot it is important to ask the participants for their comments on the exercises undertaken:

—Was the time allocated sufficient for the tasks?
—Do the tasks accurately reflect the tasks in the workplace?
—Could they be improved? If so, how?

These data can be collected using standard questionnaires and discussion. It is important to check the style, presentation and content of the materials. All of these should match the materials normally available in the workplace. Face validity of the materials is more at issue here than the outputs of the pilot event, although the outputs themselves can provide useful information on how best to improve the exercises.

- A questionnaire needs to be designed in order to send it out to participants shortly after attending the development centre. This could also check out other factors, such as biographical details of participants, the extent of their pre-briefing by line management, and post-centre development activities.

However, a number of questions will help to assess the validity of the development centre in the eyes of its participants. These questions, together with a six-point rating scale (1 low to 6 high), might usefully include:

—How effective were the introductions and briefings on the first day?
—How realistic were the development centre exercises?
—How difficult were the exercises?
—How helpful was the final feedback interview?

It is possible to analyse the results of these questionnaires in terms of percentage responses. There is reasonable face validity if the majority of participants consider the activities to have been realistic (4 and above on the rating scale). Too much or too little difficulty may also reflect upon the validity of the exercises.

- If senior managers are to be assessors on the development centre, they can also help to improve the validity of the assessments. By the time of the assessor training workshop the materials will have been well developed, although this event will also usefully help to improve validity. As observers are trained to use the exercises, it may be possible to ask for their thoughts and comments, and subsequently to make any necessary amendments.
- Assessment of content validity presents a more detailed process, requiring the collation of a large amount of data.

Each participant will be rated for each competence during each exercise. As explained elsewhere in this volume, different combinations of competences will be assessed for individual participants during an exercise, whether a written, project planning, group or presentation exercise.

Measurements of behavioural anchors making up these competences could be made against a pre-determined rating scale, for example, ranging from 1 to 6. The basis of this scale could be as follows:

1 Criteria not met.
2 Demonstrates major development needs in all areas to meet criteria.
3 Demonstrates development needs in key areas in order to meet the criteria.

4 Demonstrates a level of attainment against the main criteria, but with some minor development needs in less important areas.
5 Demonstrates an acceptable level of attainment against the criteria.
6 Demonstrates a high level of attainment against the criteria.

The results will provide an assessment matrix for the participant. For example, see Table 10.1. At the completion of the development centre these results are fed back to the participant by an assigned personal assessor. The collected results for all of the participants, together with other data made available provide the basis for validation and an aggregate performance review for the entire workforce that attended the development centre programme.

It is important to establish during the design stage of the development centre how and what data should be collected on an ongoing basis. A management system should subsequently be set up in order to run the evaluation process, and individual development centre managers need to be informed of arrangements so that items of data do not go missing.

The development centre manager needs to collect for each participant:

• A copy of the rating matrix
• Aptitude test scores
• Scores for other measures used
• Relevant background data

The background data will also be useful for research, validation and reliability purposes, including perhaps (depending upon the circumstances of the event): age, gender, management level within the organization, number of years' experience, ethnic origin and educational level.

All these data should be arranged together for each participant in a logical fashion and returned to a central management location in preparation for analysis. Names should be removed and each participant identified purely by number in order to ensure anonymity and confidentiality. When the data are collected from participants during the previous development centre, this approach, as well as the purposes of the data collection, should be explained so as to allay fears about use of the data.

Table 10.1

Exercise	Written	Planning	Group	Presentation	Overall rating
Competence 1	4	5	4	5	5
Competence 2	3	2	3	2	2
Competence 3	5	6	5	5	5
Competence 4	4	4	4	4	4
Competence 5	3	3	2	3	3

It must be emphasized that for the event to remain focused upon development, the aggregate data, including any aptitude test scores, background data, and personality test ratings (where used), must remain anonymous and confidential. No identification of any individual participant should be possible.

Analysis of the combined data requires a powerful statistical tool. A number of these are now available. One of the most effective and best known is the Statistical Package for the Social Sciences (SPSS). This software enables the construction of a spreadsheet, into which all of the data can be recorded and subjected to statistical analyses.

Column headings on the spreadsheet should identify the nature of each score entered. For example, the matrix shown above could be entered as:

Com1w   Com1p   Com1   Com1g   Com1pr   Com1   Com2w   Com2p   Com2g

and the ratings entered beneath these headings in vertical columns. Columns can also be constructed for aptitude test scores, as well as personality test scores such as the 31 dimensions of the SHL Occupational Personality Questionnaire (OPQ) if this is used during the development centre. The detailed analysis of development centre results provides not only validation data but also a rich source of information for human resource management. Examples include:

- Succession planning
- Manpower planning
- Training audit
- Evaluation of job selection criteria
- Analysis of stress levels

The spreadsheet, constructed in this manner, will tend to be long, especially if background data are included. Often these data will need to be coded so that different values are represented by numbers. Some spreadsheets have been as long as 120 variables and have involved input of the data for more than 600 development centre participants. Input, therefore, presents a mammoth task and clerical or support staff will need to input the data on a regular basis for an extensive period. However, the results are valuable and can provide substantial insights into the performance of a large workforce, and can initiate valuable organization development and change.

Validity can now be assessed through the statistical association of meaningful variables. For example, following a recent development programme for sales managers, performance in the sales presentation exercise was significantly correlated with the number of years' experience in a sales function. This indicates high validity for the exercise. Similarly, an analysis of age groups showed that the ratings given for a competence defined as 'maturity' were highest among managers in the 50–60 year age group. Again, this was statistically significant and suggests good validity for the behavioural anchors involved.

Competences which involve analytical thinking can be correlated with numerical aptitude scores, and with personality measures such as 'data rational' or 'detail conscious' of the OPQ. A competence relating to planning and organization of the workplace can be associated with the OPQ's 'forward planning' and 'conscientious'. Communication and related skills may be linked to verbal aptitude scores. If a substantial volume of aggregate data has been accumulated, together with a wide variety of variables from different sources, there is scope for very detailed analysis and a thorough validation of the development centre.

Evaluating development centres

The purposes of development centre evaluation should be as follows:

1 To measure uplift in skills in the workplace following a development centre programme.
2 To measure the uplift in terms of financial savings.
3 To use 'hard' data to demonstrate to senior managers the benefits of development centres as sound investment decisions.

In the training environment an evaluation study is often conducted during or immediately following a training event, normally through the use of questionnaires which are completed by participants. The objective of this is to establish the level of skills acquisition or behaviour change as a result of the event. Effective course validation thus appears to be a prerequisite of successful evaluation.

In order effectively to evaluate a development centre two core measures are required:

• A pre-course workplace assessment by individual line managers of the skills of participants.
• A post-course workplace assessment, again by the line manager, of the skills of participants.

Both of these should be on the same basis and should employ the competences used on the development centre itself. Questionnaires with numerical assessment of competences (1 low through to 6 high) may be used, although it is wise for these to be completed at an interview which allows the line manager to make any other relevant comments at the time. The problem with this approach alone is that although it may provide evidence of a significant shift in behaviour at work, it fails to provide a process for indicating the worth or financial value of this change.

Interviews

In order to gain this 'worth' a structured interview using the critical incident technique with line managers is required. These interviews need to be planned over a period of time about six months following a development centre programme, thus giving adequate time for participants to try out and to develop new behaviours and attitudes within the workplace. A random sample of line managers, representative of the larger sample of line management, needs to be selected, contacts made and appointments set up. Discussion will need to be confidential in view of the fact that the working performance of employees is under discussion, although in practice the line manager need not identify particular individuals and could discuss them without using names.

The interview is an important tool for gathering data and is an important step in evaluation. It is essential to gather information that is as accurate and complete as possible. Before conducting interviews, the interviewer should be thoroughly prepared and have a clear plan. Some of the planning considerations are given below:

1 The interview objectives should be explicit, to identify the costs of typical incidents of failure in the workplace before the development centre programme and to identify whether there have been changes in behaviour, skills and attitude as a consequence of the programme.
2 The target group of interviewees should be defined, for example the immediate supervisors or line managers. For evaluation purposes, these will have more accurate knowledge of participants' work performance.
3 The approach that will be used to accomplish the interview should be specified and reviewed, for example the degree of structure, number of interviewees or interviewers. Experience indicates that a one-to-one interview may be preferable.
4 Materials needed to carry out the interview should be available. Pre-designed forms with sufficient space for note-taking are required.

Not everyone can conduct a good interview, and the procedure requires a unique combination of skills, including active listening, being able to put people at ease while directing the conversation, probing for answers which the interviewee may be reluctant to provide, and systematically recording relevant information.

The critical incident method, developed by John C. Flanagan, is a systematic interview procedure for recording direct observations of human behaviours that lead to the success or failure of accomplishment of a specific task. An incident is critical if it makes a significant contribution, either positively or negatively, to the general aim of the working activity or to some work-related objective. The technique is unique in its ability to provide realistic, empirical data about actual behaviour in work situations. This approach to interviewing is considered to be a generic method because it can be used to study any job for a variety of different human resource purposes.

Five requirements need to be met when using the critical incidents technique and these are particularly important for the evaluation process:

1 Incidents must be collected from only those people who have made actual observations of the job activities and their outcomes of development centre participants.
2 The interviewee needs to be aware of the aims and objectives of the work carried out by the participant.

3 The basis for determining whether an incident is critical needs to be defined. The same rules should apply in all interviews in order to achieve objectivity and standardization.

4 The critical incidents should be collected from only those people who are closely associated with the work of participants, usually from the line managers. They are in a much better position to make judgements as to whether an incident or activity is outstanding or unsatisfactory. Participants, themselves, would make judgements which are influenced by bias.

5 To minimize problems caused by poor recollections, critical incidents should have been observed within the previous 6 to 12 months.

Flanagan argued that the procedure has considerable efficiency because of the use of only the extremes of behaviour, and that these extremes can be more accurately identified than behaviour which is more average in character. Set against this are the arguments that the technique is time consuming and may neglect a large amount of other information.

However, this latter criticism may be avoided through the definition of the terms 'competent' and 'effective' as behaviour which the interviewee would wish all employees in this situation to exhibit. Similarly, the terms 'ineffective' or 'incompetent' can be defined in the interview as referring to behaviour which if exhibited repeatedly would cause the interviewee to doubt the competence of the individual. Emphasis can then be placed upon the word 'do'.

In the case of evaluation, we need to establish not only the nature of pre-development centre failure incidents but also the costs involved, whether these include direct financial payments, time wasted for both the participant and the line manager, business lost to other customers, and costs to other units, if known. This will require extensive probing, especially where the line manager's recollections are poor. Time costs will need to be established through calculation based upon salary levels.

In many cases, minimum costs are outlined, rather than the full costs of failure. Any subsequent report should stress this, that the costs involved amount to minimum figures and that the true costs may be substantially greater. However, the minimum figures may well be substantial.

A suggested interview structure would include the following items:

- Opportunity for the line manager to discuss the nature of the work carried out by participants and the structure of the organization involved.
- Discussion of three pre-development centre critical incidents representing typical failure behaviours at the time, and recording of the associated costs.
- Ratings by the line manager of individual participants on a suitable numerical rating scale. For example 1 (low) to 10 (high) for each of the competences used during the development centre. Pre-development centre performance needs to be considered.

- Discussion of three post-development centre critical incidents representing current behaviour in the workplace, and recording of any costs, where these exist.
- Competence ratings need to be considered again using the same scale as before, although in this case the line manager needs to consider current working performance.
- Discussion of the line manager's general comments about the development centre programme and the influence of this upon workplace performance. The manager's recommendations for the future use of the event may also be useful.

A structured interview schedule for each critical incident could look like that in Figure 10.1.

Analysis   The results of a representative number of interviews will need to be subjected to detailed and thorough analysis, including content analysis, statistical data analysis and a costs analysis.

Content analysis   Content analysis will provide details of, for example:

1 The line managers and staff involved, their geographical distribution and areas of work.
2 The number and nature of the pre-development centre critical incidents and how these may be classified.
3 The number and nature of post-event behaviours and activities and how these also can be classified.
4 General comments about the programme, its influence upon workplace performance and its potential for future use.

Statistical analysis   Statistical analysis can be used to look at differences between pre- and post-development centre performance ratings, or indicators. Each participant discussed will have been given ratings for each competence, on a before-and-after basis. Thus there will be two columns of data for each competence, and these two sets of data may be subjected to statistical (t) tests in order to identify whether there is a significant difference between the means. Where there is a significant difference, one which is greater than chance, there has been an improvement in performance. If the number of participants discussed is sufficiently large and representative of the wider population of development centre participants, this means we may assume an overall improvement in performance in respect of those competences.

Costs analysis   Costs analysis enables an estimation of the financial benefits of the programme. It is necessary to consider the results of the previous statistical analysis and to identify those participants who have made an overall improvement in performance. If they are now performing at an adequate level, then the failure costs associated with them in the past have been removed. Summation of the costs across the group can subsequently be extrapolated across the same proportion of the entire workforce, resulting in an estimate of the savings made as a result of the

Evaluation Interview Form

Situation One

The background:

What were the objectives for dealing with the situation satisfactorily?

What happened and why?

What did your member of staff DO? Please give a specific account of the activities and behaviours demonstrated.

Could you determine the costs in any way?

	You	Member of staff	Other units
Financial costs:			
Time wasted:			
Other costs:			

Could you please specify how you arrived at these figures?
How would you justify them?

Figure 10.1 *Evaluation interview form*

overall programme of development centres. This may be a considerable figure, even though, as stated earlier, it is likely to represent a minimum cost of failure.

Summation of the costs will include the following items:

1 Total costs of lost business—these may be greater for a workforce which is in constant contact with business customers.
2 Total costs of money paid out to customers, to other business units within the organization, or to any other recipient, however small the

sum involved. These may sometimes appear small at first but, extrapolated across a workforce, could represent a substantial overhead for the business.

3 Costs of wasted time. Salary levels will have been elicited during the interviews with line managers, and calculations can be made based upon these, whether the cost of a wasted hour, or day, or even a week at different levels.

4 Costs for associated business units, which are frequently difficult to estimate. Where these are clearly known by the line manager, they may be entered into the equation. However, it may be best to ignore them in instances where there is uncertainty.

It is useful to contrast these total estimated costs, which have been eliminated through performance improvement in the workforce, with the direct costs of the development centres themselves. Total costs per development centre should include:

• salary costs for participants, observers and training/personnel staff involved;
• combined travel and accommodation costs;
• the costs of research, design and materials for the event.

The total costs need to be multiplied by the number of development centres held to arrive at a final figure, which may be contrasted with the earlier figure relating to the benefits of improved performance. Development centre costs present a one-off payment, while it may be argued that the calculated savings are established on a recurring basis.

Case study: The BT sales force

The business background

BT's UK sales operation is a professional sales force of 3000 sales and support staff, together with 250 managers. In 1990 the General Manager was confronted by a number of key strategic decisions on how to manage change. To improve his organization he needed to:

1 respond to a major company reorganization which transferred large business customers to another division, leaving him with a diminished customer base but identical sales targets;
2 allocate existing staff into two new sales grades in order to service the new customer base more effectively;
3 develop account management skills in the sales force, which had formerly worked from a basis of technical and product knowledge.

A project team from BT Training liaised with the General Manager and senior sales managers to identify the characteristics which staff would require in the new organization. Detailed job analysis was conducted including interviews, observations and critical incident analysis.

Areas of competence required among staff included analytical and strategic thinking skills; the ability to plan and organize work; being able to sell and to influence others; product and commercial awareness; and the ability to cooperate with and to lead others. Management abilities were classified into behaviourally anchored rating scales which were expressed as clearly recognizable skills, behaviours, knowledge and attitudes. Clear statements were required for acceptance in an organization which is task oriented and seeks to measure work performance against commercial criteria.

It was agreed that a programme of development centres should be set up as these could be 'customized' to meet business needs.

Selection and design   The objectives of the development centre were to provide:

1 information which would highlight the development and training needs of the sales population, and provide a basis for individual development planning involving line managers;
2 a wide-ranging skills audit which would provide aggregate data about skills and aptitudes in order to improve policy and decision making in the areas of manpower planning, succession planning, training and selection;
3 information about the skills profiles of individual members of the sales force and personal counselling which would allow them to make decisions about their future roles in the new organization as account executives or account managers.

A three-day development centre was designed, using 45 senior sales managers as observers. They were selected on the basis of their commitment to developing sales people. These observers underwent detailed training and selection, including pass/fail training in objective interviewing techniques, as well as having their awareness heightened of interpersonal issues and the enhancement of self-esteem among staff. An Observer Training Workshop was held for familiarization with exercises and to establish agreed rating standards.

During the design stage, exercise materials were subjected to validation by sales managers serving on the joint project team, and by a pilot event using staff with sales experience. The outcomes of both events led to amendments and improvements of the exercise materials.

Competences resulting from the job analysis were assessed by these exercises, which were designed so that they were based upon a 'storyboard' approach and so participants accumulated knowledge in a consistent fashion. This meant they did not have to absorb large quantities of new information at the beginning of each exercise. Participants also took the Graduate and Managerial Assessment (GMA) tests for both numerical and verbal reasoning ability, and the Occupational Personality Questionnaire (OPQ).

Arrangements were made so that each skill area was assessed by different observers to increase accuracy and observer reliability.

Line managers were drawn into the process by providing briefings before their people attended, and by arranging post-development centre review meetings to plan development activity when their people returned to work.

Design work was completed during autumn 1990, and the final content and process were signed off by the project team.

Implementation

A total of 635 participants took part in the development centre programme. The principles underpinning it were:

1 senior managers who acted as observers did not see their own people on an event;
2 information obtained on each individual was treated in strict confidence;
3 each participant owned and held the data collected on personal abilities. Only agreed action points for development were shared with line managers;
4 only anonymous aggregate data were collected and maintained by the UK sales operations.

Effective use of resources was made through strict scheduling of exercises and psychometrics. The development centre was structured as follows:

Day 1 An introduction by a senior sales manager to explain the purpose of the event; administration of the Occupational Personality Questionnaire; written exercise; and the GMA verbal reasoning ability test.

Day 2 The GMA numerical reasoning test; planning, group and presentation exercises; and biographical interviews conducted by a personal observer.

Day 3 Feedback by the personal observer of the results of the exercises, and OPQ and GMA feedback by a registered psychometrics practitioner.

Evaluation

Evaluation of the benefits of the development centre programme was based upon interviews with 12 senior sales managers, using the critical incidents technique as well as scale and other available performance ratings. A total of 226 staff (35 per cent of participants) were managed by these managers. Both quantitative and qualitative data, linked to content and statistical procedures, were elicited during these interviews.

The managers provided accounts of 18 instances in which staff had experienced failures at work prior to the development centres. The costs involved were investigated in detail. These costs included payments by the sales person involved or the manager in order to rectify the situation, time wasted at both levels, and any lost customers through BT customers failing to complete negotiations.

Total costs for each individual amounted to £98 000 and the costs for the sample of 18 sales staff reached £1 764 000. Extended across the UK sales organization, the overall costs amounts to £67.2 million. The figure represents direct financial costs, time costs and lost business and is the estimated saving across the organization as a result of improved performance following the development centres.

Total costs expended for each event, including salary, travel and accommodation costs, and research, design and materials, amount to £11 223. On this basis, the full opportunity cost of the programme of 15 development centres comes to £168 345. This is a one-off payment, while the savings calculated are established on a recurring basis.

Ratings given for staff performance both before and after the programme showed there had been a significant overall improvement in performance. There had been significant improvements in planning and organizing skills and in interpersonal skills. Improvements had also been found in competences relating to customer focus, planning and organizing, and job-related knowledge.

New business accounts had been opened and opportunities acquired through the development of new attitudes. Performance against sales targets showed a significant improvement, and there were six cases in which previously poor performers are now exceeding targets.

The managers said there is now a recognition by staff of the need for better ways of working. They had gained in confidence generally and this had resulted in higher levels of personal initiative and sense of purpose, sometimes through better use of prospect lists. There were significant gains in customer management, commercial awareness, planning and organizing, and sales skills.

More than 90 per cent of participants responded positively to the developmental counselling and feedback they had been given. A majority felt the exercises were valid and appropriate.

Conclusions

The benefits of the development centres have enabled the UK sales organization to respond effectively to reorganization, including the allocation of staff into a new customer-oriented structure, and have developed account management skills in the sales force.

BT's sales force is now better positioned to respond positively to changing conditions in the telecommunications market in the 1990s. Emphasis upon the quality of service to BT's customers has been a major performance outcome.

Checklist

Do's
1 Ensure you are clear of the objectives and desired outcomes of the development centre.
2 Plan validation and evaluation in a logical and systematic way during the early stages of development centre design.
3 Pilot exercises thoroughly and seek thoughtful feedback on them from people with expertise in the work area involved.

Don'ts
1 Do not collect development centre information such as ratings, scores and data in a disorganized manner—the costs include your time and potential loss of accuracy.
2 Do not be careless about the anonymity and confidentiality of development centre data.
3 Do not conduct evaluation interviews without good preparation and a clear view of the information you seek to gain.

Further reading

Jackson, T. (1989) *Evaluation: Relating Training to Business Performance*, Kogan Page, London.

Useful addresses

The company listed below can provide skills audits and evaluation studies:

Compass Training
33 Grosvenor Place
Bath
Avon BA1 6BA
Great Britain
Tel: 0225 336722 (+44 225 336722)

11 Future trends in the use of development centres

Ray Knightley, Chris Latham and Geoff Lee

Introduction

Development centres have been widely used throughout Europe, the United States and the Far East since the 1970s. This chapter looks at some of the recent trends in their application, and identifies future applications during the 1990s. The chapter consists of eight sections:

- Introduction
- Avoiding discriminatory practices
- Ethical considerations
- Future trends
- Technological applications
- Wider uses
- Case study: Development of a professional sales force in Wang (UK) Ltd
- References and further reading

Avoiding discriminatory practices

Introduction

On first sight, development centre methodology seems to remove most opportunities for discrimination in the field of employee development and training. After all, what could be fairer than a tightly programmed event in which trained observers use the same schedule of exercises and tests objectively to assess participants against set benchmarks? Compared to more arcane alternatives for judging potential, such as 'intuition', graphology and palm reading, development centre methods certainly help to keep a rein on personal prejudice when assessing the abilities of other people, and planning their development at work.

None the less, the wise organization will keep a wary eye on possibilities of bias by paying careful attention to details in the research, design and implementation stages of a development centre programme. This section looks at some of the hidden potential for discrimination in the design and implementation of development centres.

Discrimination and the law

In the field of employment, English law prohibits discrimination on the grounds of gender and race. An international comparison of similar legislation at country and state level is clearly outside the scope of this book. At present, research in the area of comparative labour law appears to be very sparse. It can be said, however, that many industrialized countries have, or are considering introducing, labour law to address discriminatory practices.

In considering the introduction of a development centre programme, practitioners would be well advised to seek advice on relevant domestic labour law early in the planning phase. In this way, the need to avoid inbuilt bias will remain in the foreground throughout the design processes and the possibility of later challenge can be greatly reduced.

Discrimination can take place either directly or indirectly. Direct discrimination occurs where an individual is treated less favourably on the grounds of race, gender, religion, age or some other factor over which the sufferer has little or no choice and which has no relevance to the ability to carry out tasks. Practices which discriminate in this way are relatively easy to identify and eliminate.

Far more subtle is discrimination which falls into the 'indirect' category. This involves applying an unjustifiable requirement which certain groups of people cannot meet. Indirect discrimination commonly occurs where a policy, although applied to everyone, is likely to affect one particular group to a disproportionate extent. It is this type of discrimination, usually neither malicious nor intentional, which can most easily occur during the design and implementation of a development centre programme.

The workings of the labour market

Doeringer and Piore (1971) described labour markets in terms of their segmentation. The same firm will have both primary sector (full-time, well paid and relatively secure) and secondary sector (casual, part-time, less skilled and lower-paid) employees. Brown (1984) showed that immigrant populations, constrained by less fluency in the host-country language, are often restricted to secondary sector jobs. Unfortunately, movement from this secondary sector is impeded by the operation of the 'merry-go-round' of a closed labour market within the primary sector.

Movement in the other direction, i.e. primary to secondary sector, is relatively common. Dex (1987) showed that many women who leave full-time jobs to have children subsequently return to part-time work, often in a completely different occupation. Thus, the secondary sector of the labour market may contain a disproportionate number of ethnic minorities and women of all races.

The workings of the labour market give rise to a number of assumptions and stereotypes which can unwittingly be built into the development centre process. As the development centre is a form of investment in a company's human capital, some form of investment appraisal will usually be carried out at either or both ends of the programme. This may result in decisions about who should attend, or to restricting development opportunities for those who have attended a centre. The danger is that some subjective, value-laden decisions are made which will discriminate against certain employees.

The role of development centre programme 'owners'

Within an organization, the 'owners' of a development centre must ensure that no bias or potential for discrimination is being built into the process. This can be done by adherence to the simple guidelines provided below. It is also useful to have an equal opportunities policy for the organization which can inform designers about the company 'view' on this issue, and provide a useful template for programme design and implementation. It is not the intention of this chapter to reiterate the best practice which was covered earlier in this book, but rather to highlight to the designer the developmental stages at which bias may enter the programme. We will look at the opportunities for bias in access, content, structure, process and outcomes.

Access

This area probably has the greatest potential for discrimination. The imposition of entry requirements can be indirectly discriminatory. For example, it has been held in England that ethnic minorities can find it difficult to comply with demands for certain certificated standards of English. Similarly, upper age limits have been judged to discriminate indirectly against immigrants and women.

It may be difficult to resist the blandishments of senior managers to put 'the right people' on development centres. English law is quite explicit in these circumstances in stating that it is unlawful for a senior person to order a subordinate to carry out a discriminatory action and much overseas anti-discrimination law similarly recognizes such possible loopholes.

Content

Some managers may see the development centre as a way of providing a helping hand for the 'deserving' among their subordinates. A study of British Civil Service managers (OMCS, 1988) showed them subjectively rating women's present performance as equal to that of the men. Future potential was, however, rated more highly for the males. The danger here is that designers direct their research on criteria for high potential towards those who are currently seen to demonstrate high potential, and that the content of the development centre may come to reflect subjective criteria, and perpetuate existing imbalances or discrimination. Elsewhere in this book, you will have read of the importance of selecting tests which identify the right qualities and aptitudes. Equally important, but less obvious, is the avoidance of tests whose outcomes are affected by irrelevant characteristics.

Structure

In her study of nursing chief officers, Hutt (1985) found that 42 per cent of women felt that domestic responsibilities had restricted their access to training and job opportunities. Inappropriate and inflexible development centre timetabling can often exclude women as effectively as a locked door. The assumption that 'worthwhile' people can put in a full day with an hour or two added, may not be shared by a female manager who has to pick up her children at a particular time.

Process   Careful training of observers is the key to eliminating bias in the managing assessment and feedback on a development centre. The observers' guidance manual must be carefully drafted to direct assessment towards explicit rather than inferred behaviours. One problem is that, while line managers in an observer role are enthusiastic in principle, they may be unwilling to commit time to observer training. There are no short cuts to effective observer training. As a general rule, those line managers who protest most at the need for training, are the ones who are in most need of it.

Outcomes   Development activity usually takes place after completion of the development centre, when participants return to the workplace, and is frequently outside the remit of the programme manager. However, there is usually some carry-over of responsibility for the provision of training and development. The law may forbid any discrimination in the provision of training but some scope is allowed in certain countries and states for what is normally termed 'affirmative action'. Under specific conditions of under-representation, employers may be permitted to arrange special programmes with the intention of addressing inequality. Providers seeking to implement such training should first seek the advice of labour lawyers or a relevant statutory body.

Conclusions   An awareness of the possibility that development centres could be instruments of discrimination in the fields of development and training is useful. The way in which a programme is designed and operated can be carefully checked to ensure that anti-discrimination laws are not contravened.

Ethical considerations

This section looks at ethical considerations in the design and delivery of development centres, emphasizing the application of ethical and professional standards.

Development centre standards   Ethics are defined in the *Collins English Dictionary* as '[the] science of morals; moral principles; rules of conduct'. This suggests that in order for a development centre process to be judged as ethical there must be rules of conduct that are explicitly and consistently applied, and these must not damage the rights of participants, observers and other stakeholders.

The standards for ethical considerations for assessment centre operations quoted in Moses and Byham (1975) are equally applicable to the development centres. These guidelines were generated by a task force of American psychologists and managers directly involved in developing, establishing or maintaining assessment centre programmes in their organizations.

The guidelines argue that an appropriate set of standards should apply which provide a definition of what is meant by an assessment (development) centre and cover the following points:

- Organizational support for the operation
- Observer training
- Participant informed consent
- Use of data from the centre
- Issues of validation

Definition of a development centre

The definition of a development centre can be derived from the work of Kerr and Davenport (1989), as a process for identifying the development needs of an individual in a collaborative and supportive environment, leading to agreed development plans which meet the needs of both the employing organization and the individual.

Meeting the 'assessment' centre standards

As discussed in earlier chapters, the methodology applied to the development centre consists of 'standardized evaluation of behaviour based on multiple inputs. Multiple trained observers and techniques are used. Judgments about behaviour are made, in part, from specially developed assessment simulations' (Moses and Byham, 1975).

The process also requires the centre to use relevant job behaviours and performance criteria, as shown in Chapter 2. Moses and Byham emphasize the need for an evaluation meeting at the end of the assessment process where judgements are pooled and an agreement is reached on the overall evaluation for each participant. This provides the basis for a final report on the performance of each participant.

The final review meeting should be designed into the development centre. However, it may not always take place if the programme is run by line managers who fall behind schedule, and the timetable slips. There are several things designers of centres can do to minimize the likelihood of this happening. For example:

1 Timetable a full day for feedback.
2 Programme in slippage time during the assessment section of the centre.
3 Explain the benefits of the evaluation meeting so that the observers are convinced of the benefits.
4 Include an overall evaluation process for the observers to comment on the development centre and provide feedback to designers and programme managers so that they do not drop sections of the development centre process because they do not like them.

Meeting the 'development' criteria

Some writers such as Ferguson (1991) and Goodge (1991) would argue that the centres described in this book are assessment centres. So is it 'ethical' to describe them as a development centre process?

A comparison between the suggested good practice for development centres, as put forward by Ferguson, and the model which is discussed in this book, shows that the only significant difference occurs over whether participants have a choice about whether to attend or not. In practice, the opportunity for participants to exercise discretion about their participation is constrained by the formal or informal requirements of the organization. In practice, the organization's views prevail, as seen in many of the case studies quoted in this book.

Goodge (1991) argues that people should be selected on to development centres. For him, a genuine development centre must include in-depth discussions on career development and people with low potential should not attend the centres.

Goodge offers a definition of development centres that reconciles these three approaches. He states that a development centre is 'An off-site process resulting in effective development action'. The issue being not the selection criteria but the objectives of the centre. Using this criterion, the discussion moves on to what type of development centre is being described by Goodge, and what is meant by 'development centre' as described in this book. What Goodge is describing is a career development centre, while Ferguson talks of personal development centres. The techniques which are presented in this book can be used for either of these types of development centre, or can be used to assess skills in a current job and identify further development needs. Consequently, a more accurate description of the principles which have been expounded in earlier chapters would be that they describe the process of a 'skills development centre'.

Goodge's definition includes the requirement to run the programme as an 'off-site process'. This arrangement is not entirely necessary, and many companies run very successful 'on site' programmes in order to reduce costs. However, there are many advantages to an 'off-site' programme, and these are summarized below.

1 Minimizing intrusions from the workplace.
2 Enabling the centre to be more of a social process.
3 Allowing participants to reflect more effectively on workplace performance.
4 Removing constraints and inhibitions which may exist when in the workplace.

Organizational support for the centre

In order to operate effectively and achieve its objectives, a development centre programme needs organizational support and resources in seven crucial areas. These are summarized below.

1 **Active support from senior managers**. This includes the provision of budgets, skilled people to design and run the programme, and a clear endorsement which signals to participants that the programme is worth while.
2 **Clear objectives and good communications**. This should include appropriate briefing which explains the purpose of the centre, how it fits the management development strategy and meets business needs, and the benefits which will be derived from running the programme.
3 **Roles and responsibilities**. The roles of participants, observers, line

managers and senior managers should be clearly defined in relation to the development centre programme. Responsibility for post-development centre activities should also be assigned.

4 **Selection criteria and training for observers**. Observer selection should be based on criteria which are appropriate to their role, and training should be a condition of their involvement in the process. It is also useful to provide ongoing monitoring of their performance and some support coaching.

5 **Participants' consent**. Moses states that 'informed consent' is a fundamental requirement of an assessment (development) centre. For this to happen, the participant must be given sufficient information prior to assessment to evaluate intelligently the nature of the programme and the consequences of attending or not attending the centre.

Attendance is often part of a development strategy for the organization, the implementation of which is that individuals are expected to participate. This does not negate the responsibility of the organization to provide information relating to the purpose of the centre, the participation criteria, the observer's background, development centre process and feedback. Chapter 6 refers to line manager and participant briefing.

6 **Use of development centre data**. This should be agreed at the design stage, and should explain the details relating to rights of access to data generated by the development centre. Development centre data should not be used for appraisal or performance review. Computerized data storage systems are subject to the Data Protection Act.

In practice, some conflicts may develop over competing needs to access development centre data, and these have to be reconciled. An organization investing time and money in a development centre programme will obviously want to make best use of the data, but this needs to be balanced against individual rights of privacy. One compromise which is often adopted involves individual ownership of personal feedback data and organizational ownership of anonymous aggregate data for the entire population of participants.

7 **'Safety nets'**. Occasionally, participants who attend development centres may learn things about themselves which they find difficult to accept, and which may trigger a personal crisis. This happens very rarely. (On one programme, which was attended by 1000 sales people during a six-month period, three people (0.3 per cent) were badly affected by the outcomes. All three were suffering from some major crisis in their personal lives before attending.)

There are two ways of dealing with this problem:

• Pre-emptive—identify people who are suffering from some personal crisis, and discourage them from attending.
• Reactive—provide a counselling referral service for anyone who needs to discuss the personal implication of feedback following development centre participation.

Conclusion   The methodology in this book can be used to design assessment or development centres. In both cases there is a need to follow a set of standards in order to ensure that the process is ethical and professional.

Future trends

External support   One trend, hopefully assisted by this book, will be the continuing use and improvement of competency-based development centres.

Concomitant to that may be a decreasing use of external consultants by company training and development specialists. Most of the competency frameworks devised in the 1980s were constructed by external consultants and the process was then handed over to the in-house personnel. In our experience and that of other companies two trends emerged:

1 **Collaboration with consultants**. Firstly, in the case of adaptable consultants, we learned about the skills and techniques by working with them and formed a link with them as approved suppliers. We could discuss new developments with them and contract out work to them with confidence when internal resources became stretched.

2 **Managing consultants**. Secondly, it could occur that the consultants would arrive with very clear allegiance to a particular approach, which they had often used and adapted through use in other companies. This could be a problem if the model was not congruent for one's needs, time-scales or organizational culture. In these circumstances it is necessary to work with and steer the 'experts'. A prime example is the use of repertory grid interviews which can seem to reveal rich data on required behaviour, until it is realized that the phrases and messages are regurgitating current initiatives on total quality, customer care, budgetary control or supportive management. You are being offered your own material as future-orientated data. In these circumstances, if your knowledge of the techniques is strong enough and the work area good, consultants become partners or leave with their methodology bruised but probably adapted again in the light of what has been learned from your organization.

An obvious warning is one of 'entryism', i.e. the competency and development centre expert who attaches himself or herself to a management development manager who is short on knowledge of the field and has objectives to meet to install processes. A relationship of dependency can occur, as the consultant explains the interdependencies and related processes on job evaluation, appraisal or 'real' obstacles that require a process consultancy intervention, e.g. teambuilding, before the work in its totality can succeed. This may all be true, but one has to take one step and ensure that it is a demonstrable success.

A similar weather-eye needs to be kept open with regard to the training of psychometricians. This is expensive, and in-house programmes rather than public courses save money. The attempt to move to 'chartered psychologists' and certificates of competence at different levels will be useful if it clarifies the taxonomy of instruments, squeezes out the substandard, and stops casual misuse. It would be unfortunate, however, to see signs of a 'closed shop' emerging to impede qualified and experienced psychometricians from practising because they do not possess a psychology degree or any new upgrading qualification.

Some companies new to the competency and development centre world, often led there by the need to identify key skills and then retain those with them in flatter organizations with fewer promotion opportunities, are now seeking to minimize the change by picking one of the many sets of competences developed by blue-chip companies. These are all very similar and the adjustment required to claim they are 'owned' by new companies is simply to check them out with their sponsors—the managers and especially board members. As we have shown in our discussion of generic and company-specific competences, this short cut is of dubious value.

Further evidence of the extension of the approach is the British Institute of Management's 1991 Code of Conduct which carries a set of six competency headings with 32 activities listed that the 'professional' manager 'should' do. The absence of BARS and empirical proof of origin is no safeguard against its potential employment as a framework.

Technological applications

This trend is already occurring, either to save money or because managers prefer to fill in competency profiles on their computers. This was the case in BT and a software version of the Personal Development Planning system is being developed for those units that find paper-based systems alien.

Development Dimensions International of Pittsburgh were early advocates. In his paper, 'The assessment center method and methodology: New applications and technologies', Dr William C. Byham (1986) could see how computers would help process data from assessment centres and they could behave as 'expert' systems by acting as job analyst—posing the questions.

Their Identifying Criteria for Success (ICS) is a self-contained, user-friendly job analysis 'expert' system. It accomplishes most of the steps involved in a conventional job-relatedness exercise, deriving a set of dimensions by asking questions through a standardized behaviour questionnaire. ICS can then produce interview guides and plans, a dimension-based job description and performance appraisal form and some statistical back-up data.

The system is useful in reducing the work of a large job analysis programme, and for geographically dispersed sites to which disks can be sent. It can save time and money. Against this there is a loss of understanding by the company's analysts and ICS will draw from a memory bank, thus the dimensions will lack the language and culture of the organization. ICS can be tailored to the organization if the budget is available.

Working with the Harris Corporation, DDI are now embarked on the most ambitious use of technology—'Touchstone'—which will be a dimension-based integrated human resources system. This will be based on databases of dimensions and organizational values, which can then drive job analysis performance, organizational planning, management, assessment, selection, and training and development planning. Some of the elements of the system—degree assessment and others as yet undecided—are to be developed. The architecture is an open systems design, it has a relational database and has all the user interface functions one would expect. It is being trialled by the National Westminster Bank.

In his monograph Dr Byham (1992) foresees that technology will go beyond the acceleration of processing centre data. He cites the example of one organization evaluating interactive situations by using computers linked to video disks—the assessee is asked multiple-choice questions and the 'subordinate' who is on the screen responds accordingly. But then, unlike the use of interactive video for training, the assessee's behaviours are compared to a pre-determined set of 'correct' responses. He also relates that there is wider use of videotaping of exercises by 100 organizations, who then send them for marking to DDI under their SDP (Skills Diagnostic Program)—thus avoiding the need for in-house assessors.

Wider uses

Goodge and Woodruff are respected consultants in this field. They see a pattern: that the 1970s saw rigid strategies of assessment centre methods being applied and as indicated above those ways of working are still around; the 1980s saw an experimentation with centres, and the example of ICL stepping back from this on grounds of cost was referred to in Chapter 2; and they see the 1990s where clients specify their needs more clearly and consultants customize and design for the appropriate participants and organizational need.

One new area into which Goodge and Woodruff have moved is the 'shop floor', where a company was performing poorly and trainer and peer feedback were used in an initially hostile environment.

Mike Holt, Training Manager of Glaxo Pharmaceuticals, also used a competency approach to increase productivity in non-management staff as well as to retain them. Team managers went through a full assessment centre and non-management staff an adapted mini version. They have a competency framework for the different levels of operator they will need in the future. At the 'team manager' level this contains an expected set of planning and organizing, continuous improvement, understanding business and analytical thinking, interpersonal effectiveness, flexibility and team-orientated working.

At Level 1 one finds work habits, job requirements and team participation, while Level 2 raises the set to approach to work, company knowledge, solving problems, people skills and team contribution. It should be easy for the reader to interpolate Level 3/4, which is the next step to team manager. The levels were then put into a matrix against the five key business functions of engineering, people, process, business and science. The four levels did equate to NVQ levels, but interestingly they had to develop much of their own assessment and training material for organizational fit. The incentives to cooperate with this are a broadening of skills, payment, as an internal assessor signs off the achievement of a competence, and NVQ transferable credits.

Other large organizations are using development centres to identify managers who have potential to work at the highest organizational levels in roles which do not yet exist. One large British company, which operates in the service sector, is identifying and developing its middle managers against learning company competences. Its purpose is to produce 'international managers' who can learn, adapt, lead multidisciplinary project teams which consist of people that they do not directly manage and which will forecast, anticipate and make balanced decisions based on a full understanding of business imperatives.

This use of competency-based and development centre methods to initiate change is illustrated by the case study below.

Case study: Development of a professional sales force in Wang (UK) Ltd

Frances Nichols describes a new form of development centre workshop used to develop the sales force at Wang (UK) Ltd. The workshop incorporates skills building experimentation and experiential learning.

This case study explains the Wang (UK) sales force experience with development centre learning, specifically applied to the skills of selling at director level within a Wang customer's company. The concept of using a development centre approach is relatively new for the sales force development team at Wang (UK) Ltd. Nevertheless it has been a popular event and successful at achieving its objectives.

Traditionally, Wang has sold proprietary office automation and computer systems to organizations which operate in a range of sectors such as the legal profession, banks, insurance companies, local government, manufacturing, health care and customer services. The information technology industry has undergone dramatic changes in the last four years, and many of the computer manufacturers have radically altered their strategic direction to accommodate rapidly falling profit margins, the saturated market-place and recession-hit customers.

Today, Wang has developed a strong alliance with IBM. The company no longer researches, designs and manufactures its own personal computers or mainframe computers. In the future, Wang would prefer to focus on providing consultancy and service to assist customers in using their current technology more productively in the office environment. Wang (UK) Ltd will provide help and support regardless of the computer make or model.

The skills required by the Wang sales people are thus very different today. The Wang sales person does not need to understand the secretary or the secretary's word processing needs any more, nor an in-depth knowledge of Wang's proprietary systems. Instead, they need to become experienced and credible business consultants, able to advise senior executives and directors of a company on the utilization of people and technology for improved productivity, by understanding the workflow processes in the office.

A development centre programme was developed in order to move the current sales force from an independent-minded 'lone ranger and box-shifter' mentality to a business-like punctual sales professional with high integrity, The content was designed specifically to ensure that participants would leave the workshop fully understanding the 'senior customer'. That is, they would try to understand how a director within a customer's organization would view their visit, and they would know the impression created by their own business attire and their letter of introduction.

Participants would complete various activities, such as planning for a meeting and giving a presentation to a senior director in a simulation exercise. Each participant would then receive feedback on his or her 'presence' in terms of business dress, presentation skills and letter-writing style so that he or she could identify personal strengths and weaknesses.

The development workshop activities focus on three areas of selling activity:

1 Why bother?
2 Why bother now?
3 Why Wang ?

These are the questions asked by any customer who is faced with a buying decision.

The skills development centre programme details are published in a brochure along with all the other training which is available as part of the sales force development programme. The full programme was launched to managers, the UK Board and the sales force during December 1991 and January 1992. Timetables are difficult to adhere to because the workshop is by design very intensive, participative and experiential. Often, great debate follows each presentation or role play. Similarly, different participants require feedback of different durations. Some are very keen to discuss their own development while others make little input.

Evaluation After each development workshop there is a considerable increase in demand for manager-driven or sales-instructor-driven personalized coaching and feedback. For many employees in the sales force of Wang (UK) Ltd, this workshop has been the first opportunity to receive personalized and objective comments on sales skills, presentation and performance. Future course design should include experiential skills development.

References and further reading

Avoiding discriminatory practices

Brown, C. (1984) *Black and White Britain: the Third PSI Survey*, Gower, Aldershot.
Dex, S. (1987) *Women's Occupational Mobility: A Lifetime Perspective*, Macmillan, Basingstoke.
Doeringer, P.B. and Piore, M.J. (1971) *Internal Labour Markets and Manpower Analysis*, D.C. Heath, Lexington USA.
Hutt, R. (1985) 'Chief Officer Profiles: Regional and District Nursing Officers', IMS Report No. 111, Institute of Manpower Studies, University of Sussex.
OMCS (1988) 'Equal Opportunities for Women in the Civil Service'. Progress report 1984–7. Office of the Minister for the Civil Service.

Ethics

Ferguson, J. (1991) 'When is an assessment centre a development centre?', *Guidance and Assessment Review*, 7 (6), 1–3.
Goodge, P. (1991) 'Development centres guidelines for decision makers', *Journal of Management Development*, 10 (3), 4–12.
Kerr, S. and Davenport, H. (1989) 'AC or DC: A Wolf in Sheep's Clothing?', *British Psychological Society*, 5 (5).
Moses, J.L. and Byham, W.C. (eds) (1975) *Applying the Assessment Center Method*, Pergamon Press Inc., Elmsford, N.Y., USA.

Future trends

Byham, W.C. (1986) *The Assessment Center Method—New Applications and Technologies*, Development Dimensions Internatinal, Pittsburgh USA.
Byham, W.C. (1992) *New Applications and Technologies*, Monograph VII, Development Dimensions International, Pittsburgh USA.
Goodge, P. (1991) 'Development centre guidelines for decision makers', *Journal of Management Development*, 10 (3), 4–12.
Holt, M. (1992) 'How to use competences to increase productivity in non-management staff and retain good staff' (Glaxo, Speke Factory). A paper delivered at the IIR Ltd Conference, Identifying, Measuring and Applying Competences, 2 June.
Jackson, L. (1991) 'Achieving change in business culture: through focused competence-based management development programmes', *Industrial and Commercial Training*, 23 (4).

Bibliography

Anderson, N. and Shackleton, V. (1990) 'Decision making in the graduate selection interview: a field study', *Journal of Occupational Psychology*, 63, 63–76.

Bateson, G. (1973a) *Steps to an Ecology of Mind*, Paladin, Boulder, Colorado USA.

Bateson, G. (1973b) 'Towards the Learning Company', *Management Education*, 20.

Beard, D. *et al* (1988) 'Definitions of Competence', Unpublished internal documents.

Beard, D. and Lee, G. (1990) 'New Connections in BT's Development Centres', *Personnel Management*. Institute of Personnel Management, London, April, 61–3.

Beer, S. (1988) *Diagnosing the System for Organizations*, John Wiley, Chichester.

Bernardin, H.J. (1978) 'Effects of rater training on leniency and halo errors in student ratings of instructors', *Journal of Applied Psychology*, 62, 422–7.

Boehm, V.R. (1985) 'Using assessment centres for management development—five applications', *Journal of Management Development*, 4 (4), 40–53.

Boyatzis, R.E. (1982) *The Competent Manager*, John Wiley, Chichester.

BPS Books (1990) *Review of Psychometric Tests for Assessment in Vocational Training*, British Psychological Society, London.

Bray, D.W. (1984) 'Fifty years of assessment centres: a retrospective and prospective view', *Journal of Management Development*, (4), 4–12.

Brown, C. (1984) *Black and White Britain: the Third PSI Survey*, Gower, Aldershot.

Burgoyne, J. (1990) 'Doubts about competences', in M. Divine (ed.) *The Photofit Manager*, Unwin Hyman, London.

Byham, C. (1980) 'The assessment center as an aid in management development', *Training and Development Journal*, 25 (12), 10–23.

Byham, C. (1986) *The Assessment Center Method—New Applications and Technologies*, Development Dimensions International, Pittsburgh USA.

Byham, C. (1992) *New Applications and Technology*, Monograph VII, Development Dimensions International, Pittsburgh USA.

Dex, S. (1987) *Women's Occupational Mobility: A Lifetime Perspective*, Macmillan, Basingstoke.

Doeringer, P.B. and Piore, M.J. (1971) *Internal Labour Markets and Manpower Analysis*, D.C. Heath, Lexington USA.

Dulewicz, V. (1989) 'Assessment centres as the route to competence', *Personnel Management*, Nov., 6.

Egan, G. (1990) *The Skilled Helper*, 4th edn., Brooks Cole, California USA.

Evarts, M. (1987) 'The Competency Programme of the AMA', *Journal of Industrial and Commercial Training*, Jan/Feb.

Feltham, R. (1988) 'Validity of a police assessment centre', *Journal of Occupational Psychology*, 61 (2), 129–44.

Ferguson, J. (1991) 'When is an assessment centre a development centre?', *Guidance and Assessment Review*, 7 (6), 1–3.

Flanagan, J.C. (1954) 'The critical incident technique', *Psychological Bulletin*, 51 (4).

Fletcher, C., Johnson, C. and Saville, P. (1989) 'A test by any other name', *Personnel and Management*, March, 46–51.

Garratt, B. (1990) *Creating a Learning Organisation*, Director Books, Woodhead Faulkner, Cambridge.

Garratt, B. (1981) 'Contrasts in Chinese and Western management thinking', *Leadership and Organisation Development Journal*, 2 (1), 17–22.

Gilbert, J.F. (1978) *Human Competence: Engineering Worthy Performance*, McGraw-Hill, New York USA.

Gill, R.W.T. (1979) 'The in-tray (in-basket) exercise as a measure of management potential', *Journal of Occupational Psychology*, 52, 185–97.

Golding, *et al.* (1989) 'Management Competence Standards in Europe', Training Agency, Sheffield.

Goodge, P. (1988) 'Task-based assessment', *Journal of European Industrial Training*, 12 June.

Goodge, P.M. (1987) 'Assessment centres: time for deregulation', *Management Education and Development*, 18, Part 2.

Goodge, P. (1991) 'Development centre guidelines for decision makers', *Journal of Management Development*, 10 (3), 4–12.

Green, S. (1986) 'A critical assessment of RVQ', *Personnel Management*, 18 (7).

Griffiths, P.J. and Allen, B. (1987) 'Assessment centres: breaking with tradition', *Journal of Management*, 6 (1).

Herriot, P. (1988) 'Selection at a crossroads', *Psychologist*, October, 388–92.

Hirsch, P. (1987) *Pack Your Own Parachute*, Addison-Wesley, Wokingham.

Hofstede, G. (1980) *Culture's Consequences*, Sage Publications Ltd., London.

Hogg, B. (1989) 'The AMA Competency Programme'.

Hogg, B. (1991) 'European Managerial Competences' (unpublished MSc thesis), BT/UMIST.

Holland, P.W. and Rubin, D.B. (1982) *Test Equating*, Academic Press, London.

Holt, M. (1992) 'How to use competences to increase productivity in non-management staff and retain good staff' (Glaxo, Speke Factory). A paper delivered at the IIR Ltd Conference, 'Identifying, Measuring and Applying Competences', 2 June.

Honey, P. (1988) *Improve Your People Skills*, Institute of Personnel Management, London.

Hornby, D. and Thomas, R. (1989) 'Towards a Better Standard of Management', *Personnel Management*, January.

Hunter, J.E. and Hunter, R.F. (1984) 'Validity and utility of alternative predictors of job performance', *Psychologist Bulletin*, 96, 72–98.

Huntley, S. (1990) 'Johari Window—How blind are we to its uses', *Training and Development Journal*, June, 17–21.

Hutt, R. (1985) 'Chief Officer Profiles: Regional and District Nursing Officers', IMS Report No. 111, Institute of Manpower Studies, University of Sussex.

Jackson, L. (1991) 'Achieving change in business culture: through focused competence-based management development programmes', *Industrial and Commercial Training*, 23 (4).

Jackson, T. (1989) *Evaluation: Relating Training to Business Performance*, Kogan Page, London.

Janz, T. (1982) 'Initial comparisons of patterned behaviour description interviews versus unstructured interviews', *Journal of Applied Psychology*, 67, 577–80.

Johnson, C.E., Wood, R. and Blinkhorn, S.F. (1988) 'Spuriouser and spuriouser: the use of ipsative personality tests', *Journal of Occupational Psychology*, 61 (2), 153–62.

Jones, A. (1989) 'Assessment centres and measurement efficiency: evaluation of the need for change'. Paper presented at the Fourth West Congress on the Psychology of Work and Organisation, Cambridge UK.

Kennedy, P. (1991) 'Effective Strategies for Defining, Identifying and Applying competences.' A paper to the IRR conference in London, 13 June.

Kerr, S. and Davenport, H. (1989) 'AC or DC: A wolf in sheep's clothing?', *British Psychological Society*, 5 (5), 1.

Kolb, D.A. (1984) *Experiential Learning*, Prentice Hall, New Jersey USA.

Landy, F.J. (1980) *Psychology of Work Behaviour*, Chapter 5, Dorsey Press, Homewood, Illinois USA.

Latham, G.P. *et al.* (1980) 'The situational interview', *Journal of Applied Psychology*, 65, 422–47.

Lumsden, J. (1979) 'Test theory', *Annual Review of Psychology*, 27, 154–80.

MacKinnon, D.W. (1980) *How Assessment Centers Were Started in the United States: The OSS Assessment Program*, Development Dimensions International, Pittsburgh USA.

Mant, A. (1977) *The Rise and Fall of the British Manager*, Macmillan, London.

Martin, P. and Nichols, J. (1987) *Creating a Committed Work Force*, Institute of Personnel Management, London.

Menthe, B. de (1987) *Japanese Etiquette and Ethics in Business*, Phoenix Publishing Associates, Canaan, New Hampshire USA.

Morgan, G. (1988) *Riding the Waves of Change*, Jossey Bass, San Francisco USA.

Moses, J.L. and Byham, W.C. (eds)(1975) *Applying the Assessment Center Method*, Pergamon Press Inc., Elmsford, N.Y. USA.

Moss Kanter, R. (1991) 'Companies Need to Have a Global Perspective', *Personnel Management*, May, 16.

Nevis, E.C. (1983) 'Cultural assumptions and productivity: the United States and China', *Sloan Management Review*, Spring, 17–29.

OMCS (1988) 'Equal Opportunities for Women in the Civil Service'. Progress report 1984–87. Office of the Minister for the Civil Service.

Orpen, C. (1985) 'Patterned behaviour description interviews versus unstructured interviews: a comparative validity study', *Journal of Applied Psychology*, 70, 774–6.

OSS Assessment Center (1948) *Assessment of Men*, Johnson Reprint Corp. (Harcourt Brace & Jovanovich Inc.) New York USA.

Owens, W.A. (1976) 'Background data', in M.D. Dunnette (ed.) *Handbook of Industrial and Organizational Psychology*, Rand McNally, Chicago USA.

Pedler, M., Boydell, T. and Burgoyne, J. (1989) 'Towards the learning company', *Management Education and Development*, 20, Part 1, 1–8.

Pedler, M., Burgoyne, J. and Boydell, T. (1986) *A Manager's Guide to Self Development*, McGraw-Hill, Maidenhead.

Pedler, M., Burgoyne, J. and Boydell, T. (1990) *The Learning Company*, McGraw-Hill, Maidenhead.

Powers, M. (1989) 'Enhancing Managerial Competence: the AMA Competence Programme', *Journal of Management Development*, 6 (4).

Redding, S.G. (1980) 'Definition as an aspect of culture: exploratory view of the Chinese case', *Journal of Management Studies*, May, 127–49.

Ricks, D.A. (1983) *Big Business Blunders: Mistakes in Multinational Marketing*, Dow Jones-Irwin, Homewood, Illinois USA.

Sackett, P.R. and Ryan, A.M. (1985) 'A review of recent assessment centres research', *Journal of Management Development*, 4 (4), 13–27.

Schon, D.A. (1971) *Beyond the Stable State*, Random House, London.

Smith, J.M. (1981) 'The Paradox of Talent', Occasional Research Paper, Coutts Career Consultants, London.

Smith, M. and Robertson, I. (1990) *Advances in Selection and Assessment*, John Wiley, Chichester.

Smith, M., Gregg, M. and Andrews, D. (1979) *Selection and Assessment: A New Approach*, Pitman, London.

Smith, M., Gregg, M. and Adams, D. (1989) *Selection and Assessment—A New Appraisal*, Pitman, London.

Stewart, A. and Stewart, V. (1981) *Tomorrow's Managers Today*, Institute of Personnel Management, London.

Toplis, J., Dulewicz, V. and Fletcher, C. (1987) *Psychological Testing: A Practical Guide*, Institute of Personnel Management, London.

Training Agency (1990), MCI Standards on Training, Training Agency, Sheffield.

Weisner, W.H. and Cronshaw, S.P. (1988) 'A meta-analytic investigation of the impact of interview format and structure on the validity of the employment interview', *Journal of Occupational Psychology*, 61, 275–90.

Wexley, N. and Youtz, G,. (1985) *Organisational Behaviour for the FLMI Insurance Education Program*, Dow Jones-Irwin, Homewood, Illinois USA.

Wingrove, J., Jones, A. and Herriot, P. (1985) 'The predictive validity of pre- and post-discussion assessment centre ratings', *Journal of Occupational Psychology*, 58, 189–92.

Wright, P.M., Lichtenfels, P.A. and Pursell, E.D. (1989) 'The situational interview: additional studies and meta-analysis', *Journal of Occupational Psychology*, 62, 191–9.

Yih-Heng Jou, J. and Kai Sung (1990) 'Chinese value systems and managerial behaviour', *International Journal of Psychology*, 25, 619–27.

Index

Further titles in the McGraw-Hill Training Series

THE BUSINESS OF TRAINING
Achieving Success in Changing World Markets
Trevor Bentley   ISBN 0-07-707328-2

EVALUATING TRAINING EFFECTIVENESS
Translating Theory into Practice
Peter Bramley   ISBN 0-07-707331-2

DEVELOPING EFFECTIVE TRAINING SKILLS
Tony Pont   ISBN 0-07-707383-5

MAKING MANAGEMENT DEVELOPMENT WORK
Achieving Success in the Nineties
Charles Margerison   ISBN 0-07-707382-7

MANAGING PERSONAL LEARNING AND CHANGE
A Trainer's Guide
Neil Clark   ISBN 0-07-707344-4

HOW TO DESIGN EFFECTIVE TEXT-BASED OPEN
LEARNING: A Modular Course
Nigel Harrison   ISBN 0-07-707355-X

HOW TO DESIGN EFFECTIVE COMPUTER-BASED
TRAINING:
A Modular Course
Nigel Harrison   ISBN 0-07-707354-1

HOW TO SUCCEED IN EMPLOYEE DEVELOPMENT
Moving from Vision to Results
Ed Moorby   ISBN 0-07-707459-9

USING VIDEO IN TRAINING AND EDUCATION
Ashly Pinnington   ISBN 0-07-707384-3

TRANSACTIONAL ANALYSIS FOR TRAINERS
Julie Hay   ISBN 0-07-707470-X

SELF-DEVELOPMENT
A Facilitator's Guide
Mike Pedler and
David Megginson   ISBN 0-07-707460-2

DEVELOPING WOMEN THROUGH TRAINING
A Practical Handbook
Liz Willis,
Jenny Daisley   ISBN 0-707-707566-8

DESIGNING AND ACHIEVING COMPETENCY
A Competency-Based Approach to Developing People and
Organizations
Editors: Rosemary Boam
and Paul Sparrow   ISBN 0-07-707572-2

TOTAL QUALITY TRAINING
The Quality Culture and Quality Trainer
Brian Thomas   ISBN 0-07-707472-6

CAREER DEVELOPMENT AND PLANNING
A Guide for Managers, Trainers and Personnel Staff
Malcolm Peel   ISBN 0-07-707554-4

SALES TRAINING
A Guide to Developing Effective Salespeople
Frank S. Salisbury   ISBN 0-07-707458-0

CLIENT-CENTRED CONSULTING
A Practical Guide for Internal Advisors and Trainers
Peter Cockman, Bill Evans
and Peter Reynolds   ISBN 0-07-707685-0

TRAINING TO MEET THE TECHNOLOGY CHALLENGE
Trevor Bentley   ISBN 0-07-707589-7

IMAGINATIVE EVENTS Volumes I & II
Ken Jones
          ISBN 0-07-707679-6   Volume I
          ISBN 0-07-707680-X   Volume II
          ISBN 0-07-707681-8   for set of Volume I & II